QUAKER MARRIAGE CERTIFICATES

PASQUOTANK, PERQUIMANS, PINEY WOODS,
AND SUTTONS CREEK
MONTHLY MEETINGS, NORTH CAROLINA, 1677-1800

Compiled By Gwen Boyer Bjorkman

HERITAGE BOOKS, INC.

Published 1988 By

HERITAGE BOOKS INC.
1540E Pointer Ridge Place, Bowie, Maryland 20716
(301)-390-7709

ISBN 1-55613-169-0

TABLE OF CONTENTS

For half a century researchers have consulted
William Wade Hinshaw's Encyclopedia of American
Quaker Genealogy (volume one) for early North
Carolina Quaker marriage records. The Encyclopedia,
however, omitted a vitally important component of
many of those records: the names of those witnesses
who signed Friends' marriage certificates. Gwen
Bjorkman now supplies those names in her abstracts
of certificates from the three monthly meetings
which existed before 1800 in northeastern North
Carolina, the birthplace of the Society of Friends
in the state.

After the 1672 missionary endeavors of William
Edmundson and George Fox, two monthly meetings
developed in the Albemarle region. One meeting
covered Pasquotank and Little River, while the other
served Perquimans. The monthly meeting in
Pasquotank (later called Symons Creek Monthly
Meeting) drew its membership from both Pasquotank
and Perquimans counties; it was ultimately laid down
in 1854. The somewhat stronger monthly meeting in
Perquimans had members in Perquimans and Chowan
counties and--for a time--in areas as distant as
Northampton County. In the mid eighteenth century
the Perquimans Monthly Meeting was frequently called
Wellses Monthly Meeting, and in 1794 it took the
name Piney Woods Monthly Meeting which it has
retained to the present. From 1794 until 1835 the
eastern part of Perquimans County was served by the
short-lived Suttons Creek Monthly Meeting.

The minute books and registers of the three monthly
meetings of Pasquotank, Perquimans, and Suttons
Creek contain copies of numerous marriage
certificates. Although there are some textual
variations, the certificates generally adhere to the
recommendations of George Fox as to content.
Grooms, brides, and their fathers are named. Places
of residence and of marriage are stated along with
the wedding dates. References are customarily made
to the two declarations of intention and the
subsequent approval by a monthly meeting which were
prerequisites of any Quaker marriage. Certificates

describe the manner in which couples joined hands and spoke their promises to be faithful spouses. Lastly, the certificates bear the signatures of newlyweds and of the relatives, friends, and visitors who subscribed their names in witness to the marriages having been accomplished.

Not all the subscribing witnesses were North Carolinians (many Virginians may be noted), nor were they all Quakers. The name of Paul Palmer, the first Baptist minister in North Carolina, appears in Perquimans along with government officials (and Anglicans) Thomas Harvey, Henry Clayton, and Richard Everard. (It cannot be determined whether the last was Governor Everard or his son.) Attendance by such public figures may have been merely a neighborly act, but their presence may have imparted a sanction to Quaker marriages which were (until 1778) often regarded as irregular if not illicit. Curiously, North Carolina's earliest marriage statute--ratified in 1670--seemed to prefigure Quaker marriage customs when it allowed couples to repair to the governor or a councillor "before him declareing that they do joyne together in the holy state of Wedlock And doe accept one the other for man and wife" in the presence of three or four neighbors.

As shown by the extant marriage certificates from the Albemarle meetings, all Friends' marriages in North Carolina took place in dwelling houses until the first public meeting houses were erected in the first decade of the eighteenth century. Pasquotank certificates subsequently referred to meeting houses at Little River (at Woodville in Perquimans County), Symons Creek (near Nixonton), Newbegun Creek (near Weeksville), and the Narrows of Pasquotank River (near Elizabeth City). In Perquimans there were marriages at the Upper Meeting House (later called Wellses), in the Narrows of Perquimans River; the Lower Meeting House (later Old Neck), near Francis Tomes'; and the meeting houses at Piney Woods (near Belvidere) and Suttons Creek. The Suttons Creek meeting houses included Suttons Creek, Wellses, and Vosses Creek; all were in central Perquimans within a few miles of present-day Winfall. (The certificates, by the way, illustrate a Quaker custom of identification, as in saying "the meeting house at Little River" rather than "Little River Meeting House.") A few of the certificates recorded marriages which took place outside the jurisdictions of the Albemarle meetings.

All the marriage certificates for the Pasquotank, Perquimans, and Suttons Creek monthly meetings are recorded copies. No original certificates seem to have been preserved by the meetings, and only a precious few originals can now be found anywhere. The recorded certificates were subject to all the potential for error which hand copying entailed. Further problems could arise when certificates were recorded many years after the marriages. It should be noted particularly that all the certificates in the volume "Eastern Q[uarter] Piney Woods M[onthly] M[eeting] Vol I Records" were entered in or after 1852 when the meeting attempted to replace some of its records which had been destroyed by fire. Unfortunately, many of those records could not be recovered from private sources and no certificate is to be had for many of the marriages allowed by the Perquimans meeting. Losses of certificates from Pasquotank are also evident, and a few marriages known for Suttons Creek are not represented by certificates in the extant records.

The study of early North Carolina Quaker records comes naturally to Gwen Bjorkman, who is descended from many of the ancient Friends. Her account of several Quaker ancestors won the 1987 prize in the National Genealogical Society's Family-History Writing Contest. Together with the concern of a descendant she brings to her work the competence of a skilled researcher. In publishing thorough abstracts of Quaker marriage certificates for northeastern North Carolina, she renders a major and invaluable service to genealogists. Her abstracts preserve more nearly the original form and language of the record than did Hinshaw, and they correct mistakes in the Encyclopedia. Henceforth, researchers will consult Bjorkman rather than Hinshaw for these marriage records.

Raymond A. Winslow, Jr.
Hertford, North Carolina

All of the original Minutes of the Monthly Meetings
of the Society of Friends in North Carolina are
available in microfilm on interlibrary loan from the
North Carolina Friends Historical Collection at
Guilford College, Greensboro, North Carolina. In
this abstract of the records, the page numbers are
in the same order as on the microfilm. All of the
marriage certificates through 1800 have been copied
and some after 1800. There are still many later
certificates that were not copied. There are also
various other lists of names that were included in
the Minutes, but not included by Hinshaw, that have
been abstracted for this book. One of the original
marriage certificates is copied in full on page 145.

The names have been copied as written, with the
exception of capitalization of the first letter of
the first name and the surname. When it occurs, the
"ff" has been changed to a single "F" as in Francis
and the "i" has been changed to a "j" as in
Benjamin. A doubtful reading is followed by a
question mark in brackets. One problem with the "h"
or "k" reading for Nicholson/Nickolson has not been
resolved or marked with a question mark.

Some rearrangement of the information in the
marriage certificate has been made for uniformity
and minor punctuation has been added. The Quaker
dates have been abbreviated to numerals in the order
of day, month, year. Any information supplied that
was not in the original, or was in a different
location in the original, is inside brackets.
Abbreviations used are dau for daughter, decd for
deceased, m for month, and cont. for continued.

My thanks are extended to Carole Treadway of
Guilford College and Raymond A. Winslow, Jr. of
Perquimans County for their assistance in this
research, and especially to Mr. Winslow for the
introduction which adds so much to our understanding
of these important family records.

Gwen Boyer Bjorkman
Bellevue, Washington

Eastern Quarter, Symons Creek Monthly Meeting
(Pasquotank) Misc. Records from 1678.

Page 11 Zacarias son to Zacarias NIXON of the
County of Notingham in the Paresh of north mascom,
and Elezabeath PAGE daughtter of Isacke PAGE desesed
of the county of allbamarll...the 2 day of the
fifth[?] month 1681...

[Column 1]
Henry WHITE
Charls PROUS
Arnould WHITE
Soloman POOLE
Timothy MAIDS
Willam TRAVIS
Jeramia SIMONS
[Column 2]
Jonathan TAILLER
Rubin WILLIS
Joseph GOODMAN

[Column 2 cont.]
Willam JACSON
Ane PROWS
Ane MEAIDS
Ruth TORNER
[Column 3]
Elezabeath JACSON
Sary TRAVIS
Ane SIMONS
Margreat POOLE
Recorded by me
Henry WHITE

Page 12 Samuell CHARLLS the son of Willam CHARLLS
of poquemench Rever, and Elezabeath MORISON
daughtter of John MORISON of Lettle Rever...the 6
day of the tenth month [1696] at the house of Henry
WHITE...

[Column 1]
Henry WHITE
Francis TOOMS
Samuell NIKELLSON
Jeams DAVIS
Joseph NEKELLSON
Isarell SNELLIN
Willam MORE
Gaberell NEWBEY

[Column 2]
Damaris WHITE
Elizabeth NIXON
Mary TOOMS
Elizabeth NIKELLSON
[Column 3]
Samuell CHARLLS
Elizabeth CHARLLS

Page 13a Thomas CATERIGHT of pascotanke presenke,
and Grace HALLEY of lettle Rever in the same
presenke...this 4 day of the 4 month 1693...

[Column 1]
Henry WHITE
Thomas SYMONS
Jeremyah SYMONS
Callib BUNDEY
Wilam TORNER
Joseph COMMANDR
[Column 2]
Rebeaca SIMONS

[Column 2 cont.]
Damaris WHITE
Ane SIMONS
Elezabeath NIXON
[Column 3]
Thomas T CATRIGHT
his marke
Grece HALLEY

Page 13B   Arnould WHITE son of Arnould WHITE of
lettle Rever, and Phetheny WELLSON the daughter of
Micall WILLSON of pascotank...at a meeting apinted
for that porpose the sixt day of the tenth month
[1696] at the house of Henry WHITE...

[Column 1]

Henry WHITE
Jeramiah SIMONS
Samuell NIKELLSON
Francis TOOMS
Isarell SNELIN
Jeams DAVIS
John NEKELSON
Joseph NEKELSON
Gabrell NEWBEY
Joh RAPER

[Column 2]

Ann SIMONS
Damaris WHITE
Elezabeth NIXON
Mary TOOMS
Elizabeth NEKELLSON
Margreat RAPER

[Column 3]

Arnould WHITE
Phetheny WHITE

Page 14   John WHITE the son of Henry WHITE of lettle
Rever, and Elezabeth NEWBEY daughter to John NEWBEY
and daughter in law to Mathew CALLIN of the same
Rever...at a meeting apinted for that porpose at the
house of Mathew CALLEY the 14, 11m, 1696...

[Column 1]

Henry WHITE
John SIMONS
Mathew CALLEY
Jeramiah SIMONS
Jeams DAVIS
Robert WHITE
Arnond WHITE

[Column 1 cont.]

Jeams WHITE

[Column 2]

Magdelen CALLEY
Damaris WHITE
Ane SIMONS
Elezabeath NIXON
Elezabeath DAVIS

Page 16   John SIMONS of lettle Rever of the province
of Caralina in the presenke of pascotank son to
Thomas SIMONS, and Damaris WHITE daughter to Henry
WHITE of the same County and presenke ...at the
house of Henry WHITE the 8 day of the 6m, 1700...

[Column 1]

Henry WHITE
Thomas SIMONS
Jeramiah SIMONS
Robart WHITE
Arnould WHITE
Gabrill NEWBEY
Joseph PERCE
Jeams WHITE
Calib BUNDY
Jeams NEWBEY
Stephen SCOTE

[Column 2]

John SIMONS
Damaris WHITE
  now SYMONS
Rebeaca SIMONS
Elezabeth NIXON
Damaris WHITE
Elizabeath CHARLLS
Damaris PERSE

Recorded pr
Henry WHITE

Page 17 Arnould WHITE and Jane PIKE widow both of
pascotank Pricint...this 9th of ye 4th month in ye
year 1720...at ye publike meeting house at Litle
River...

[Column 1]
Martha SYMONS
Damaris WHITE
Margret RAIPER
Mary PIKE
Ann PIKE
Elesabeth NIXON
Sarah WHITE
Mary MORRIS
Elesabeth WHITE
Ann BUNDEY
Mary WHITE
Ruth GLAISTER
Mary PRICHERD
Sarah EAGAR
Sarah GLAISTER
Jean MARTIN
Sarah WHITE
   [Column 2]
Damaris SYMONS

[Column 3]
Arnould WHITE
the marke of
Jean I PIKE
   now WHITE
Benjamen PRICHARD
Robart WHITE
Thomas PRICHARD
John PIKE
Henry WHITE
Arnould WHITE Junr
John SYMONS
Josaway WHITE
Zachariah NIXON
Jeams NEWBEY
William BUNDEY
John MORRIS
Aron MORRIS
Recorded by
   John SYMONS

Page 18 Joseph NEWBEY son of Gabariel NEWBEY of
paquamens, and Elesabeth NIXON daughter of Zachariah
and Elesabeth NIXON of Litle River...at ye publike
meeting house att Litle River...on the first day of
the first month in the year accourding to ye English
acount 1715/6...

[Column 1]
Zachariah NIXON
Gabriel NEWBEY
Thomas PAGE
William NEWBEY
John MORRIS
Henery WHITE
Benjamen EDEY
Thomas NEWBEY
Edward NEWBEY
John NEWBEY
Matthew PRICHARD
Edward MAYO
Recorded by
   John SYMONS
   [Column 2]
Richard RATLIVE

[Column 2 cont.]
Damaris WHITE
Damaris SYMONS
   [Column 3]
Joseph NEWBEY
Elesabeth NIXON
   now NEWBEY
Mary NEWBEY
Elesabeth NIXON
Damaris RATLIVE
Ann HENDLEY
Mary TOMS
Ruth GLAISTER
Mary GLASTER
Mary MAYO
Mary MORRIS
Elesabeth CHARLS

[Column 2 cont.]
Humphrey WAIDY
Jeams DAVICE Senor
John SYMONS

[Column 3 cont.]
Rebaca SYMONS
Hanah NIKOLSON
Elesabeth NIKOLSON

Page 19 Jeams NEWBEY of the precint of pascotanke in ye province of North Carolinah, and Elesabeth DAVICE of ye place aforsd... this 18th of ye 5th month in the year 1719...in the publicke Meeting house at Litle River...

[Column 1]
Matthew PRICHARD
Zachariah NIXON
Samuel NICKOLSON
John NEWBEY
John SYMONS
Samuel CHARLS
Henry WHITE
John MORRIS
Joseph COMANDER
Regersted pr
  John SYMONS
[Column 2]
Mary GLAISTER
Elesabeth NEWBEY
Mary MORRIS
Elesabth NIXON Juner
Robart DAVICE
Robart WHITE

[Column 2 cont.]
Arnould WHITE
Christophar NICKOLSON
Thomas MOUNTAQUA
William BARRY
Thomas SYMONS
[Column 3]
Jeams NEWBEY
Elesabeth DAVICE
  now NEWBEY
Damaris WHITE
Elesabeth WHITE
Rebaca WHITE
Ann NICKOLSON
Damaris SYMONS
Elesabeth NIXON
Elesabeth CHARLS
Elesabeth MOUNTAQUA
Mary WHITE

Page 20 Johnathan WHITE son of Robart WHITE, and Ann PIKE daughter of Samuel PIKE of the county aforesaid [Albarmarle] decesed...this tenth day of ye second month called Aprel in the year 1729...at the publick meetting house at Litle River...

[Column 1]
Mary GLASTER
Mary MORRIS Senr
Mary MORRIS juner
Jeams NEWBEY
Charls OVERMAN
John MORRIS
Jos. JORDAN
Stephen DELAMAR
Daniel CHANCY
John OVERMAN
Regestered Per
  John SYMONS

[Column 2 cont.]
Abigal OVERMAN
Mary JORDAN
Isabell HENLY
Elisabeth PRICTHARD
Martha PRICTHARD
[Column 3]
Johnathan WHITE
Ann PIKE now WHITE
Robart WHITE
Jean WHITE
Arnould WHITE
Joseph WHITE

[Column 2]
Zachariah NIXON
Stephen SCOTE
Thomas MOUNTAQUA
Benja. PRICHARD
Thomas PRICHARD
Elesabeth PRICHARD

[Column 3 cont.]
John PIKE
Mary PIKE
Henry WHITE
Joshua WHITE
Susana PIKE
Johnathan PIKE
Sarah WHITE

Page 33 Samll. BUNDY of Pascotank Precinct Planter
& Tamer SYMONS Daughter of Jeremiah SYMONS Planter
of the place afore Said...5th day of the X month
1696 at the house of Henry WHITT...

[Column 1]
Francis TOOMS
Eserell SNELLELL
Danaris WHITE
Elezabeth WHIT
Joseph COMMANDER
[Column 2]
Samuel S B BONDEY
    his marke
Tamer T S SIMONS
    her marke

[Column 3]
Jeramiah SIMONS
Calleb BUNDEY
Thomas SIMONS
Henry WHITE
Jeams DAVIS
Samuell NECALS

Page 175 A meting...at the house of Elezabeaths
NIXONS the 11 day of the 5 month 1699 then the said
Joseph PERSE son to John PERSE of Poquemench did
publekly and solemly take Damaris NIXON...who was
daughter to Elezabeath NIXON of little Rever...

[Column 1]
Necoles SEMMONS
Caleb BUNDEY
Henry WHITE
John MORIS
Danell AKEHURST
Willam TORNER
John NECALLS
Robert WHITE
Jeams WHITE
Nathanell NECALLS
Thomas SIMONS

[Column 1 cont.]
Jeramiah SIMONS
[Column 2]
Mary SEMMONS
Elezabeath NIXON
Damaris WHITE
Elezabeath CHARLS
Rebeaca SIMONS
Phelocresta JORDEN
Ane SIMONS
Margreat RAPER

Page 179 [disownment of Edward MAYO] ...giveen
forth from our quarterly meeting and signed by us
this first day of the 7 month 1688
    [Column 1]
    Henry WHITE

[Column 1 cont.]
Willam BONDY
Crestofer NEKELLSON
Arnold WHITE
Danell AKEHURST
Zacarias NIXON
John [torn]
   [Column 2]
Jeramiah SIMONS
Tho LEAPER

[Column 2 cont.]
Tho SIMONS
Willam TORNER
Robert HERMON
John WHITE
Stephen HANCOK
   [Column 3]
Elezabeath NIXON
Damaris WHITE
Ane LEPER

Page 180 At a meeting at the house of Henry WHITE
this 24 of the 5 mo [1690]...Calib BUNDY son to
Willam BUNDY, and Jeane MANERS daughter to Perigrene
MANERS both of the county of Albamarle in the
provence of Carolina...   [Column 2]
   [Column 1]   Callib C B BUNDEY
William BUNDY   his mark
Henry WHITE   Jean X MANERS
Thomas SYMONS   her mark
Joseph COMANDER   Mary BUNDEY
Jeremiah SYMONS   Ane WILLSON
Zacharias NIXON   Damaris WHITE
William HOGBIN   Elezabeath NIXON
Willam TORNER   Dorathy COMANDER
Samuell NICALLS   Ruth TORNER
                          Margret HOGBIN

Page 181 At a meeting at the house of Arnould WHITE
the 24 of the 4 month 1679...Solloman POOLE Sone to
Richard POOLE in Medlesexe in londan benig about
therty yere ould, and Margrete WHITE daughter to
Henry WHITE of the County of allbamarll a gerl
aboute 17 yere or therabout...
   [Column 1]   [Column 1 cont.]
Henry WHITE   Sary TRAVIS
Timothy MEADS   Francis HUNTE
Francis TOOMS   Rebecka SIMONS
Charlls PROUS   Ane MEAIDS
Willam SMEITH   Elezabeath JACSON
Johnathan TAILLER   Jeams HUNTER
Arnould WHITE   [Column 2]
Georg TAILLER   Solloman POOLL
Willam TRAVIS   Margrete WHITE
Willam BREAD
Willam JACSON   Regesttered by me
Crestofer OULLDFEELD   Henry WHITE
Mary WHITE   Regestter to the meeting

Page 183 At a meeting at the house of Henry WHITE
this 26 of the 4 month 1690...Jeams DAVIS son to
Willam DAVIS, and Elezabeath WHITE Daughter to Henry
WHITE of the County of allbamarll...

[Column 1]
Henry WHITE
Zacharias NIXON
Thomas SYMONS
Jeremiah SYMONS
William HOGBIN
William TORNER
Henry PLATT
John DEARE
[Column 2]
Damaris WHITE

[Column 2 cont.]
Rebeaca SIMONS
Elezabeath NIXON
Ane SIMONS
Ruth TORNER
Margret HOGBIN
[Column 3]
Jeams X DAVIS
    his marke
Elezabeath X WHITE
    her marke

Page 184 Timothy MEAIDS and Ane BLESSING do take
one another and are man and wife...it Being the 4
day of the 4 month 1677...

[Column 1]
Henry WHITE
John HUNTE
Arnould WHITE
Willam TRAVIS
Willam TORNER
Dorathy HARVY
Mary WHITE
Sary TRAVIS
Fransis HUNT
Ruth TORNER

[Column 1 cont.]
Elezabeath SHERAD
Elinor TAILLER
[Column 2]
Timothy MEAIDS
Ane A BLESSING
    her marke

Regestered by me
Henry WHITE
from the oreginall

Eastern Quarter, Symons Creek Monthly Meeting
(Pasquotank) Volume II Marriages

Page 6 Joshua TRUBLOOD son of Abel, and Mary HENLEY
dau of Joseph, both of Pasquotank...7, 7m, 1790...in
their publick Meeting House at Newbegun Creek...

[Column 1]
Joseph HENLEY
Joseph TRUBLOOD
[Column 2]
Joshua TRUBLOOD
Mary TRUBLOOD
Page 7
[Column 3]
Joseph TRUBLOOD
Joshua PERISHO
Edwd. EVERIGIN

[Column 4 cont.]
Lydia MORRIS
Elisabeth BUNDY
Cristopher NICHN.
Joseph BUNDY
John SYMONS
Miliscent WHITE
Elias ALBERTSON
Aaron MORRIS Jr
[Column 5]
Mary NICHOLSON

[Column 3 cont.]
Rubn. KEATON
John MCDONALD
Zachariah WHITE
Fred. B. SAWYER
John NICHOLSON
Miriam PRITCHARD
    [Column 4]
Aaron MORRIS

[Column 5 cont.]
Miliscent NICHON.
Elizabeth TOMS
Lucretia HENLEY
Lydia MORRIS
Naomi NEWBY
John TRUBLOOD
Jemima TRUBLOOD
Vilaty GLASGOW

Page 11 John BELL of Pasquotank, and Sarah BUNDY
dau of Josiah of Perquimans...30, 12m, 1789...in
their meeting place near the head of Little River...

[Column 1]
Jonathan MORRIS
Lyda NIXON
Sarah COSAND
    [Column 2]
Naomi NEWBY
Mary BUNDY
Mary BUNDY
George BUNDY
Caleb BUNDY
Lyda MORRIS
Christopher NICH:
Mary NIXON
Sarah NICHOLSON
    [Column 3]
Josiah BUNDY
Mary BUNDY

[Column 3 cont.]
Benjamin BUNDY
Sarah BUNDY
Miriam BELL
Caroline BELL
Charles MORGAN
Peninah BUNDY
Elizabeth SYMONS
    [Column 4]
John BELL
Sarah BELL
Mary MORRIS
Nathan MORRIS
Nathan BUNDY
Lyda MORGAN
Absalon SYMONS
Abraham SYMONS

Page 20-21 Jesse SYMONS and Melisant MORRIS relict
of Benjamin decd...20, 1m, 1791...at the Meeting
House at Symons Creek...

[Column 1]
Nathan MORRIS
Benjamin MORRIS
Rebekah PEARSON
Rebekah GILBERT
Aaron MORRIS
Mathew SYMONS
Margaret DAVIS
Caleb TRUBLOOD
Charles MORGAN
Josiah GILBERT
John PRICE
    [Column 2]
John SYMONS

[Column 2 cont.]
Silas DRAPER
Thomas DRAPER
Penelope MORRIS
Absala SYMONS
Josiah BUNDY
Meliscent MORGAN
Josiah DRAPER
Miriam DRAPER
Jonathan MORRIS
Ann METCALF
    [Column 3]
Jesse SYMONS
Meliscen SYMONS

Page 22-23 Abraham SYMONS son of John decd, and
Mary CHARLES dau of Samuel and Abigail CHARLES decd
...25 4m, 1790...in the Meeting House at Symons
Creek...

[Column 1]
Benjamin WHITE
Joshua MORRIS
Caleb TRUBLOOD
Chrsr. NICHOLSON
Abraham BOSWELL
Benjamin OVERMAN
Elizabeth EARL
Onias OVERMAN
John NICHOLSON
Miriam PRITCHARD
Nehemiah WHITE

[Column 2]
John PRICE
Mary WINSLOW
Jonathan PRICE
Mordecai MORRIS
Absala SYMONS

[Column 2 cont.]
Rebekah DAVIS
Josiah GILBERT
Joshua MORRIS
William OVERMAN
Ann SYMONS
Thomas MORRIS
Thomas MORRIS

[Column 3]
Abraham SYMONS
Mary SYMONS
Sarah WILSON
Joseph WILSON
Mathew SYMONS
Sarah SYMONS
Abraham SYMONS
Elizabeth SYMONS
Benjamin CHARLES
Josiah GILBERT

Page 24 James MORGAN son of James of Pasquotank,
and Hannah GRIFFIN dau of Joseph of Chowan...16, 3m
called March, 1768...in Perquimons County...at
pinewoods meeting house...

[Column 1]
Charles MORGAN
Thomas SAINT
Sarah NEWBY
Guley WHITE
Amos GRIFFIN
Caleb ELIOTT

[Column 2]
William GRIFFIN
Reuben GRIFFIN
John EVENS

[Column 2 cont.]
Mariam GRIFFIN
Leadoh GRIFFIN
Robrt EVENS

[Column 3]
James MORGAN
Hannah MORGAN
Thomas OVERMAN
John GRIFFIN
Hannah MORGAN

Page 29 Josiah TRUEBLOOD son of Amos, and Elisabeth
ARNOLD dau of William, all of the Counties of
Pasquotank and Perquimons...14, 3m called March,
1759...at Little River in their publick meeting
place in the county of Perquimons...

[Column 1]
Josiah TRUEBLOOD
Elisabeth TRUEBLOOD
Page 30

[Column 3 cont.]
Phineus NIXON
Mary NICHOLSON
Miriam OVERMAN

[Column 2]
William ARNOLD
Amos TRUEBLOOD
Mary ARNOLD
Abel TRUEBLOOD
Joshua TRUEBLOOD
Caleb TRUEBLOOD
Joseph NEWBEY
Saml NEWBY
John ANDERSON
Joshua MORRIS
Joseph ROBINSON
Patience NEWBY
Mary NIXON
[Column 3]
Thomas NICHOLSON
Samuel ANDERSON
Abigail CHARLES
Elihu ALBERTSON
Naomi NEWBY
Joshua PERISHO

[Column 3 cont.]
Elisabeth HENLEY
Thos. HOLLOWELL Junr
Benjamin NEWBY
Elisabeth BUNDY
Joseph NICHOLSON
[Column 4]
Thomas ROBINSON Junr
Joshua OVERMAN
Zachariah NIXON
Thomas ROBINSON
Josiah WINSLOW
William ARNOLD
Mary MORRIS
John NIXON
Sarah ROBINSON Junr
Sarah ANDERSON
Joseph JORDAN
Jane JORDAN
Sarah PRICHARD
Ruth TRUEBLOOD

Page 31 Mordecai MORRIS son of Joshua, and Abigail
OVERMAN dau of Nathan, both of Pasquotank...28, 4m,
1773...at the Meeting House at Newbegun Creek...

[Column 1]
Sarah NICHOLSON
Benjn. WHITE Senr
Abram SYMONS
Miriam SANDERS
Joseph SYMONS
Nathan MORRIS
Benjn. MORRIS
Demcy[?] CONNER
Robt. JORDAN
John WINSLOW
Caleb SAWYER
Thomas OVERMAN
Nathan OVERMAN
[Column 2]
Benjamin WHITE
Joseph HENLEY
Josiah WINSLOW
Miriam PRICHARD
Miriam MORRIS
Elisabeth PYPER[?]
John MORRIS
Thos. PRICHARD

[Column 2 cont.]
Sarah PRICHARD
Nathan OVERMAN
Mary OVERMAN
Thomas NICHOLSON
Ephraim OVERMAN
John SYMONS
[Column 3]
Mordecai MORRIS
Abigail X MORRIS
        her mark
Joshua MORRIS
Clarkey MORRIS
Mary MORRIS Senr
Rebekah NICHOLSON
Aaron MORRIS Senr
Jeremiah GILBERT
Aaron MORRIS Junr
Joseph MORRIS Junr
John HENLEY
Thomas GILBERT
Elisabeth GILBERT
John SYMONS Junr

Page 34-35 Charles OVERMAN son of Charles of
Pasquotank, and Mary ALBERTSON dau of Benjamin of
Perquimans...19, 3m, 1791...at the Meeting House
near Suttons Creek...

[Column 1]
Charles OVERMAN
Mary OVERMAN
  [Column 2]
Benjn. ALBERTSON
Sarah ALBERTSON
Joseph JONES
Mary JONES
Sarah JONES
William ALBERTSON
Miriam WHITE
Phineas ALBERTSON
Judith HOLLAWELL
Armajah LAMB
  [Column 3]
Joseph LASEY
Elisabeth TOMS
Samuel ANDERSON

[Column 3 cont.]
John TRUBLOOD
Jemima TRUBLOOD
Thomas ALBERTSON
James NIXON
John TOMS
Mary TOMS
Martha TOMS
  [Column 4]
William OVERMAN
[?] NIXON
Joseph ANDERSON
Mary ANDERSON
Sarah ANDERSON
Benn. ANDERSON
Nixon ELLIOTT
James OVERMAN
Jesse TRUBLOOD

Page 43 Benjamin PRICHARD son of Joseph decd of
Pasquotank, and Peninnah WHITE dau of Caleb of
Perquimans...22, 12m, 1779...at the meeting house in
Piney Woods...

[Column 1]
Francis WHITE
Exum NEWBY
Wm. NEWBY
Josiah WHITE
Sarah WHITE
Jonathan PARKER
Nathan MORRIS
Thomas WINSLOW
  [Column 2]
Elizabeth PARKER
George WALTON
Leah SANDERS
Sarah METCALFE
Margret KNOX
Benjn. WHITE
Miles WHITE
Nathan WHITE

[Column 3]
Lyddia WHITE
Jacob HILL
Chalkley ALBERTSON
Thomas PALIN
Thomas NEWBY
Aaron MORRIS
Margt. MORRIS
Matthew WHITE
  [Column 4]
Benjamin PRICHARD
Peninnah PRICHARD
Caleb WHITE
Rebekah WHITE
Sarah NICHOLSON
Rachel WINSLOW
Thomas WHITE
Thomas KNOX

Page 45 Joseph NEWBY son of Gabriel of Perquimans,
and Elizabeth NIXON dau of Elizabeth NIXON of Little

River...1, 1m, 1715...in their publick Meeting place
at Little River...

[Column 1]
Hannah NICHOLSON
Elisabeth NICHOLSON
Damaris WHITE
Richard RATLIFF
Henry WAIDEY[?]
James DAVIS Senr
John SYMONS

[Column 2]
Edward MAYO
Zachariah NIXON
Gabriel NEWBY
Thomas PAGE
William NEWBY
John MORRIS
Henry WHITE
Mary MAYO
Mary GLAISTER

[Column 2 cont.]
Mary MORRIS
Elisabeth CHARLES
Rebekah SYMONS

[Column 3]
Joseph NEWBY
Elisabeth NEWBY
Elisabeth NIXON
Mary NEWBY
Elisabeth NIXON
Damaris RATLIFF
Ann HENLEY
Mary TOMES
Ruth GLAISTER
Thomas NEWBY
Edward NEWBY
Tamer NEWBY
John NEWBY
Matthew PRICHARD

Page 46 William EVERIGIN Cordwainer, and Mary WHITE
Spinster dau of Henry WHITE decd, both of
Pasquotank...22, 1m called March, 1722...in their
publick Meeting place at Little River...

[Column 1]
James NEWBY
Anna Lutitie[?] LOW[?]
Mary NICHOLSON
Hannah NICHOLSON
Thomas SYMONS

[Column 2]
Edward MAYO Jun
Damaris RATLIFF
Mary MORRIS
Rebecca SYMONS
Pressilla SYMONS
Mary NICHOLSON
Mary MAYO
Ruth GLAISTER
Naomy WHITE

[Column 3]
Samuel CHARLES
John SYMONS

[Column 3 cont.]
Matthew PRICHARD
Edward MAYO
Benja PRICHARD
Matthew ALLEN
Joseph NEWBY
John HENLEY
Stephen SCOTT

[Column 4]
W. EVERIGIN
Mary WHITE
  now EVERIGIN
Damaris WHITE
Elisabeth NIXON
Henry WHITE
Arnold WHITE
John MORRIS
Zachariah NIXON

Page 47 James MORGAN son of James of Pasquotank,
and Hannah GRIFFIN dau of Joseph of Chowan...16, 3m
called March, 1768...in Perquimons county at Piny

woods Meeting house...

[Column 1]
Jane BAILY
Joshua OVERMAN
Charles OVERMAN
Benjm. NEWBY
Martin[?] MORGAN

[Column 2]
Susannah BAILEY
Caleb BUNDY
Joseph NEWBY
Thomas OVERMAN
Joseph MURPHEY
Huldah BUNDY
Sarah NEWBY
John PIERCE
Benj. OVERMAN
James OVERMAN
Morgan OVERMAN
James GRIFIN

[Column 3]
Lydia GRIFFIN
Robert EXUM

[Column 3 cont.]
Charles MORGAN
Thomas SAINT
Sarah NEWBY
Guby WHITE
Amos GRIFFIN
William GRIFFIN
Wm. BONDS
Caleb ELLEOTT
Joseph WHITE

[Column 4]
James MORGAN
Hannah MORGAN
Thos. OVERMAN
John GRIFFIN
Hannah MORGAN
Demsey BUNDY
William GRIFFIN
Ruben GRIFFIN
John EVINS
Miriam GRIFFIN

Page 48   James MORGAN son of James, and Milisent
SYMONS dau of Jehosophat all of Pasquotank...2, 4m,
1783...at the Meeting House near the head of Little
River...

[Column 1]
Joshua BOSWELL
Elizabeth OVERMAN
Joseph GRIFFIN
Mary BUNDY
Miriam BUNDY
Miriam MORGAN
Martha GRIFFIN
Nathan MORRIS

[Column 2]
Sarah NICHOLSON
John SYMONS Senr
Jesse[?] SYMONS
Aron MORRIS
Gabriel COSAND
Absala SYMONS
Zach NIXON
Mary NIXON[?]
William ROBINSON
Sarah NICHOLIN[?]

[Column 2 cont.]
Rachel NICHOL[?]
Sarah BU[?]DEY
Charles OVERMAN

[Column 3]
James MORGAN
Miliscent X MORGAN
       her mark
Charles MORGAN
Benjm. MORGAN
Lemul[?] MORGAN
Nathan SYMONS
Sarah METCALFE
Lydia MORRIS
Josiah BUNDY
Margt. BUNDY
Penelope SYMONS
Elizabeth SYMONS
Chalkley ALBERTSON
Elizabeth ABERSON[?]

Page 50-51   Abel TRUBLOOD and Elizabeth PIPER Relict
of Nathan, both of Pasquotank...2, 12m, 1778...at
the Meeting House at Little River...

[Column 1]
Benjamin TRUBLOOD
Charles OVERMAN
Elizabeth OVERMAN
Joseph MCADAMS
Caleb TRUBLOOD
James NEWBY
Sarah NEWBY
Keziah NEWBY
Josiah BUNDY

[Column 2]
Caleb TRUBLOOD
Aaron TRUBLOOD
John NIXON
Barnaby NIXON
Joshua PERISHO
Thomas NICHOLSON
Sarah NICHOLSON
John TRUBLOOD

[Column 3]
Abel TRUBLOOD
Elizabeth TRUBLOOD

Page 52   Edmond WHITE son of Joseph decd of
Perquimans, and Mary MORRIS dau of Aaron of
Pasquotank...29, 2m, 1792...at the Meeting House
near Newbegun Creek...

[Column 1]
Mordecai MORRIS
James NIXON
Thomas PRITCHARD
Zachariah NIXON
John SYMONS
Charles OVERMAN
Ann MORRIS

[Column 2]
Aaron MORRIS Junr
Miriam MORRIS
Josiah WHITE
Sarah NICHOLSON
Sarah OVERMAN
Thomas MORRIS
Joseph MORRIS Junr
Seth WHITE

[Column 3]
Edmond WHITE
Mary WHITE
turn over for the rest
Page 53
[Column 4]
Miliscent WINSLOW
Susannah CLARY
Jonathan PRICE
Aaron MORRIS

[Column 4 cont.]
Lyddia MORRIS
William ROBINSON
Sarah WHITE
Wyke NEWBY
Samuel NIXON
[Column 5]
Elizabeth WHITE
Thomas NIXON
Joseph MORRIS
Mary NICHOLSON
Elizabeth SYMONS
Lovey SAWYER
Elizabeth RELFE
Elizabeth PRITCHARD
John NIXON
John PRITCHARD
[Column 6]
William OVERMAN
Christopher NICHOLSON
Malachi SAWYER
Fred. B. SAWYER
Josiah GILBERT
Thomas NICHOLSON
Abigail MORRIS
Margaret NIXON
Sarah ROBINSON

Page 54   Jonathan PRICE son of Benjamin decd, and
Susanna MORRIS dau of John decd, both of
Pasquotank...29, 11m, 1786...in their publick
Meeting place near Newbegun Creek...

[Column 1]
Susannah PRICE
Susannah CLARY
Mary NICHOLSON
[Column 2]
Aaron MORRIS
John PRICE
Betty PRICE
[Column 3]
Jonathan PRICE
Susannah PRICE
Page 55 [Column 4]
Thomas JORDAN

[Column 4 cont.]
Joseph MORRIS Junr
Jonathan MORRIS
Elizabeth SYMONS
[Column 5]
John H[?] SYMONS
Jeremiah GILBERT
Thomas PALIN
Christopher NICHOLSON
[Column 6]
Elizabeth NICHOL[?]
Sarah SYMONS
Mary MORRIS

Page 56   Isaac OVERMAN son of Ephraim decd, and
Isbel TRUEBLOOD Relict of Fisher TRUEBLOOD decd,
both of Pasquotank...16, 9m, 1792...near the narrows
of Pasquotank in their public meeting place...

[Column 1]
Ephraim TRUEBLOOD
Abel TRUEBLOOD
Mary TRUEBLOOD
[Column 2]
Margret TRUEBLOOD
Elezabeth TRUEBLOOD
Naomi NEWBY
Pennina TRUEBLOOD
James TATLOCK
[Column 3]
Isaac TRUEBLOOD

[Column 3 cont.]
Joshua PERISHO Ju[?]
John TRUEBLOOD
James RUSSELL
Joseph TRUEBLOOD
[Column 4]
Isaac OVERMAN
Isbel OVERMAN
David BOWLES
Kasia BOWLES
Miles TRUEBLOOD
Jonathan TRUEBLOOD

Page 58   Nathan MORRIS son of Joshua decd, and Mary
BELL dau of Lancelot, both of Pasquotank...28, 6m
(June), 1780...at the meeting house near Little
River Bridge...

[Column 1]
Thomas ROBINSON
Elizabeth ROBINSON
George WALTON
Mary WALTON
Sarah METCALFE
Josiah BUNDY
Mary BUNDY
John SYMONS Junr

[Column 3]
Sarah WILSON
Jesse HILL
Elisabeth PRICHARD
Nicholas NICHOLSON
Zachariah NIXON
Sarah NICHOLSON
Chalkley ALBERTSON
Josiah WINSLOW
Christopher NICHOLSON

[Column 1 cont.]
John SYMONS
Thomas JORDAN
Margaret JORDAN
Jacob HILL
Moses HILL
Isaac OVERMAN
    [Column 2]
Ruth MORRIS
Miriam MORRIS
Rebekah MORRIS
Joshua PERISHO
Devotion DAVIS
Peirce NIXON
Thomas NICHOLSON
Miriam MORRIS
Robt. MCMORINE
Saml. COOPER
Richard HARBERT
William ROBINSON
Sarah ROBINSON
Mary NIXON

[Column 3 cont.]
Mary NICHOLSON
Rachel WILSON
Abigail MORRIS
Thomas OVERMAN
Hannah MORGAN
    [Column 4]
Nathan MORRIS
Mary MORRIS
Lancelot BELL
Mary MORRIS Senr
Sarah BELL
Margaret BELL
Mordecai MORRIS
Jonathan MORRIS
Aaron MORRIS Junr
Clarkey POOL
Joseph NICHOLSON
John BELL
Benjamin WHITE
Aaron MORRIS Senr
Elisabeth SYMONS
Joseph WILSON

Page 62 John OVERMAN and Sarah PRICHARD Relict of
Matthew...26, 2m, 1783...in their Meeting place at
Newbegun Creek...

    [Column 1]
Caleb TRUEBLOOD
John SYMONS Junr
Jos. HENLEY
Aaron MORRIS
Lyddai MORRIS
Lyddai DAVIS
Jeremiah GILBERT
Jonathan MORRIS
Thomas PALIN
    [Column 2]
Sarah SMALL
Wm. OVERMAN
James OVERMAN
Mary SMITH
Zachariah MORRIS
James WHITE

    [Column 2 cont.]
Elizabeth TRUEBLOOD
Penelope SYMONS
Sarah OVERMAN
Rebekah GILBERT
    [Column 3]
John OVERMAN
Sarah OVERMAN
John SYMONS
Abram SYMONS
Rebekah PEARSON
Sarah METCALFE
Abel TRUEBLOOD
Elisabeth JONULE[?]
Elisabeth WHITE
Miriam PRICHARD
Ann WHITE
John SMITH

Page 66 John TRUEBLOOD son of Daniel of Pasquotank,
and Jemima NIXON dau of Phineas decd...4, 2m,
1778...at a meeting near the head of Little River...

[Column 1]
Thomas NICHOLSON
Phineas LAMB
Frederick NIXON
Phineas NIXON
Benjn. TRUEBLOOD
Joseph TRUEBLOOD
Hannah NIXON
James OVERMAN
Benjamin MORRIS
John MORRIS

[Column 2]
Sarah NICHOLSON
Benjn. ALBERTSON
Zachariah NIXON
William ARNOLD
Abigail NIXON
Sarah NEWBY
Josiah BUNDY
Joseph NICHOLSON

[Column 2 cont.]
Benjamin PRICHARD
Thomas JORDAN
Jane JORDAN
Sarah NICHOLSON

[Column 3]
John TRUEBLOOD
Jemima TRUEBLOOD
Daniel TRUEBLOOD
Mary NIXON
Sarah ALBERTSON
Pierce NIXON
Barnaby NIXON
Jesse TRUEBLOOD
Joshua PERISHO
Elizabeth PERISHO
Hannah NIXON
Kezia NIXON
Meliscent NEWBY

Page 67 James NIXON son of Frances decd, and
Elizabeth CLARY dau of Thomas PRITCHARD decd and
relict of William CLARY decd, both of Pasquotank
...24, 7m, 1793...at the meeting house near Newbegin
Creek...

[Column 1]
Sarah COPELAND
Chrisr. NICHOLSON
Aaron MORRIS

[Column 2]
Thomas NIXON
John CLARY
Rachel NIXON

[Column 3]
John PRITCHARD
Samuel NIXON
Thomas PRITCHARD

[Column 4]
James NIXON
Elizabeth NIXON

Page 68 Thomas PALIN son of Thomas decd, and
Elisabeth SQUIRES dau of Roger, both of Pasquotank
...27, 12m called December, 1775...at the meeting
place at Newbegun Creek...

[Column 1]
Ruth OVERMAN
Jacob HILL
Mary NICHOLSON
John PALIN

[Column 2]
Joseph HENLEY
Nathan OVERMAN
Aaron MORRIS

[Column 2 cont.]
Caleb SAWYER
John SYMONS Junr

[Column 3]
Thomas PALIN
Elisabeth PALIN
Henry PALIN
Mary PALIN
Elisabeth DAVIS

[Column 2 cont.]
Elisabeth PYPER
Aaron MORRIS Junr

[Column 3 cont.]
Archibald DAVIS

Page 70 Aaron MORRIS and Mary PRICHARD, both of
Pasquotank...20, 6m called August, 1724...in their
publick meeting place at Pasquotank...

[Column 1]
Hannah SCOTT
Naomi WHITE
Sarah GLAISTER
Ann PIKE
Joshua SCOTT
Mary MAYO Junr
Ann MAYO

[Column 2]
Joshua THOMES
Charles OVERMAN
Mary GLAISTER
Elisabeth TOMES
Elisabeth MORRIS
Elisabeth PRICHARD
Ruth GLAISTER

[Column 3]
Henry WHITE
Edward MAYO Senr
Mary MAYO
Stephen SCOTT
Thomas SYMONS
Edwd. MAYO Junr
Thomas PRICHARD

[Column 4]
Aaron MORRIS
Mary MORRIS
John MORRIS
Benjn. PRICHARD
Mary MORRIS Senr
Matthew PRICHARD
Zachariah NIXON
John SYMONS

Page 71 Josiah BUNDY son of Joseph, and Miriam
PERISHO dau of Joshua, both of Pasquotank...28, 2m,
1793...at a publick meeting held near the Narrows of
Pasquotank...

[Column 1]
Joshua PERISHO
Joshua PERISHO Junr
Caleb TRUEBLOOD
Joseph TRUEBLOOD
Joseph PERISHO
Aaron TRUEBLOOD
Josiah TRUEBLOOD
Aaron MORRIS

[Column 2]
Anna PERISHO
Penninah TRUEBLOOD

[Column 2 cont.]
Elizabeth TRUEBLOOD
Isbell OVERMAN
Miriam SCOTT
John TRUEBLOOD
Sarah TATLOCK
Isaac OVERMAN
James TATLOCK
John TRUEBLOOD

[Column 3]
Josiah BUNDY
Miriam BUNDY

Page 73 Joshua WHITE son of Joshua decd of
Perquimans, and Mary NICHOLSON dau of Christopher of
Pasquotank...27, 3m, 1793...at the meeting house
near Newbegun Creek...

[Column 1]
Mary MORE
John WHITE
John SYMONS
[Column 2]
Christopher NICHOLSON
Mary NICHOLSON

[Column 2 cont.]
Jacob WHITE
Zachariah WHITE
Thomas WHITE
[Column 3]
Joshua WHITE
Mary WHITE

Page 75 Joseph BUNDY son of Joseph decd, and
Elisabeth HENLEY dau of Joseph, both of
Pasquotank...1, 2m called February, 1786...in their
meeting place at Newbegun Creek...

[Column 1]
Zachariah NIXON
Mary PRICHARD
John WHITE
Thomas Elwood HENLEY
[Column 2]
John SYMONS Junr
Sarah SYMONS
Sarah METCALFE
Thomas PALIN
Moredecai MORRIS
Thomas JORDAN
James MUBAIN [?]
Joseph MORRIS
Mary LACKEY [?]
Elisabeth NICHOLSON
Susannah MORRIS
Meliscent NICHOLSON

[Column 2 cont.]
John NICHOLSON
[Column 3]
Joseph BUNDY
Elisabeth BUNDY
Joseph HENLEY
Mary NICHOLSON
Meliscent WHITE
Josiah BUNDY
Sarah SYMONS
Mary HENLEY
John OVERMAN
Sarah OVERMAN
Abigail MORRIS
Lucretia HENLEY
Aaron MORRIS
Lyddia MORRIS

Page 77 Joseph NIXON son of Pierce of Perquimons,
and Elizabeth MURPHEY dau of Joseph of
Pasquotank...26, 6m, 1793...at the meeting house
near the head of little river...

[Column 1]
Margaret NIXON
Wm. ALBERTSON
Jonathan MORRIS
John NIXON
Dorothy NIXON
Sarah NICHOLSON
Sarah COSAN
Margaret SAWYER
Miriam WHITE
Mary OVERMAN
Phinehas ALBERTSON
Sarah NIXON

[Column 2]
Joseph GRIFFIN
Martha GRIFFIN
Miles MURPHEY
Zach. NIXON
Josiah BUNDY
Ludia NIXON
John NIXON
William MURPHEY
Charles OVERMAN
Gabriel COSAN
Nathan MORRIS
Mary MORRIS

[Column 1 cont.]
Thomas NICHOLSON
Phinehas NIXON
Mary BUNDY
Josiah GILBERT
John MORRIS

[Column 2 cont.]
Wm. OVERMAN
[Column 3]
Joseph NIXON
Elizabeth NIXON

Page 79-80   John HENLEY son of Jesse of Randolf
County, and Keziah NIXON dau of Phinehas decd and
Mary NIXON of Perquimons...21, 9m, 1788...at the
meeting house at Little River...

[Column 1]
Abigail NIXON
Dorithy NIXON
Aaron COSAND
Mary HENLEY
Joseph HENLEY
Charles OVERMAN
Gabriel COSAND
[Column 2]
Naom NEWBY
Miriam WHITE
Phinehas ALBERT.
Thomas NICHOLSON
Sarah NICHOLSON
Zach. NIXON

[Column 2 cont.]
William ARNOLD
John NIXON Sen
Chalkley ALB.
Aaron MORRIS
[Column 3]
John HENLEY
Kezia HENLEY
Jemima TRUBLOOD
Hannah NIXON
B: ALBERTSON
John TRUBLOOD
Margaret NIXON
Mary ALBERTSON

Page 80-81   Enoch NEWBY son of Joseph of Pasquotank
decd, and Mary NICHOLSON dau of Nicholas of
Perquimons...27, 1m called January, 1790...at Little
River Meeting House in Perquimans County...

[Column 1]
Sarah COSAN
Nathan MORRIS
Joseph NICHOLSON
Zachariah NIXON
Josiah BUNDY
Charles OVERMAN
Caleb DAVIS
Caleb BUNDY
Sarah BELL
Mary BUNDY
[Column 2]
John NIXON
Margaret NIXON
Naomi NEWBY
Nathan NIXON
Samuel NIXON

[Column 2 cont.]
Mary BUNDY
Mary MORRIS
John SMITH
Mary SMITH
Samuel NICHOLSON
Gabril COSAND
[Column 3]
Enoch NEWBY
Mary NEWBY
Sarah NICHOLSON
Nicholas NICHOLSON
Christopher NICHOLSON
Caleb BUNDY
Dorothy NIXON
Thomas NICHOLSON
John BELL

Page 83 John NIXON son of Zachariah of Perquimons, and Ann MORRIS dau of Aaron Junr of Pasquotank... 1, 10m, 1794...near Newbegun Creek at their public meeting place...

[Column 1]
William ROBINSON
Chris. NICHOLSON
Chris. MORRIS
Thomas MORRIS
Joseph MORRIS
William NIXON
Miles JENNINGS
Henley NICHOLSON
William SYMONS
John PRITCHARD

[Column 2]
Mal[?] WILSON
Fred. B. SAWYER
Reub. KEATON
Thomas PRITCHARD
Benjn. PRITCHARD
Nathan MORRIS
Zach. NIXON
Thomas MORRIS
Thomas RELFE
Joshua MORRIS

[Column 3]
Wm. OVERMAN

[Column 3 cont.]
Edmd. WHITE
Thos. NICHOLSON
James NIXON
Mary NICHOLSON
Elizabeth SYMONS
John SYMONS
Aaron MORRIS Senr[?]
Charles OVERMAN
Mary OVERMAN
Meriam PRITCHARD
Mary MORRIS

[Column 4]
John NIXON
Ann NIXON
Zach. NIXON
Aaron MORRIS Junr
Miriam MORRIS
Sarah WHITE
Mary WHITE
Margaret MORRIS
Margaret NIXON
Lavinia SKINNER
Ann COTTON
Dolley COTTON

Page 84 Thomas JORDAN son of Joseph of Perquimons decd, and Margaret MORRIS dau of John of Pasquotank decd...29, 7m called July, 1778...at Newbegun Creek in their Publick meeting place...

[Column 1]
Sarah BELL
Sarah OVERMAN
Thomas BELL
Mordecai MORRIS
Nathan MORRIS
Rebekah PEARSON
Sarah PRICHARD

[Column 2]
Rebekah MORRIS
Eliphelet[?] SCOTT
Kezia MORRIS
Miriam MORRIS
Mary BELL
Benjn. PRICHARD

[Column 4]
Thomas JORDAN
Margaret JORDAN
Mary MORRIS
Aaron MORRIS
Margaret MORRIS
Ruth MORRIS
Joshua PERISHO
Lancelot BELL
Page 85
[Column 5]
John PRICE
John SYMONS Junr
Jacob HILL
Thomas PRICHARD

[Column 2 cont.]
William DAVIS
[Column 3]
Christopher NICHOLSON
Ruth OVERMAN
Mary NICHOLSON
Joseph JONES
Joseph NICHOLSON
Susannah MORRIS
Clarkey POOL

[Column 5 cont.]
Joseph HENLEY
James OVERMAN
Thomas OVERMAN
[Column 6]
David DAVIS
Robert HILL
Aaron MORRIS Jun
Martha BAILEY
Sarah NICHOLSON
Elizabeth GILBERT

Page 85-86 Isaac BOSWELL and Elizabeth NIXON dau of
John all of Perquimons...13, 8m, 1758...at our
public Meeting place on the head of Little River...

[Column 1]
William ALBERTSON
Joseph NICHOLSON
Josiah WINSLOW
John ANDERSON
Thomas ROBINSON
Joshua MOORE
Mehetabel NICHOLSON
Mary MORGAIN
Hannah BAILEY
Izebel BOSWELL
[Column 2]
Hannah MUNDEN
Thomas OVERMAN
Miriam NICHOLSON
Huldah HILL
Joshua PERISHO
Hannah MUNDEN
Elizabeth BOSWELL

[Column 2 cont.]
Thomas NICHOLSON
Josiah BUNDY
Joshua MORRIS
John HASKIT
[Column 3]
Isaac X BOSWELL
    his mark
Elizabeth X BOSWELL
    her mark
John NIXON
Miriam NEWBY
Zachariah NIXON
Hannah NIXON
Phinehas NIXON
Mary NIXON
Rebeckah NIXON
Mary MOORE

Page 86-87 Joshua BOSWELL son of Isaac, and Miriam
NICHOLSON dau of Joseph, both of Perquimons...6, 4m,
1783...at their Meeting house at Little River in
Perquimons County...

[Column 1]
Sarah NICHOLSON
Sarah BARBER
Mary NIXON
Isaac WILLIAMS
Demsey BUNDY
Thomas HENBY
Joseph BUNDY
Anna HASKIT

[Column 2 cont.]
Levi MUNDEN
Abigail NIXON
Henry WHITE
Samuel STAFFORD
[Column 3]
Joshua BOSWELL
Miriam X BOSWELL
    her mark

[Column 2]
John NIXON
Pierce NIXON
Josiah BUNDY
Joshua ALBERTSON

[Column 3 cont.]
Elizabeth BOSWELL
Isaac BOSWELL
Ruth BOSWELL
Zachariah NIXON
Mary NIXON

Page 89 William TRUEBLOOD son of Josiah of
Pasquotank, and Elisabeth NEWBY dau of Mark decd of
Perquimons...17, 8m, 1785...at the Old Neck Meeting
House in Perquimons...

[Column 1]
Phineas ALBERTSON
[Column 2]
Saml. NIXON
Zach. NEWBY
Caleb TRUEBLOOD
W: NEWBOULD
Joshua TRUEBLOOD
Thomas NIXON
Thomas NEWBY
Thomas SAINT
Joseph RATLIFF
Robert NEWBY

[Column 3]
William TRUEBLOOD
Elisabeth TRUEBLOOD
Jonathan NEWBY
Mourning NEWBY
Polley NEWBY
Kezia PRITLOW
Isaac OVERMAN
James NIXON
Mary NEWBY
Mary MOORE
William ARNOLD

Page 91 Isaac OVERMAN son of Ephraim, and Miriam
TRUEBLOOD dau of Josiah, both of Pasquotank...25,
1m, 1784...at a publick meeting held near the
Narrows of Pasquotank...

[Column 1]
Bailey JACKSON
Reuben MADREN
Judith MORRIS
James SCOTT
John TATLOCK
William PROBY
Demsey NASH
Polley WESTON
Susannah NORRIS
Peggy PROBEY
[Column 2]
Isabel TRUEBLOOD
Benjamin TRUEBLOOD
Elisabeth TRUEBLOOD
Joshua TRUEBLOOD
Jehu CARTWRIGHT
Ahaz CARTWRIGHT
Polley TRUEBLOOD

[Column 2 cont.]
Peggy TRUEBLOOD
James GRIFFIN
Thomas SIMPSON
Miriam PERISHO
Caleb TRUEBLOOD
[Column 3]
Isaac OVERMAN
Miriam OVERMAN
Ephraim OVERMAN
Josiah TRUEBLOOD
Ephraim OVERMAN Junr
William TRUEBLOOD
Abel TRUEBLOOD
Elisabeth TRUEBLOOD
Joshua PERISHO
Caleb TRUEBLOOD
Joseph TRUEBLOOD
John TRUEBLOOD
Mary TRUEBLOOD

Page 92   James NEWBY and Elisabeth DAVIS both of
Pasquotank...18, 5m called July, 1719...in the
publick meeting house at Little River...

[Column 1]
Matthew PRICHARD
Zachariah NIXON
Samuel NICHOLSON
John NEWBY
John SYMONS
Samuel CHARLES
Henry WHITE
Thomas SYMONS
Joseph COMMANDER
[Column 2]
Mary GLAISTER
Elisabeth NEWBY
Mary MORRIS
Elisabeth NIXON Junr
Robert DAVIS
Robert WHITE

[Column 2 cont.]
Arnold WHITE
Christ. NICHOLSON
Thomas MONTAGUE
William BUNDY
[Column 3]
James IN NEWBY
Elisabeth X DAVIS
(now NEWBY)
her mark
Damaris WHITE
Elisabeth WHITE
Rebecca WHITE
Ann NICHOLSON
Damaris SYMONS
Elisabeth NIXON
Elisabeth CHARLES

Page 93   John MORRIS son of Aaron and Mary, and Mary
NICHOLSON dau of Thomas and Mary...20, 1m called
January, 1762...in Perquimons County in their
publick Meeting place at Little River...

[Column 1]
Elisabeth NEWBY
Phineas NIXON
Sarah HENBY
Caleb TRUEBLOOD
Joseph MORRIS
Elisabeth NEWBY
Hannah OVERMAN
Elisabeth MORRIS
Susannah BAILEY
Rebekah NIXON
Bathsheba BAILEY
Elisabeth BUNDY
[Column 2]
Naomi NEWBY
Joseph NICHOLSON
Mary BUNDY
Susannah DODD
Christopher OVERMAN
John OVERMAN
Huldah HILL
Mary NICHOLSON Junr
Mehitabel NICHOLSON

[Column 3]
Joseph NEWBY Senr
Sarah BARROW
Nicholas NICHOLSON
Leah HOLLOWELL
Rachel WILSON
Eliphal SCOTT
Miriam HILL
Hannah OVERMAN
Samuel NEWBY
Miriam BELL
Thomas ROBINSON
[Column 4]
John MORRIS
Mary MORRIS
Aaron MORRIS
Mary MORRIS
Thomas NICHOLSON
Mary NICHOLSON
Joshua MORRIS
Christopher NICHOLSON
Joseph MORRIS Junr
Joseph BUNDY

[Column 2 cont.]
Miriam TRUEBLOOD
Miriam ROBINSON

[Column 4 cont.]
Lancelot BELL

Page 94 Aaron MORRIS son of Aaron of Pasquotank,
and Margaret NICHOLSON dau of Thomas of
Perquimons...30, 11m called November, 1768...at a
Meeting house near Little River Bridge...

[Column 1]
Sarah ALBERTSON
John SYMONS Junr
Aaron MORRIS
Joseph NICHOLSON
Mary NICHOLSON Junr
Zachariah NIXON Junr
Charles OVERMAN Junr
Chalkley ALBERTSON
James NEWBY
Jesse MOORE
Eliphalet SCOTT
Rowland ROBINSON
John WINSLOW
Joseph MCADAM
Thomas NICHOLSON

[Column 2]
John SYMONS
John MOORE
Sarah MOORE
Sarah BOGUE
Thomas ROBINSON
Margaret ROBINSON
Miriam ROBINSON
Helena ELLIOTT
Robert MUNDEN
Sarah ALBERTSON
Mary NIXON
Mordecai MORRIS
William ROBINSON
Samuel WINSLOW
Benjn. ALBERTSON

[Column 3]
Joshua PERISHO
Miriam PERISHO
Mary TRUEBLOOD
Elisabeth GILBERT
William ALBERTSON
Sarah ALBERTSON
Patience NEWBY
Deborah HEATON
Naomi NEWBY
Thomas GILBERT
Phineas NIXON
Samuel NEWBY
Thomas DRAPER
Elisabeth NEWBY

[Column 4]
Aaron MORRIS
Margt. MORRIS
Aaron MORRIS
Mary MORRIS
Thomas NICHOLSON
Mary NICHOLSON
Joshua MORRIS
John MORRIS
Mary MORRIS
Rachel WILSON
Leah HOLLOWELL
Lancelot BELL
Miriam BELL
Christopher NICHOLSON
Nicholas NICHOLSON
Sarah NICHOLSON

Page 95 Thomas SYMONS son of Thomas decd, and Jane
BUNDY dau of Josiah, both of Pasquotank...12, 12m,
1765...in their publick Meeting House at Little
River...

[Column 1]
Josiah BUNDY
Aaron MORRIS

[Column 2 cont.]
Jeremiah GILBERT
Ann SYMONS

[Column 1 cont.]
John SYMONS
Richard POOL
Nathan OVERMAN
[Column 2]
Jehoshaphat SYMONS
Elisabeth SYMONS

[Column 2 cont.]
John SYMONS
Rebekah LOW
[Column 3]
Thomas SYMONS
Jane X SYMONS
her mark

Page 96 Aaron MORRIS son of Aaron decd, and Lyddia
DAVIS widow dau of Jehoshaphat SYMONS decd, both of
Pasquotank...27, 2m, 1782...in their Meeting House
on Newbegun Creek...

[Column 1]
Mary SMITH
Sarah SYMONS
Thomas PALIN
Jonathan MORRIS
James OVERMAN
Samuel SMALL
Aaron TRUEBLOOD
Miriam PERISHO
[Column 2]
William ALBERTSON
Joseph HENLEY
Aaron MORRIS Junr
Sarah SYMONS
Mordecai MORRIS
Ann WHITE
Abigail MORRIS
Nathan MORRIS
John SMITH
[Column 3]
Nathan SYMONS

[Column 3 cont.]
Absala SYMONS
Penelope SYMONS
Melicent SYMONS
Elisabeth SYMONS
John SYMONS
Sarah PRICHARD
Rebekah PEARSON
Christopher NICHOLSON
Miriam WHITE
[Column 4]
Aaron MORRIS
Lyddia MORRIS
Mary MORRIS
Sarah METCALFE
Joshua PERISHO
Joseph MORRIS
John SYMONS Junr
Lyddia DAVIS
Rebekah MORRIS

Page 97 Charles OVERMAN son of Charles and Ann of
Perquimons, and Elisabeth LOW dau of John and Hannah
of Pasquotank...24, 4m, 1771...in their publick
Meeting House in Perquimons County at the head of
Little River...

[Column 1]
Mordecai NEWBY
Levi MUNDEN
Peirce NIXON
Nicholas NICHOLSON
Helena ELLIOTT
Mary NIXON
Jemima NIXON
Thomas NICHOLSON

[Column 3]
Mary JONES
Naomi NEWBY
Elisabeth NEWBY
Thomas ROBINSON
Zachariah NIXON
Sarah NICHOLSON
Rebekah LOW
Elisabeth ALLEN

[Column 1 cont.]
Thomas JORDAN
[Column 2]
Chalkley ALBERTSON
Joseph JONES
Joseph NICHOLSON
Barnabe NIXON
Aaron MORRIS
Thomas NICHOLSON
Phineas NIXON
Samuel NEWBY
Ephraim BAGLEY
Joseph NEWBY
Joseph NICHOLSON
John NIXON
Jane NIXON

[Column 3 cont.]
Christopher NICHOLSON
Mary NICHOLSON
Joseph MCADAM
Benjn. NEWBY
[Column 4]
Charles OVERMAN
Elisabeth X OVERMAN
her mark
Charles OVERMAN Senr
Ann OVERMAN
Joshua OVERMAN
Elisabeth OVERMAN
Francis ALBERTSON
Rebekah ALBERTSON
Barna LOW

Page 98 Joseph NICHOLSON son of Thomas, and Mehitabel NIXON dau of Zachariah decd...11, 6m called June, 1755...in Perquimons County in their publick Meeting place at the old neck...

[Column 1]
Nathan NEWBY
Francis NIXON
Joshua FLETCHER
Zachariah NIXON
Francis TOMS
Mathew JORDAN
Elisabeth JORDAN
Miriam NICHOLSON
Ralph FLETCHER
[Column 2]
Elisabeth SAINT
Richard SANDERS
Thomas PEIRCE
Joshua MOORE
Joseph NEWBY
Joseph ROBINSON
Christopher NICHOLSON
Aaron HILL
Jonathan PHELPS

[Column 3]
Miriam HILL
Francis TOMS
Dorothy PHELPS
Sarah ROBINSON
Kezia NEWBY
Elisabeth ELLIOTT
Joseph RATLIFF
Daniel SAINT
Joseph OUTLAND
[Column 4]
Joseph NICHOLSON
Mehitabel X NICHOLSON
her mark
Thomas NICHOLSON
Elisabeth NIXON
Mary NICHOLSON
Patience NEWBY
Thomas OVERMAN
Mary MOORE
Mourning NEWBY

Page 99 Lancelot BELL of Cumberland in Great [?], and Miriam NICHOLSON dau of Thomas of Perquimans...14, 3m called March, 1759...at Little River Meeting House...

[Column 1]
Elisabeth OVERMAN
John OVERMAN
Joshua MORRIS
Mary MORRIS
[Column 2]
John NIXON
Miriam HILL
Caleb TRUEBLOOD
John ANDERSON
Sarah ROBINSON
Saml. ANDERSON
Zachariah NIXON
Josiah WINSLOW
Thos. ROBINSON Junr
Thos. ROBINSON
Joshua OVERMAN
[Column 3]
Sarah ROBINSON Junr
Thos. OVERMAN
Miriam OVERMAN
Rachel WILSON
Leah HOLLOWELL
Mehetable NICHOLSON
Elisabeth NEWBY
Joseph NICHOLSON

[Column 3 cont.]
Joshua PERISHO
Thos. HOLLOWELL
[Column 4]
Thos. LOW
Aaron HILL
Nicholas NICHOLSON
Phineas NIXON
Patience NEWBY
Naomi NEWBY
Mary NICHOLSON Junr
Mary NICHOLSON y Younger
Huldah HILL
Ruth DAVIS
Mary NIXON
[Column 5]
Lancelot BELL
Miriam BELL
Thomas NICHOLSON
Mary NICHOLSON
Sarah BARROW
Joseph NEWBY
Samuel NEWBY
Joseph ROBINSON
Christopher NICHOLSON
Nicholas ASHBURN

Page 100 Joshua MORRIS son of Aaron of Pasquotank,
and Mary WINSLOW Relict of John of Perquimons...
1, 5m called May, 1755...at Symons Creek in their
public Meeting place at the Monthly Meeting...

[Column 1]
Ann SYMONS
Joseph BORDEN
Joshua SCOTT
Tabitha SCOTT
Joseph ROBINSON
[Column 2]
John SYMONS
Abel TRUEBLOOD
Jehoshaphat SYMONS
Daniel TRUEBLOOD
Mary MORRIS
Elisabeth NEWBY
Susannah NICHOLSON

[Column 3]
Benjn. MORRIS
Barnabe NIXON
Christ. NICHOLSON
Samuel NEWBY
John ROBINSON
Joshua TRUEBLOOD
Amos TRUEBLOOD
[Column 4]
Joshua MORRIS
Mary X MORRIS
  her mark
Aaron MORRIS
Thomas SYMONS
Thos. PRICHARD
Jos. PRICHARD

Page 101 Benjamin MORRIS son of Joseph, and
Elisabeth OVERMAN dau of Jacob both of
Pasquotank...9, 10m, 1763...at the upper Meeting
house on Little River...

[Column 1]
Miriam HILL
Joshua MORRIS
Elisabeth NEWBY
Mourning OVERMAN
Mourning TRUEBLOOD
Lancelot BELL
John SYMONS
Elisabeth MANN
[Column 2]
Joseph MORRIS
Jacob OVERMAN
Sarah MORRIS

[Column 2 cont.]
Samuel NEWBY
Phineas NIXON
Caleb TRUEBLOOD
Martha OVERMAN
[Column 3]
Benjamin MORRIS
Elisabeth X MORRIS
        her mark
Charles OVERMAN
Ann OVERMAN
Mary OVERMAN

Page 102 John NIXON son of John decd, and Jane
SYMONS widow, dau of Josiah BUNDY decd, all of
Perquimons...27, 3m called March, 1771...in the
County of Perquimons at the head of Little River...

[Column 1]
Thomas NICHOLSON
Josiah BUNDY
Joshua BUNDY
Caleb BUNDY
Sarah BUNDY
Mary NIXON
Mary LOW
[Column 2]
Thomas NIXON
Jane JORDAN
Hannah BAILEY
Charles OVERMAN
Thomas JORDAN
Jemima NIXON
Thomas NEWBY
Phineas NIXON

[Column 3]
Rebekah SYMONS
Susanna NIXON
Joseph NICHOLSON
Naomi NEWBY
Mary NIXON Senr
Elisabeth BUNDY
Sarah PEARSON
Joseph MCADAM
Margaret JORDAN
[Column 4]
John NIXON
Jane X NIXON
        her mark
Zachariah NIXON
Ezra NIXON
Elisabeth SYMONS
Thomas ROBINSON
Helena ELLIOTT

Page 103 Joseph NICHOLSON son of Thomas of
Perquimans, and Rebekah LOW Relict of John LOW of
Pasquotank...23, 6m called June, 1771...in
Pasquotank County...at Symons's Creek...

[Column 1]
Mary SYMONS

[Column 3 cont.]
Mary MORRIS

[Column 1 cont.]
Mary MORRIS
Miriam OVERMAN
Elisabeth GILBERT
   [Column 2]
Elisabeth OVERMAN
Caleb TRUEBLOOD
Sarah WOOD
John SYMONS Junr
Miriam GILBERT
Miriam WHITE
Nathan OVERMAN
Aaron MORRIS Minr
Clarkey MORRIS
Mordecai MORRIS
Elisabeth EARLL
Mirium WOOD[?]
   [Column 3]
Chalkley ALBERTSON
Mourning TRUEBLOOD
Rhoda WARNER
Mary LOWE
Benjn. WHITE
Anna WHITE
Huldah WHITE
Martha OVERMAN
Hannah MORGAN

[Column 3 cont.]
Charles OVERMAN
   [Column 4]
John MORRIS
Carolina NICHOLSON
Mathew PRICHARD
Miriam BELL
Margaret MORRIS
Aaron MORRIS
Mary NICHOLSON
Ruth OVERMAN
Rachel WILSON
Ann SYMONS
Zachariah NIXON
Thos. GILBERT
   [Column 5]
Joseph NICHOLSON
Rebekah NICHOLSON
Thomas NICHOLSON
John SYMONS
Lancelot BELL
Nicholas NICHOLSON
Abram SYMONS
Mary OVERMAN
Sarah HOLLOWELL
Mary MORRIS
Sarah PRICHARD

Page 104   John LOW and Rebekah SYMONS dau of Thomas
decd, both of Pasquotank...13, 6m called June,
1765...in their publick Meeting place near Symons's
Creek...

[Column 1]
Mary MORRIS
Martha OVERMAN
Ann SYMONS
Elisabeth SYMONS
Mary OVERMAN
Martha WHITE
   [Column 2]
Aaron MORRIS
Caleb TRUEBLOOD
Nathan OVERMAN

[Column 2 cont.]
Mary SYMONS
Richard WOOD
Thomas OVERMAN
   [Column 3]
John LOW
Rebekah LOW
Jehoshaphat SYMONS
Joseph NEWBY
Abram SYMONS
Thomas SYMONS

Page 106   Benjamin MORRIS son of Joseph of
Pasquotank, and Meliscent DRAPER dau of Peter decd
of Perquimons...15, 11m, 1772...at a General Meeting
at Wells's Meeting House...

[Column 1]
William ALBERTSON
Jesse BOGUE
Jonathan PEARSON
John SYMONS
Silas DRAPER
Thomas DRAPER
    [Column 2]
Sarah HOLLOWELL
Elisabeth PEARSON
Benjn. ALBERTSON
Icabod PEARSON
Robert EVANS
Miriam LACEY
John MOORE
Mary MOORE
Morgan PEARSON
    [Column 3]
Mary MORRIS
Sarah STIDHAM

[Column 3 cont.]
Mary HARRELL
Chalkley ALBERTSON
Rhoda PEARSON
Jemima PEARSON
Zachariah MORRIS
Sarah ALBERTSON
Miriam PEARSON
Jane BUNDY
    [Column 4]
Benjamin MORRIS
Meliscent MORRIS
Joseph MORRIS
Hannah DRAPER
Joseph DRAPER
Rachel WILSON
Moses BUNDY
Sarah MOORE
Sarah MORRIS
Miriam LAMB

Page 107 Nathan PEARSON of Pasquotank son of Peter,
and Rebekah NICHOLSON Relict of Joseph decd...26,
12m called December, 1773...in their Meeting house
near Little River Bridge in the County of
Perquimons...

[Column 1]
Chalkley ALBERTSON
Elisabeth ALBERTSON
Benjn. ALBERTSON
Sarah ALBERTSON
Charles OVERMAN
Elisabeth OVERMAN
Joseph MCADAM
Nathan OVERMAN
    [Column 2]
Thomas OVERMAN
Joseph NEWBY
Aaron MORRIS
John SYMONS Junr
Josiah BUNDY
John MOORE
Jonathan PEARSON
Levi MUNDEN
Ann SANDERS

[Column 3]
Sarah PRICHARD
Christopher NICHOLSON
Mary NICHOLSON
Zachariah NIXON
Jonathan PEARSON
Robert EVANS
Joshua MORRIS
William HILL
Mary HILL
    [Column 4]
Nathan PEARSON
Rebekah PEARSON
Peter PEARSON
John SYMONS
William PEARSON
Levi PEARSON
Miriam PEARSON
Elezebeth EVANS
Ruth WILSON
Mary MOORE
Abram SYMONS

Page 108   James GRIFFIN of Chowan, and Hannah
KINNEON of Perquimons...16, 5m called May, 1770...on
Suttons Creek in their publick Meeting place...

[Column 1]
Abigail ALBERTSON
John HENBY
Elisabeth WELLS
Mary ANDERSON
Samuel NEWBY
William ALBERTSON
John OVERMAN
Hannah OVERMAN
   [Column 2]
William BOGUE
Kezia BOGUE
Abigail COSAND
Benjn. KINNEON

[Column 2 cont.]
John ANDERSON
Chalkley ALBERTSON
Amos BOSWELL
Benjn. ALBERTSON
Sarah ALBERTSON
   [Column 3]
James GRIFFIN
Hannah / GRIFFIN
     her mark
James GRIFFIN
Elisabeth BOGUE
Benjn. NEWBY
Ruth NEWBY

Page 109   Nathaniel SUTTON of Perquimons, and
Elisabeth CHANCEY of Pasquotank...9, 1m, 1725/6...
at the publick meeting house at Pasquotank...

[Column 1]
Joshua SCOTT
Ruth GLAISTER
Isabel HENLEY
Sarah GLAISTER
Hannah BUNDY
Mary MAYO
   [Column 2]
William CHANCEY
Stephen SCOTT
Jos. REDING
Thomas DAVIS
Edwd. MAYO
Stephen DELEMAN

[Column 2 cont.]
Hannah SCOTT
Sarah OVERMAN
   [Column 3]
Nathaniel N S SUTTON
      his mark
Elisabeth SUTTON
William CHANCEY
Jer: SYMONS
Daniel CHANCEY
Zachariah CHANCEY
John SYMONS
George SUTTON

Page 110   John SYMONS Senr, and Elisabeth GILBERT
widow and Relict of Thomas decd both of
Pasquotank...23, 3m, 1780...at their Publick Meeting
house at Symons's Creek...

[Column 1]
Thomas JORDAN
Margaret JORDAN
Ruth MORRIS
Joshua WHITE
John SYMONS Junr
Nathan MORRIS
Jeremiah GILBERT

[Column 2 cont.]
Joseph MORRIS
Mary ADAMS
Ama NEWTON
Absala SYMONS
Jane JORDAN
   [Column 3]
John SYMONS

[Column 1 cont.]
Nathan SYMONS
Jonathan MORRIS
Thomas SYMONS
Benjn. PRICHARD
Thomas HILL
[Column 2]
Richard WOOD
Rebekah PEARSON
Miriam MORRIS
Mary MORRIS
Sarah PRICHARD
Aaron MORRIS
Aaron MORRIS Junr
Joshua PERISHO
Caleb TRUEBLOOD
Benjn. WHITE

[Column 3 cont.]
Elisabeth SYMONS
Martha OVERMAN
Miriam PERISHO
Mary LACKEY
Mary TRUEBLOOD
Sarah SYMONS
Rebecca MORRIS
Benjamin MORRIS
Meliscent MORRIS
Clarkey POOL
John SMITH
Mary SMITH
Daniel TRUEBLOOD
Nathan PEARSON
Abram SYMONS

Page 111   James NEWBY of Pasquotank planter son of
James, and Naomi WHITE dau of Henry Sr. decd...12,
5m, 1732...in the house of John NIXON, it being the
place where their fourth day meeting is...

[Column 1]
Jonathan WHITE
Aaron MORRIS
Mary MORRIS
Joseph GRIFFIN
Aaron HILL
[Column 2]
Benja: NEWBY
John MORRIS
Robert WHITE
Zachariah NIXON
Thos. MOUNTICUE
Nathaniel NICHOLSON
Thomas SYMONS
[Column 3]
Susannah SYMONS
Jane MARTIN
Elisabeth NIXON
William SANDERS
John SYMONS

[Column 3 cont.]
Michael MURPHEY
Joshua MOORE
Samuel NEWBY
[Column 4]
Elisabeth NIXON
Ann BUNDY
Ann SYMONS
Susannah NEWBY
Elisabeth NEWBY
Miriam WHITE
Susannah PIKE
[Column 5]
James I N NEWBY
    his mark
Naomi NEWBY
James NEWBY
Elisabeth MOUNTICUE
Mary MORRIS
Elisabeth THOMAS

Page 112   John SYMONS of Little River son of Thomas,
and Damaris WHITE dau of Henry, all of Pasquotank
precinct...8, 6m, 1700...at a publick meeting at the
house of Henry WHITE...

[Column 1]
Rebekah SYMONS
Elisabeth NIXON
Damaris WHITE
Elesabeth CHARLES
Damaris PEARSE
Henry WHITE
Thomas SYMONS
Jeremiah SYMONS
Robert WHITE
Arnold WHITE

[Column 1 cont.]
Will NEWBY
Joseph PEIRCE
James WHITE
Caleb BUNDY
John WHITE
James NEWBY
Stephen SCOTT
[Column 2]
John SYMONS
Damaris WHITE

Page 113 James WHITE son of Benjamin, and Ann
PRICHARD dau of Matthew decd, both of
Pasquotank...31, 10m, 1781...at Newbegun Creek in
their publick meeting place...

[Column 1]
Ephrm. OVERMAN
James WHITE
Aaron MORRIS
[Column 2]
Sarah SYMONS
Thomas OVERMAN
Thamar OVERMAN
Elisabeth PRICHARD
Jos. NICHOLSON
Obadiah OVERMAN
Benjn. PRICHARD
Joseph HENLEY
[Column 3]
Isaac OVERMAN
Nathan OVERMAN
Thomas SYMONS
John SMITH
Mordecai MORRIS

[Column 3 cont.]
Mary NICHOLSON
Sarah SYMONS
Mary SMITH
Penelope SYMONS
Abigail MORRIS
[Column 4]
James WHITE
Ann X WHITE
  her mark
Benjn. WHITE
Miriam WHITE
Sarah PRICHARD
Rebekah PEARSON
John SYMONS
John SYMONS J
Elisabeth SYMONS
Samuel WHITE

Page 115 Thomas NIXON son of Phineas, and Sarah
SMITH dau of John both of Perquimons...30, 3m called
March, 1768...in Perqus. County at their publick
meeting place at Wells's...

[Column 1]
Thomas NICHOLSON
Sarah NEWBY
Huldah NEWBY
Elisabeth LAMB
William HILL
Mary NICHOLSON Junr
Peirce NIXON

[Column 2 cont.]
Rebekah ARNOLD
Isaac LAMB
Joseph MCADAM
Charles OVERMAN Junr
Chalkley ALBERTSON
[Column 3]
Thomas NIXON

[Column 1 cont.]
Mary NEWBY
Mary NICHOLSON
Sarah HOLLOWELL
Samuel NEWBY
Elisabeth JORDAN
[Column 2]
Phineas NIXON
Rachel CANNON
Jeremiah CANNON
Sarah ALBERTSON
Benjn. ALBERTSON
Jemima NEWBY
William ARNOLD

[Column 3 cont.]
Sarah NIXON
Joseph SMITH
Samuel SMITH
Leah SMITH
William WHITE
Joseph WHITE
Joseph MURPHEY
John ANDERSON
Joseph HASKITT
Joseph SKINNER
Sarah CANNON
Rachel SMITH
Thomas NEWBY

Page 117   Josiah ALBERTSON son of Elihu, and Sarah
NEWBY dau of William, both of Perquimons...8, 3m
called March, 1775...at the Week day Meeting house
on Suttons Creek...

[Column 1]
John OVERMAN
Joseph ANDERSON
Aaron COSAN
Samuel ANDERSON
Hannah HENBY
Elisabeth ALBERTSON
Samuel CHARLES
[Column 2]
Francis ALBERTSON
Sarah ARNOLD
Absala WILSON
Gabriel COSAN
Wm. ALBERTSON
Eliza: HALL
Ben: ALBERTSON
Sarah ALBERTSON
[Column 3]
Lyddia ALBERTSON

[Column 3 cont.]
Sarah ALBERTSON
Sarah ALBERTSON
Abigail COSAND
Mary ALBERTSON
Chalkley ALBERTSON
Elisabeth ALBERTSON
Miriam ALBERTSON
Joshua MORRIS
[Column 4]
Josiah ALBERTSON
Sarah ALBERTSON
William NEWBY
Jemima NEWBY
Joshua ALBERTSON
Isabel MOORE
Elisabeth NEWBY
Thomas MOORE
John ANDERSON

Page 119   Henry WHITE of Perquimons weaver, and Ruth
KEATON of Pasquotank dau of Henry decd...23, 3m
called may, 1727...in their publick meeting house at
Pasquotank...

[Column 1]
Ruth GLAISTER
Anna Letitia LOW
Sarah GLAISTER
Mary MAYO

[Column 3 cont.]
Thomas SYMONS
Edwd. MAYO
Samuel BUNDY Sen
Thos. MONTAGUE

[Column 1 cont.]
Ephraim OVERMAN
Elisabeth TOMES
[Column 2]
Samuel NEWBY
John HENLEY
Zachariah CHANCEY
Joshua WHITE
Mary GLAISTER
Hannah SCOTT
[Column 3]
John SYMONS

[Column 3 cont.]
Joshua SCOTT
Stephen SCOTT
[Column 4]
Henry WHITE
Ruth R KEATON
 her mark
Naomi WHITE
Anne SYMONS
Miriam KEETON
John BUNDY
John MORRIS

Page 120 Thomas HALLAM of Perquimons, and Elisabeth
WHITE of Pasquotank widow...27, 2m, 1721...at the
meeting house at Little River...

[Column 1]
Mary WHITE
Rebecca SYMONS
Sarah DAVIS
Mary MORRIS
Elisabeth NIXON Senr
Rachel SYMONS
Ruth GLAISTER
John SYMONS
[Column 2]
Fran[?] FOSTER
Arnold WHITE
Arnold WHITE
Robert DAVIS
Joshua TOMES
Samuel CHARLES

[Column 2 cont.]
William SYMONS
Matthew ALLEN
Zachariah NIXON
Matthew PRICHARD
[Column 3]
Thomas T HALLAN
 his mark
Elisabeth / WHITE
 her mark
James NEWBY
John NEWBY
Damaris WHITE
Robert WHITE
Henry WHITE

Page 121 Thomas NICHOLSON son of Christopher, and
Sarah NIXON widow and relict of Thomas decd of
Perquimons...24, 1m called January, 1773... in
Perquimons County in their publick meeting place at
or near Little River Bridge...

[Column 1]
Jemima NIXON
Orpah GRIFFIN
Josiah BUNDY
Samuel NEWBY
Mordecai NEWBY
John SANDERS
Jane JORDAN
Thomas JORDAN

[Column 3]
William HILL
Chalkley ALBERTSON
Elisabeth ALBERTSON
Elisabeth NEWBY
Joshua MORRIS
Hannah OVERMAN
Zachariah NIXON
Mary NIXON

[Column 1 cont.]
Margt. JORDAN
Moses HILL
Mary NIXON
Sarah BUNDY
Ruth MUNDY
John NIXON
Jane NIXON
Rowland ROBINSON
John SMITH
[Column 2]
Anna WHITE
Joseph MCADAM
Helena MCADAM
Wm. ALBERTSON
Thomas ROBINSON
Margaret ROBINSON
Barnabe NIXON
Benjamin ARNOLD
Sarah ARNOLD
Benjamin WHITE
Hannah NIXON
John ANDERSON
John LANCASTER
Wm. MCCORMICK
Joseph JONES
Neil SNODGRASS
Benjn. ALBERTSON
Sarah ALBERTSON

[Column 3 cont.]
Sarah WHITE
Mourning TRUEBLOOD
John SYMONS
Caleb TRUEBLOOD
Kezia BOWLES
Carolina NICHOLSON
John OVERMAN
Gabriel COSAND
Joseph NEWBY
Benjamin NEWBY
Mary BUNDY
[Column 4]
Thomas NICHOLSON
Sarah NICHOLSON
Jeremiah CANNON
Rachel CANNON
Mary NIXON
Christopher NICHOLSON
Nicholas NICHOLSON
Sarah NICHOLSON
Rebekah NICHOLSON
Lancelot BELL
Mary NICHOLSON
Miriam BELL
Margaret MORRIS
Aaron MORRIS
Mary HILL
Penina NIXON
Kezia NIXON
Sarah HOLLOWELL

Page 122 Gabriel COSAND of Perquimons, and Sarah
NEWBY relict of Thomas decd of Pasquotank...29, 10m
called October, 1779...in the County of Perquimons
at their publick meeting place at Little River...

[Column 1]
Elisabeth NEWBY
Elisabeth TRUEBLOOD
Charles MORGAN
Joshua ALBERTSON
Benjn. MORGAN
Sarah NICHOLSON
[Column 2]
Miriam MORRIS
Jos. NICHOLSON
Josiah BUNDY
Thomas DRAPER

[Column 3 cont.]
Thomas OVERMAN
Orpa GRIFFIN
Benjn. TRUEBLOOD
Meliscent MORRIS
Mary ALBERTSON
Sarah ROBINSON
Sarah NICHOLSON
[Column 4]
Gabriel COSAND
Sarah S COSAND
her mark

[Column 2 cont.]
Charles OVERMAN
Elisabeth OVERMAN
Caleb TRUEBLOOD
   [Column 3]
Mary ALBERTSON

[Column 4 cont.]
Aaron COSAND
Hannah COSAND
John ANDERSON
Benjn. ALBERTSON

Page 123 Nehemiah WHITE, planter, and Thamar
OVERMAN, Spinster, dau of Charles, both of
Pasquotank...18, 3m called may, 1732...at their
publick meeting house, at Little River...

[Column 1]
John SYMONS
Miriam WHITE
Mary MORRIS Junr
   [Column 2]
Samuel NEWBY
Danl. CHANCEY
Thomas OVERMAN
Jonathan WHITE
John PIKE
William SANDERS
Aaron HILL
Aaron MORRIS

[Column 3]
Nehemiah WHITE
Thamar T O now WHITE
      her mark
Charles OVERMAN
Joshua WHITE
John OVERMAN
William CHANCEY
Abigail PIKE
Ann OVERMAN
Stephen SCOTT

Page 124 Jonathan WHITE son of Robert, and Anne
PIKE dau of Samuel decd, both of Albemarle
County...10, 2m called April, [1729]...at the
Publick meeting house on Little River...

[Column 1]
Mary GLAISTER
Mary MORRIS Senr
Mary MORRIS Junr
James NEWBY
Charles OVERMAN
John MORRIS
Jos. JORDAN
Stephen DELAMARE
Danll. CHANCEY
Jno. OVERMAN
Martha PRICHARD
   [Column 2]
Zachariah NIXON
Stephen SCOTT
Thomas MOUNTAGU
Benjn. PRICHARD
Thomas PRICHARD
Elisabeth PRICHARD

[Column 2 cont.]
Sarah WHITE
Abigail OVERMAN
Mary JORDAN
Isabel HENLEY
Elisabeth PRICHARD
   [Column 3]
Jonathan WHITE
Ann PIKE now WHITE
Robert WHITE
Jane WHITE
Arnold WHITE
Joseph WHITE
John PIKE
Mary PIKE
Henry WHITE
Joshua WHITE
Susanna PIKE
Jonathan PIKE

Page 125   James WHITE of Pasquotank, planter, and
Miriam KEATON, spinster, dau of Henry decd...9, 1m
called March, 1731/2...in their publick meeting
house at Little River...

[Column 1]
Jonathan WHITE
Miriam OVERMAN
Thomas SYMONS
Aaron MORRIS
Mary MORRIS
John SYMONS
  [Column 2]
Ann SYMONS
Ruth WHITE
Sarah POTTLE
James NEWBY
Samuel NEWBY

[Column 2 cont.]
James NEWBY
Richard THOMAS
John OVERMAN
  [Column 3]
James X WHITE
     his mark
Miriam X WHITE
     her mark
Elisabeth THOMAS
Robert WHITE
Abraham WHITE
Elisabeth SYMONS

Page 126   Samuel BUNDY of Pasquotank, and Jane MORE
of Perquimons...8, 4m, 1731...at the publick meeting
house at Perquimons...

[Column 1]
Zachariah NIXON
Gabriel NEWBY
Wm. HILL
Joseph NEWBY
Thomas HOLLOWELL
William HAIG
Jesse NEWBY
James NEWBY
Joshua ELLIOTT
  [Column 2]
Mary HENBY
Elisabeth NIXON
Leah SMITH
Rachel WHITE
Ann BUNDY
Sarah WHITE
Sarah HILL
Hannah ELLIOTT
Susannah GRIFFIN

[Column 2 cont.]
Elisabeth NEWBY
Huldah NEWBY
Elisabeth BLANCHET
Mary HILL
  [Column 3]
Samuel BUNDY
Jane J BUNDY
William MOORE
Abllam[?] MOORE
Joshua MOORE
John MOORE
Samuel BUNDY
Samuel MOORE
John SYMONS
Thomas WINSLOW
Joseph WINSLOW
William BOGUE
Elisabeth WINSLOW

Page 127   Jonathan MORRIS son of Joshua decd, and
Penelope SYMONS dau of Jehoshaphat decd, both of
Pasquotank...26, 1m, 1786...near Symons's Creek in
their publick meeting place...

[Column 1]
Miriam PERISHO
Jeremiah GILBERT
Abigail MORRIS
John OVERMAN
Sarah WILSON
Charles MORGAN
Martha OVERMAN
Betty PRICE
    [Column 2]
Jane JORDAN
Elisabeth SYMONS
Joshua PERISHO Junr
Christ. NICHOLSON
John SANDERS
Thomas SYMONS
Miriam PRICHARD
Jesse HILL
Mark DELON
Caleb TRUEBLOOD
Joshua PERISHO
Sarah OVERMAN
    [Column 3]
Mary MORRIS
Aaron MORRIS

[Column 3 cont.]
Absala SYMONS
Josiah BUNDY
Mary BUNDY
Benjamin WHITE
James MORGAN
Melisent MORGAN
Rebekah PEARSON
Sarah SYMONS
John PRICE
Thomas JORDAN
Margaret JORDAN
    [Column 4]
Jonathan MORRIS
Penelope MORRIS
John SYMONS Junr
Mordecai MORRIS
Nathan MORRIS
Jesse SYMONS
Zachariah MORRIS
Sarah METCALFE
Lyddia MORRIS
John SYMONS
Joseph WILSON

Page 129   Thomas MORRIS son of Joseph, and Lucretia
HENLEY dau of Joseph, both of Pasquotank...12, 11m,
1794...in a publick assembly near newbegun Creek...

[Column 1]
Joseph MORRIS
Aaron MORRIS Jur
James WHITE
Nathan MORRIS
Aaron MORRIS
John SYMONS
John JOHNSTON
Thomas MORRIS
Sarah SYMONS
Joshua MORRIS
Mark MORRIS
    [Column 2]
Sarah ROBINSON
Elizabeth TRUEBLOOD
Miriam MORRIS
Abigail MORRIS
Sarah OVERMAN

[Column 2 cont.]
Mary MORRIS
Penninah PRITCHARD
Hannah PRITCHARD
Sarah MORRIS
    [Column 3]
Joseph HENLEY
Joseph MORRIS Senr
Joseph BUNDY
Joshua TRUEBLOOD
Mary TRUEBLOOD
Margaret HENLEY
Elisabeth TRUEBLOOD
Margaret MORRIS
William ROBINSON
    [Column 4]
Thomas MORRIS
Lucretia MORRIS

Page 130   Jonathan MORRIS son of Joshua decd, and
Lydia NIXON dau of John, both of Perquimons...19,
10m called October, 1794...at their public meeting
place near the head of Little River...

[Column 1]
Wm. OVERMAN
Caleb BUNDY
Nathan BUNDY
Zach. NIXON
[Column 2]
Mary MORRIS
Abigail MORRIS
Mary MORRIS
Miriam BELL
John NIXON
Josiah BUNDY
[Column 3]
John NIXON
Mordecai MORRIS
Nathan MORRIS
Elizabeth WILSON
Sarah NIXON
John MORRIS
[Column 4]
Jonathan MORRIS
Lydia MORRIS

Page 131
[Column 5]
Abigail NIXON
Joseph NIXON
Joshua MORRIS
Josiah GILBERT
[Column 6]
Margaret NIXON
Caleb TRUEBLOOD
Charles OVERMAN
Mary OVERMAN
[Column 7]
Sarah BELL
Nathan BAGLEY
Chas. NICHOLSON
Abraham SAUNDERS
[Column 8]
Josh. PERISHO
Stephen WHITE
Wm. MURPHY

Page 133   Obadiah SMALL son of Obadiah of
Pasquotank, and Elisabeth SYMONS dau of Thomas decd
of Perquimons...21, 1m, 1786...at their meeting
house near the head of Little River in Perquimons...

[Column 1]
Jonathan MORRIS
Absala SYMONS
Levi MUNDEN
Penelope SYMONS
Thos. SYMONS
Thos. NICHOLSON Junr
[Column 2]
Sarah SYMONS
Caleb BUNDY
Sarah BUNDY
Geo: METCALFE
Abra SYMONS
John SYMONS
Gabriel COSAND

[Column 3]
Thomas OVERMAN
Sarah METCALFE
Mary BUNDY
Meliscent MORGAN
Obadiah SMALL
Samuel SMALL
Sarah SMALL
[Column 4]
Obadiah SMALL
Elisabeth SMALL
Josiah BUNDY
Lyddia BUNDY
Kezia NIXON
Benjamin SMALL
Lyddia NIXON

Page 134 Caleb TRUEBLOOD son of Amos, and Mary
CONNER dau of John decd all of Pasquotank...18, 10m
called October, 1758...at Newbegun Creek in their
publick meeting place...

[Column 1]

Thomas NICHOLSON
Thomas PRICHARD
Aaron MORRIS
Daniel TRUEBLOOD
Joseph PRICHARD
Mary TRUEBLOOD
Mary SCOTT

[Column 2]

Tobitha SCOTT
Benj. MORRIS
Mary MORRIS
Joseph JORDAN
Penelope JORDAN
Josiah TRUEBLOOD

[Column 2 cont.]

Joshua TRUEBLOOD
John OVERMAN

[Column 3]

Jemima TRUEBLOOD

[Column 4]

Caleb TRUEBLOOD
Mary TRUEBLOOD
Eilizabeth JEPSON
Saml. SCOTT
Miriam OVERMAN
Joshua SCOTT
Abel TRUEBLOOD
Robt. WILLIAMS

Page 136 Caleb BUNDY son of Caleb decd of
Pasquotank, and Rachel NICHOLSON dau of Nicholas of
Perquimons...30, 11m called November, 1785...in
Perquimons County in their publick meeting place
near the head of Little River...

[Column 1]

Thomas HOLLOWELL
Toms WHITE
Elisabeth SANDERS
Nathan MORRIS
Mary MORRIS
Thomas OVERMAN
Lemuel[?] MORGAN

[Column 2]

Jonathan PRICE
Meliscent MORGAN
Zachariah NIXON
Gabriel COSAND
Miriam WHITE
Charles OVERMAN
Sarah OVERMAN
Elisabeth OVERMAN

[Column 3]

Hannah SANDERS
Demsey BUNDY
John BUNDY
Elisabeth HALL
Sarah NICHOLSON
Mary BUNDY
Josiah BUNDY
Thomas ROBINSON

[Column 4]

Caleb BUNDY
Rachel BUNDY
Miriam BUNDY
Nicholas NICHOLSON
Sarah NICHOLSON
Benjamin BUNDY
Sarah BUNDY
Mary NICHOLSON
Eliphel[?] SCOTT

Page 138 William CLARY son of Barnes decd of Surry
Virginia, and Elisabeth NICHOLSON Relict of Joseph
late of Pasquotank and dau of Thomas PRICHARD of

Pasquotank...28, 2m called February, 1787...in their
publick meeting place near Newbegun Creek...

[Column 1]
John SYMONS Junr
Christopher NICHOLSON
Miriam CLARY
Joseph MORRIS
Mordecai MORRIS
Christ. NICHOLSON

[Column 2]
John PRICHARD
Joseph BUNDY
David Gilbert TODD
Mary MORRIS Junr
Joseph HENLEY
Aaron MORRIS Junr

[Column 3]
Elisabeth PRICHARD
Thomas PRICHARD Junr
Miriam MORRIS
Aaron MORRIS
Lyddia MORRIS
Thomas PALIN

[Column 4]
William CLARY
Elisabeth CLARY
John CLARY
Charles CLARY
Zachariah WHITE
Susannah CLARY

Page 140 Joseph MORRIS son of Benjamin of
Pasquotank, and Sarah HASKITT dau of John of
Perquimons...21, 5m, 1788...in the County of
Perquimons in their publick meeting place at Little
River...

[Column 1]
John NIXON
Thomas HILL
John NIXON
Charles OVERMAN
Sarah NICHOLSON

[Column 2]
Abraham BOSWELL
Mary MORRIS
Levi MUNDEN
Sarah METCALFE
Jesse HASKITT
Josiah BUNDY

[Column 2 cont.]
Gabriel COSAN

[Column 3]
Joseph MORRIS
Sarah X MORRIS
  her mark
Ann HILL[?]
Mary HASKITT
Benjamin MORRIS
Nathan MORRIS
Christopher WILSON
William HASKITT

Page 142 Jesse HILL son of Aaron decd, and Mary
PRICHARD dau of Benomi decd, both of Pasquotank...
1, 3m called March, 1786...near Newbegun Creek in
their publick meeting place...

[Column 1]
Meliscent NICHOLSON
Anne HILL
Elisabeth BUNDY

[Column 2]
Mary NICHOLSON
Elisabeth GYPSON
Miriam MORRIS

[Column 3 cont.]
Aaron MORRIS
Lyddia MORRIS
Aaron MORRIS
Elias ALBERTSON
Jonathan PRICE
Sarah OVERMAN
John SYMONS

[Column 2 cont.]
Joseph BUNDY
Sarah CAPS
Samuel WHITE
Ann WHITE
Susanna MORRIS
   [Column 3]
Jonathan MORRIS
Susannah PRICE

[Column 4]
Jesse HILL
Mary HILL
Joseph HENLEY
Thomas HILL
Thomas PALIN
Samuel SMALL
Obadiah SMALL
Elisabeth SMALL

Page 143 Thomas OVERMAN son of Thomas, and Sarah
HALL dau of Stephen, all of Pasquotank...28, 4m,
1784...in their publick meeting House in Perquimons
County near the head of Little River...

[Column 1]
Demsey BUNDY
Charles OVERMAN
Elisabeth OVERMAN
Joshua ALBERTSON
Nathan MORRIS
Mary MORRIS
   [Column 2]
Josiah BUNDY
Peirce NIXON
John NIXON
Elisabeth BOSWELL
Jane NIXON
Caleb BUNDY

[Column 3]
Zachariah NIXON
Sarah NICHOLSON
Sarah BARBER
Joseph MCADAM
Ruth BOSWELL
William ROBINSON
   [Column 4]
Thomas OVERMAN
Sarah X OVERMAN
   her mark
Elisabeth HALL
Miriam MORRIS
Mary[?] NEWBY
   (Widow of M[?])

Page 144 Zachariah NIXON son of John and Dorithy
decd, and Mary WHITE dau of John and Sarah all of
Perquimons...15, 9m called September, 1771...at
their publick meeting place at Wells's...

[Column 1]
Benjamin SMITH
Chalkley ALBERTSON
Thos. WHITE
Peirce NIXON
Caleb TOMS
   [Column 2]
Benjn. ALBERTSON
Rosanna HARMON
Phineas NIXON
Thomas SAINT
Sarah HOLLOWELL

[Column 4]
Miriam ROBINSON
Miriam MURDAUGH
Helena ELLIOTT
Rachel WHITE
Wm. WHITE
Miriam PEIRCE
Elisabeth SAINT
Thos. OVERMAN
   [Column 5]
Zachariah NIXON
Mary NIXON

[Column 3]
Elisabeth WHITE
Joseph MCADAM
Josiah WHITE
Elisabeth JONES
Joseph WHITE
Daniel SAINT

[Column 5 cont.]
Sarah WHITE
John NIXON
Jane NIXON
William WHITE
Ezra NIXON

Page 146 Charles WHITE son of John and Sarah of
Perquimons, and Sarah EARLL dau of John and
Elisabeth of Pasquotank...20, 1m, 1788...at their
Publick Meeting House near Symons's Creek...

[Column 1]
Margaret NIXON
Thomas SYMONS
Naomi NEWBY
Pleasant WINSLOW
Mary TRUEBLOOD
Christ. NICHOLSON
Matthew SYMONS

[Column 2]
Mary MORRIS
Rachel WHITE
Elisabeth WALTON
Absala SYMONS
Caleb TRUEBLOOD
William ROBERTS
Joshua TRUEBLOOD

[Column 3]
John NIXON
Pharaby WHITE
John SYMONS
Jonathan PRICE
Benjn. WHITE
Thomas NICHOLSON

[Column 4]
Charles WHITE
Sarah WHITE
John EARLL
Elisabeth EARLL
Sarah WHITE
Thomas WHITE
Sarah SYMONS

Page 148 Josiah BUNDY son of Joseph decd, and
Elisabeth MORGAN dau of Charles decd, both of
Perquimons...26, 12m, 1781...at their publick
meeting place at Little River...

[Column 1]
Zachariah NIXON
Sarah NICHOLSON
Sarah BARBER
Mary NIXON Ju[?]

[Column 2]
John NIXON
Joshua BOSWELL
Peirce NIXON
Nathan BAGLEY
Joshua ALBERTSON

[Column 2 cont.]
Jesse HASKITT
Elizabeth BOGUE

[Column 3]
Josiah BUNDY
Elisabeth X BUNDY
            her mark
Josiah BUNDY
John HASKITT
Caleb BUNDY
Joseph BUNDY

Page 150 Aaron MORRIS son of Benjamin decd of
Pasquotank, and Miriam ROBINSON dau of Joseph late
of Nansemond Virginia decd...28, 3m called March,

1773...in their publick meeting place at the house
of Thomas TROTTER in the County of Nansemond...

[Column 1]

Samuel BUFKIN
[?] NEWBY Jr[?]
Jacob F RANDOLPH
George SPARLING
John JORDAN Junr
William ROBINSON
Mourning ROBERTS

[Column 2]

Eady DAKERS
Elezebeth MOORE
Moses BUNDY
Sarah HOLLOWELL
Sarah NICHOLSON
Joseph RANDOLPH
Elizabeth JORDAN
Thomas NEWBY

[Column 2 cont.]

Demsey CONNER
Thomas TROTTER
Robert JORDAN

[Column 3]

Aaron MORRIS
Miriam MORRIS
Elisabeth TROTTER
Sarah ROBINSON
Aaron MORRIS
Ann ROBINSON
Rachel ELLIOTT
Chalkley ALBERTSON
Richard BACON Senr
Thomas NICHOLSON Junr
Margret WHITE
Lyddia SHEPHERD

Page 151   John PRICE and Bettey ANDERSON dau of John
and Sarah of Perquimons...9, 10m, 1782...in
Perquimons County in their publick meeting place at
Old Neck...

[Column 1]

Samuel ANDERSON
Josiah ALBERTSON
Sarah ALBERTSON
Samuel CHARLES
Gulielma CHARLES
William CLARY
Aaron COSAND
Joshua FLETCHER

[Column 2]

Nathan NEWBY
Elisabeth RATLIFF
Chalkley ALBERTSON
Jonathan PRICE
William PRICE

[Column 2 cont.]

John ANDERSON
Ralph FLETCHER
Molley FLETCHER
Ann CORNWELL

[Column 3]

John PRICE
Betty -- PRICE
   her mark
John ANDERSON
John TOMS
Mary TOMS
Susannah PRICE
Mary ANDERSON
Cornelius RATLIFF

Page 153   James WHITE son of James, and Elisabeth
SYMONS dau of Joseph decd both of Pasquotank...23,
10m, 1768...in Pasquotank County at Symons's Creek..

[Column 1]

Josiah TRUEBLOOD
Benja. WHITE Senr
Aaron MORRIS Senr
Benja. WHITE Senr

[Column 2]

James / WHITE
   his marke
Elisabeth / WHITE
   her mark

[Column 1 cont.]
John WHITE
Aaron MORRIS Junr
Sarah COMMANDER
John SYMONS
John SYMONS Junr
John MORRIS
Richard WOOD
Sarah WOOD
Mary MORRIS
Elizabeth GILBERT
Clarkey MORRIS

[Column 2 cont.]
Miriam OVERMAN
John OVERMAN
Mourning TRUEBLOOD
Miriam WHITE
Jane SYMONS
Miriam GILBERT
Miriam TRUEBLOOD
Rebekah LOW
Mary OVERMAN
Sarah PRICHARD
Caleb TRUEBLOOD

Page 154 Richard THOMAS of Perquimons, and
Elisabeth HALLAM of Pasquotank a widow of Little
River...23, 6m, 1722...at the Meeting house at
Little River...

[Column 1]
John BUNDY
Christopher NICHOLSON
Henry WHITE
John HENBY
Robert WHITE
John MORRIS
Thomas OVERMAN
John OVERMAN
Abraham WHITE

[Column 2]
Richard T THOMAS
        his mark
Elisabeth HALLAM now
        her X mark THOMAS
James NEWBY
Rebekah WHITE
Damaris WHITE
Elisabeth NEWBY
John SYMONS
Sarah WHITE

Page 155 John TRUEBLOOD son of Daniel of
Pasquotank, and Mary GRIFFIN dau of William decd of
Perquimons...1, 8m, 1793...at the meeting house at
Piny Woods...

[Column 1]
John SMITH
Joshua PERISHO Junr
Exum NEWBY
Jesse TRUEBLOOD
Isaac OVERMAN
Martha NEWBY
Joshua TRUEBLOOD
Josiah WHITE
Caleb WINSLOW
Thomas WHITE
Isaac WILSON
Caleb WHITE
John CORNWELL
Amos GRIFFIN
Jacob WINSLOW

[Column 2 cont.]
Margaret MOORE
Betsy WHITE
Sarah WHITE
Mary WHITE
Lydia CORNAL
Milescent WHITE
Nathan PARKER
Josiah GRIFFIN Junr
Edmund WHITE
[Column 3]
John TRUEBLOOD
Mary X TRUEBLOOD
        her mark
Elizabeth GRIFFIN
Gulielma GRIFFIN

[Column 1 cont.]
Thomas WHITE
    [Column 2]
Sarah WHITE
Rebeccah WHITE
Sarah PARK
Sarah PARKER
Ann WINSLOW

[Column 3 cont.]
James GRIFFIN
Elizabeth LAMB
William GRIFFIN
John WINSLOW Junr
Job PARKER
Samuel MOORE

Page 156 William MURPHEY son of Joseph decd of
Pasquotank, and Martha OUTLAND dau of Joseph decd of
Perquimons...19, 11m, 1794...in perquimons county in
their public Meeting place Near the head of Little
River...

[Column 1]
Zach. NIXON
Josiah BUNDY
Miles MURPHEY
Dorothy MURPHEY
Jos. NICHOLSON
Margaret NIXON[?]
Nathan MORRIS
Gabriel COSAN
Jonathan MORRIS
Margaret MURPHEY
Gulielma BUNDY
    [Column 2]
Sarah OUTLAND
Sarah NICHOLSON
Ann NIXON
Mary NEWBY
Lydia EVANS
Mary OVERMAN

[Column 2 cont.]
Miriam GRIFFIN
Joseph NIXON
Mary PRICE
Enoch NEWBY
    [Column 3]
Martha GRIFFIN
Joseph GRIFFIN
Wm. OVERMAN
Miriam WOOD
Thos. NICHOLSON
Josiah GILBERT
Mary MORRIS
Josiah GILBERT
Phinehas NIXON
Sarah NIXON
    [Column 4]
William MURPHEY
Martha MURPHEY

Page 157 Nathan BUNDY son of Josiah of Perquimons,
and Ruth MORRIS dau of Aaron Senr of Pasquotank
...19, 8m called August, 1795...at their public
meeting place near Newbegun Creek Bridge...

[Column 1]
Sarah PRITCHARD
Mary NICHOLSON
Thomas NICHOLSON
Joshua PERISHO
Mordecai MORRIS
Aaron MORRIS
[?] OVERMAN
    [Column 2]
Elizabeth SYMONS

[Column 2 cont.]
Hannah PRITCHARD
John SYMONS
    [Column 3]
Josiah BUNDY
Aaron MORRIS
Lydia MORRIS
Lydia MORGAN
Mary BUNDY
Thomas MORRIS

[Column 2 cont.]
Abraham SAUNDERS
Miriam MORRIS
Lydia DAVIS
Mark MORRIS
Josiah BUNDY
Penninah PRITCHARD

[Column 3 cont.]
Christopher MORRIS
Isaac MORRIS
[Column 4]
Nathan BUNDY
Ruth BUNDY

Page 158   William DAVIS son of Thomas, and Lyddia
SYMONS dau of Jehoshaphat decd, both of
Pasquotank...26, 4m called April, 1780...at Newbegun
Creek in their publick meeting place...

[Column 1]
Joseph HENLEY
Aaron MORRIS
Aaron MORRIS Junr
Henry PALIN
Christ. NICHOLSON
Mary NICHOLSON
John SMITH
James OVERMAN
[Column 2]
Abba MORRIS
Miriam GILBERT
Jonathan MORRIS
Mordecai MORRIS
Joseph NICHOLSON
Sarah PRICHARD
Rebeckah PEARSON[?]
Mary MORRIS
Elisabeth NICHOLSON
Sarah DAVIS
Nathan MORRIS

[Column 3]
Jeremiah GILBERT
Elisabeth SYMONS
Miriam MORRIS
Mary SMITH
Henry PENDLETON
Thos. PRICHARD
Ann OVERMAN
Elisabeth PRICHARD
Sarah SYMONS
Thos. SYMONS
[Column 4]
William DAVIS
Lyddia DAVIS
Thomas DAVIS
Lyddia DAVIS
Sarah METCALFE
Mary BUNDY
Ann LOWRY
John SYMONS Junr
Nathan SYMONS
John SYMONS

Page 159   Peter SYMONS son of John decd, and Mary
MACE dau of Francis and Anne, all of Pasquotank
...10, 7m, 1746...at the meeting house on the head
of Little River...[recorded 10, 8m, 1789]

[Column 1]
Joseph ROBINSON
Mary ROBINSON
Joshua WHITE
Hannah COLLISON
Lyddia SYMONS
Miriam HILL
[Column 2]
John NIXON

[Column 2 cont.]
Mary WHITE
Joshua MORRIS
[Column 3]
Peter SYMONS
Mary X SYMONS
  her mark
Francis MACE
Anna MACE

[Column 2 cont.]
Barnabe NIXON
Mary MORRIS
Ruth BUNDY
Robert DAVIS
John SYMONS
Mary SYMONS
Miriam SYMONS
Ann SYMONS

[Column 3 cont.]
Samuel NEWBY
Thomas SYMONS
Damaris SYMONS
Joseph NEWBY
Aaron MORRIS
Thomas OVERMAN
Naomi NEWBY

Page 160 Peter SYMONS son of John of Pasquotank,
and Priscilla BUFFKIN dau of Leaven of Nansemond,
Virginia...10, 8m, 1750...at the meeting house on
the head of Little River...

[Column 1]
Benja MORRIS
John WINSLOW
Joseph SYMONS
Miriam SYMONS
Nathan OVERMAN
Mary NICHOLSON
Rachel HILL
Phineas NIXON

[Column 2]
John ANDERSON
Samuel NEWBY
Jehoshaphat SYMONS
Mary MORRIS
Ann SYMONS
Miriam SYMONS

[Column 2 cont.]
Mary OVERMAN
Mary WILLIAMS
Joseph SCOTT
John ROBINSON

[Column 3]
Peter SYMONS
Priscilla X SYMONS
          her mark
John BUFFKIN
Dorithy NIXON
Lyddia MATTHEWS
John SYMONS
John NIXON
Joseph NEWBY
Thomas SYMONS

Page 161 Thomas NICHOLSON son of Christopher decd,
and Sarah SYMONS relict of John decd, both of
Pasquotank...19, 3m called March, 1800...at their
publick meeting near Newbeggin Creek...

[Column 1]
Will: SYMONS
Aaron MORRIS
John NIXON
Chrisr. NICHOLSON
Mary SHEPHERD
Aaron MORRIS
Edmd. WHITE
Zach. NIXON Junr
C.[?] SHEPHERD
Will: ROBINSON
Rob[?]
Robt. PERRY

[Column 2 cont.]
Eliza PARKER
Margaret MORRIS
Pharaba SYMONS
Will NIXON
Mary NICHOLSON
Mary WHITE
Miriam MORRIS
James NEWBY
Will: T. MUSE
Phins. NIXON
Henly NICHOLSON

[Column 2]
Zacha. NIXON
Mary NIXON

[Column 3]
Thomas NICHOLSON
Sarah NICHOLSON

Page 162   Benjamin BUNDY son of Caleb decd, and
Sarah BELL dau of Lancelot decd, both of
Pasquotank...23, 10m, 1785...at their meeting house
near Little River in the County of Perquimons...

[Column 1]
Joseph BUNDY
Caleb TRUEBLOOD
Thomas OVERMAN
James MORGAN
Abigail NIXON
Thomas JORDAN
Margaret JORDAN
[Column 2]
Chalkley ALBERTSON
Sarah ALBERTSON
Sarah BARBER
Miriam WHITE
Peninnah NIXON
Penelope SYMONS
Ruth BOSWELL
Aaron MORRIS
Benjn. WHITE
Jonathan MORRIS

[Column 3]
Elisabeth HALL
Caleb BUNDY
Caroline BELL
Rachel NICHOLSON
Thomas HILL
Mourning NEWBY
Lyddia BUNDY
Sarah NICHOLSON
Elisabeth SYMONS
Christ. NICHOLSON
[Column 4]
Benjamin BUNDY
Sarah BUNDY
Miriam BUNDY
John WINSLOW
Demsey BUNDY
Mary MORRIS
Sarah NICHOLSON
Nathan MORRIS
Sarah OVERMAN

Page 164   Charles MORGAN of Pasquotank, and Lyddia
BUNDY dau of Josiah of Perquimans...25, 1m,
1786...in their publick meeting place near the head
of Little River in the County of Perquimons...

[Column 1]
Aaron MORRIS
Sarah COSAND
Jonathan MORRIS
Caleb TRUEBLOOD
Jesse SYMONS
Levi MUNDEN
Thomas JORDAN
George METCALFE
[Column 2]
Caleb BUNDY
Sarah BUNDY
Sarah SYMONS
James MORGAN

[Column 3]
Thomas OVERMAN
James OVERMAN
Elisabeth SMALL
Obadiah SMALL
Zachariah NIXON
Sarah MORGAN
Ruth BOSWELL
[Column 4]
Charles MORGAN
Lyddia MORGAN
Sarah BUNDY
Mary BUNDY
Elisabeth SYMONS

[Column 2 cont.]
Melescent MORGAN
Gabriel COSAND
Sarah BUNDY

[Column 4 cont.]
Sarah METCALFE
Penelope SYMONS
Lyddia MORRIS
Demsey BUNDY

Page 165 Samuel STAFFORD son of Samuel, and Abigail COSAND dau of Gabriel, all of Pasquotank...31, 10m, 1781...in their publick meeting House in Perquimons County, near the head of Little River...

[Column 1]
Aaron LOW
Sarah NICHOLSON
Charles OVERMAN
Elisabeth OVERMAN
[Column 2]
Miriam MORRIS
Mary NEWBY
Geo: DILLWYN[?]
Sarah NICHOLSON
Rachel CANNON
Mary BUNDY
Elisabeth SYMONS
Miriam NICHOLSON
Rachel NICHOLSON
Jane BAILY

[Column 2 cont.]
Elisabeth BAILY
[Column 3]
Samuel STAFFORD
Abigail X STAFFORD
    her mark
Gabriel COSAND
Sarah COSAND
Josiah STAFFORD
Naomi WADSWORTH[?]
Joel[?] PARKER
Orpah LOW
Demsey BUNDY
Zachariah NIXON
Josiah BUNDY

Page 166 Henry PALIN son of Thomas decd, and Ann OVERMAN dau of Nathan decd, both of Pasquotank...27, 9m called September, 1780...at Newbegun Creek in their publick Meeting place...

[Column 1]
Joseph NICHOLSON
Elisabeth NICHOLSON
John PRICE
James WHITE
Robert HILL
Jesse HILL
Archibald DAVIS
Jonathan MORRIS
Thomas SYMONS
Joseph MORRIS
James OVERMAN
Jesse CARTWRIGHT
[Column 2]
Miriam WHITE
Lyddia DAVIS
John SYMONS

[Column 2 cont.]
Jeremiah GILBERT
Joseph WILSON
Elisabeth SYMONS
Rebekah MORRIS
Miriam PALIN
Elisabeth PALIN
[Column 3]
Hanry PALIN
Ann PALIN
Thomas PALIN
Miriam GILBERT
Nathan OVERMAN
Thomas OVERMAN
Jacob HILL
Thomas HILL
Mordecai MORRIS

[Column 2 cont.]
Ephraim OVERMAN
Sarah PRICHARD
Meliscent MORRIS

[Column 3 cont.]
Abigail MORRIS
Mary OVERMAN

Page 168 Aaron TRUEBLOOD of Pasquotank son of
Joshua decd, and Meliscent BLANSHARD dau of Ephraim
of the County of North Hampton...18, 9m, 1785...at a
publick meeting held at Richsquare in North Hampton
County...

[Column 1]
Joshua TRUEBLOOD
Caleb TRUEBLOOD
Jonathan BLANSHARD
Mary PARKER[?]
    [Column 2]
Aaron TRUEBLOOD
Meliscent TRUEBLOOD
Ephraim BLANSHARD

[Column 2 cont.]
Alice BLANSHARD
Jesse BLANSHARD
Peninah BLANSHARD
Ephraim BLANSHARD
John PEELLE
Richd. JORDAN
Thos. WHITE

Page 170 John COX son of John, and Miriam MORRIS
dau of Joseph, both of Pasquotank[?]...26, 9m,
1782...in their publick meeting place at Symons's
Creek...

[Column 1]
Richard WOOD
John SYMONS
Jesse TRUEBLOOD
Nathan MORRIS
Elisabeth MORRIS
Miriam PERISHO
Josiah GILBERT
Mary TRUEBLOOD
John PRICE
James OVERMAN
    [Column 2]
Joseph MORRIS
Joshua PERISHO
Jeremiah GILBERT
Caleb TRUEBLOOD
Jonathan MORRIS

[Column 2 cont.]
Rebekah MORRIS
Rachel WILSON
Joseph WILSON
Sarah WILSON
Susannah PRICE
    [Column 3]
John X COX
  his mark
Miriam X COX
  her mark
Jemima WHITE
Sarah COX
Mary MORRIS
Martha WHITE
Elisabeth SYMONS
Susannah PRICE

Page 171 Charles MORGAN son of James, and Susannah
NIXON dau of Barnabe decd, both of Perquimons...1,
5m called May, 1771...in Perquimons County in their
Publick meeting house on the head of Little River...

[Column 1]
Thos. OVERMAN

[Column 3]
John NIXON

[Column 1 cont.]
Benjamin MORGAN
Joseph MCADAM
Phineas NIXON
Thomas NICHOLSON
Thomas ROBINSON
[Column 2]
Benjamin NEWBY
Hannah NIXON
Elisabeth NEWBY
Elisabeth SYMONS
Barnabe NIXON
Benjn. OVERMAN
Ezra NIXON
James MORGAN

[Column 3 cont.]
Charles OVERMAN
Mary NIXON
Hannah NIXON
Helena ELLIOTT
Jemima NIXON
Thomas OVERMAN
[Column 4]
Charles MORGAN
Susannah MORGAN
Susannah BAILEY
Naomi NEWBY
Zachariah NIXON
Mary NIXON
Rebekah NIXON
Thomas NIXON

Page 172   Caleb TRUEBLOOD son of Josiah of
Pasquotank, and Peninnah BLANSHARD dau of Ephraim of
North Hampton...16, 10m, 1785...at a publick meeting
held at Richsquare in North Hampton County...

[Column 1]
Thomas WHITE
Pharaby KNOX
Margrate KNOX
Mary PARKER
Jesse BLANSHARD
Anna GRIFFIN
Peninnah PARKER
[Column 2]
Caleb TRUEBLOOD
Peninnah TRUEBLOOD

[Column 2 cont.]
Alice BLANSHARD
Ephraim BLANSHARD
Jonathan BLANSHARD
Melescent TRUEBLOOD
Isabel TRUEBLOOD
Joseph TRUEBLOOD
Richd. JORDAN
Jno. PEELLE
Ephraim BLANSHARD
Josiah BROWNE

Page 174   Peirce NIXON son of Phineas, and Peninnah
SMITH dau of John decd, both of Perquimons...16, 12m
called December, 1770...in the County of Perqs. in
their publick meeting place at Well's...

[Column 1]
Elisabeth SAINT
Thomas NICHOLSON
John NIXON
Jemima NIXON
Margaret WHITE
Caleb TOMS
Isaac LAMB
[Column 2]
Jos. WHITE
Hercules SAINT

[Column 2 cont.]
Sarah ALBERTSON
Zachariah NIXON
Thomas SAINT
[Column 3]
Peirce NIXON
Peninnah NIXON
Daniel SAINT
Barnabe NIXON
Benjan. ALBERTSON
Jemima NEWBY

[Column 2 cont.]
John ANDERSON
William TOWNSEND
Phineas NIXON
Rachel CANNON
Rachel SMITH
Leah SANDERS

[Column 3 cont.]
Kezia NIXON
Chalkley ALBERTSON
Zach. NEWBY
Mordecai MORRIS
Benjamin SMITH

Page 175 Zachariah WHITE son of Joshua of
Perquimans decd, and Miliscent NICHOLSON dau of
Christopher of Pasquotank...31, 3m, 1790...in their
publick Meeting place at Newbegun Creek...

[Column 1]
Eilzh. TOMBS
Vilette GLASGO
Aaron MORRIS
[Column 2]
Lyda HALL
Chrisr. NICHON.
James WHITE
Lyda[?] MORRIS
[Column 3]
Moorning WHITE
Aaron MORRIS
Francis WHITE

[Column 3 cont.]
Miriam MORRIS
Mary MORRIS
[Column 4]
Mary NICHOL
Joseph HENLEY
John NICHOLSON
Thomas NICHOLS
Mary WHITE
[Column 5]
Zachariah WHITE
Meliscent WHITE
Christopher NICH.

Page 178 Ephraim OVERMAN son of Ephraim, and Ruth
TRUEBLOOD dau of Josiah both of Pasquotank...28, 2m,
1782...at a publick meeting held near the narrows of
Pasquotank...

[Column 1]
Jonathan BLANSHARD
Jesse TRUEBLOOD
Joshua TRUEBLOOD
[Column 2]
Abel TRUEBLOOD
Elisabeth TRUEBLOOD
Miriam PERISHO
Joshua PERISHO
David BOLES
Benjn. TRUEBLOOD
Elisabeth TRUEBLOOD
Miriam PERISHO
John TRUEBLOOD
Jemima TRUEBLOOD
Margaret TRUEBLOOD
Fisher TRUEBLOOD
Isabel TRUEBLOOD

[Column 2 cont.]
Peninah BLANSHARD
[Column 3]
Ephraim OVERMAN
Ruth OVERMAN
Ephraim OVERMAN
Josiah TRUEBLOOD
Elisabeth TRUEBLOOD
Thomas OVERMAN
Caleb TRUEBLOOD
Miriam TRUEBLOOD
Isaac OVERMAN
Keziah BOLES
William TRUEBLOOD
Joseph TRUEBLOOD
Mary TRUEBLOOD
Sarah MCKEEL

Page 180 Jeremiah GILBERT, and Rebekah MORRIS
Relict of Joshua, both of Pasquotank...20, 10m
called October, 1782...near Symons's Creek in their
publick meeting place...

[Column 1]
James OVERMAN
Jonathan MORRIS
Thomas OVERMAN
Abram WHITE
Thomas JORDAN
Margaret JORDAN
Jane JORDAN

[Column 2]
Elisabeth SYMONS
Caleb TRUEBLOOD
Richard WOOD
Benjn. WHITE
John SYMONS Junr
Nathan OVERMAN
Nathan MORRIS
Mary MORRIS

[Column 3]
Miriam COX
Melisent MORRIS
Ann WHITE
Margaret DAVIS
Miriam MORRIS
Mary OVERMAN
Sarah PRICHARD
Aaron MORRIS

[Column 4]
Jeremiah GILBERT
Rebekah X GILBERT
         her mark
Jemima WHITE
John SYMONS
Mordecai MORRIS
Joshua PERISHO
Mary MORRIS
Miriam PERISHO

Page 182 Joseph WILSON son of John of Pasquotank
decd, and Sarah CHARLES dau of Samuel of Perquimans
decd...11, 6m called June, 1780...at Symons's Creek
in their Publick Meeting place...

[Column 1]
Wm. CLARY
Nathan MORRIS
Nathan SYMONS
Elisabeth SYMONS
Jacob HILL
Melisent MORRIS
Moses HILL

[Column 2]
Thomas PRITCHARD
Thomas OVERMAN
Miriam MORRIS
Thomas JORDAN
Margaret JORDAN
Hannnah HENBY
Melicent MORRIS
Melicent NICHOLSON

[Column 3]
Richard WOOD
Huldah WHITE

[Column 3 cont.]
Mary NICHOLSON
Mary MORRIS
Clarkey POOL

[Column 4]
Lancelot BELL
Jesse HILL
Chalkley ALBERTSON
Benjamin WHITE
Henry PAILEN
Caleb TRUBLOOD
Anne TRUBLOOD
Robert HILL

[Column 5]
Joseph WILSON
Sarah WILSON
Rachel WILSON
Elisabeth CHARLES
Samuel CHARLES
John ANDERSON

[Column 3 cont.]
Aaron MORRIS Junr
Aaron COSAN
Christopher NICHOLSON

[Column 5 cont.]
Elisabeth ANDERSON
Thomas HILL
Joseph ANDERSON

Page 184 Cyprian SHEPHERD son of John of Gates
County, and Mary MORRIS dau of Mordecai of
Pasquotank...16, 7m called July, 1795...in their
public meeting place near Symons's Creek...

[Column 1]
James WHITE
Thomas OVERMAN
Sarah WHITE
John SYMONS
Sarah SYMONS
Joseph WILSON
Sarah WILSON
Josiah GILBERT
Thomas JORDAN
Margaret JORDAN
Elizabeth SYMONS
Margaret WHITE
Thomas GILBERT

[Column 2]
Hannah PRITCHARD
Penninah PRITCHARD
Reuben KEATON
Wm. ROBINSON
Thomas MORRIS
Thomas MORRIS
John MORRIS
Nathan MORRIS
Jonathan MORRIS
Thomas MORRIS

[Column 2 cont.]
Josiah GILBERT
Wm. FAULK
Stephen ROGERS
Thos. ACKISS
Hosea SMITH

[Column 3]
Mordecai MORRIS
Abigail MORRIS
Stephen SHEPHERD
Sarah OVERMAN
Priscilla SHEPHERD
Sarah PRITCHARD
Joshua MORRIS
Mary ANDERSON
Nathan MORRIS
Nathan OVERMAN
Elizabeth OVERMAN
Rebeckah GILBERT
Benjamin ANDERSON
Miriam MORRIS

[Column 4]
Cyprian SHEPHERD
Mary SHEPHERD

Page 185 Benjamin ANDERSON son of Joseph decd, and
Mary MORRIS dau of Joshua decd, both of
Perquimons...22, 2m, 1795...at the meeting House at
Little River...

[Column 1]
Sarah GILBERT[?]
Sarah ANDERSON
Sarah TOMS
Mary MORRIS
Armejah LAM
Joshua MORRIS

[Column 2]
Jeremiah GILBERT

[Column 3]
John. ANDERSON
Mordecai MORRIS
Nathan MORRIS
John MORRIS
Joseph WILSON
Sarah WILSON

[Column 4]
Benjamin ANDERSON

[Column 2 cont.]
Josiah BUNDY
Abby[?] MORRIS
Anna PRITCHARD
Gabrial COSAN
Elizabeth SYMONS

[Column 4 cont.]
Mary ANDERSON
Mary ANDERSON
Rebecah GILBERT
Chalkley ALBERTSON

Page 186   Joshua B. MORRIS son of Mordecai, and
Margaret HENLEY dau of Joseph decd, both of
Pasquotank...28, 4m, 1796...at their publick meeting
place neare the narrows of Pasquotank...

[Column 1]
Penninah PRITCHARD
Nathan OVERMAN
Elizabeth OVERMAN
Elizabeth NEWBY
Elizabeth TRUEBLOOD
Mary NICHOLSON
Abigail TRUEBLOOD
Hannah PRITCHARD
Anna PRITCHARD
Josiah GILBERT
Abigail GILBERT
Thomas MORRIS
Mary MORRIS

[Column 2]
Mordecai MORRIS
Cyprian SHEPHERD
Nathan MORRIS
Joshua TRUBLOOD
Thomas RELF
Thomas OVERMAN
Leucretia MORRIS
Mary TRUBLOOD
Naomi [?]
William ROBINSON
[Column 3]
Josua MORRIS
Margaret MORRIS

Page 187-188   Francis WHITE of Pasquotank son of
John decd of Perquimons, and Sarah JORDAN dau of
Josiah decd of Perquimons...8, 10m called October,
1794...at their publick meeting place at Wells's...

[Column 1]
Samuel NIXON
Margaret NIXON
Joseph MOORE
Robert WATKINS
Susanna CLARY
William WHITE
John PRITCHARD
Thomas WHITE
Joseph WHITE
Thomas ROTINSON
Christofer NICHOLSON
[Column 2]
Elizabeth JORDAN
Lidia CORNWELL
Dorathy WATKINS

[Column 2 cont.]
Thomas JORDAN
Josiah JORDAN
Exum NEWBY
John CLARY
William WHITE
Mourning WHITE
Lida WHITE
Ann CORNWELL
Sarah COPELAND
Josiah WHITE Junr
Thomas WHITE
Thomas NICHOLSON
[Column 3]
Frances WHITE
Sarah WHITE

Page 189   Miles MURPHEY son of Joseph, and Dorothy
EVANS dau of Robert, all of Pasquotank...28, 4m,
1790...at their public meeting place near the head
of Little river...

[Column 1]
Jonatn. MORRIS
Sarah COSAND
Nathan MORRIS
Alexr. BROWN
Benjn. MORGAN
[Column 2]
William MURPHEY
William HALL
Zach. NIXON
Josiah BUNDY
John NIXON Junr
Naomi NEWBY
Joseph EVANS
Thomas EVANS
Mary LASEY
William PEARSON
Sarah EVANS

[Column 2 cont.]
Mary MORRIS
Gabriel COSAND
[Column 3]
Lydia EVANS
Martha GRIFFIN
Robert EVENS
James MORGAN
John BUNDY
Nathan NIXON
Elizabeth MURPHEY
Joseph GRIFFIN
Elizabeth SAWER
Margaret SAWER
Rachel JISSOP
[Column 4]
Miles MURPHEY
Dorothy MURPHEY

Page 191   John LAURENCE son of John and Mary of
North Hampton County, and Margaret NIXON dau of
Zachariah and Mary of Perquimons...22, 1m, 1797...at
the usual meeting place at little river in
perquimons County...

[Column 1]
Elizabeth NIXON
Sarah NICHOLS
Enoch NEWBY
William NIXON
Mary MORRIS
Eizabeth NEWBY
Nicholas NICHN.
Margaret [?]
Nathan MORRIS
Sarah NIXON
[Column 2]
Zacha. NIXON
Elizabeth MORRIS
Exum NEWBY
Jos. PARKER
James NEWBY
Naom NEWBY
Jas. NIXON

[Column 2 cont.]
Charles OVERMAN
Mary OVERMAN
[Column 3]
Jno. NIXON
Josiah BUNDY
Jno. NIXON
Ann NIXON
Sarah NICHOLSON
Sarah NIXON
Benjamin BUNDY
Abraham SANDERS
[Column 4]
Jno. LAURENCE
Margare LAURENCE
Thomas WHITE
Jno. D. WHITE
Margaret WHITE
Za.[?] NIXON

Page 192   Joshua PERISHO son of Joshua of
Pasquotank, and Elizabeth GRIFFIN dau of William
decd of Perquimons...11, 8m, 1796...at the Meeting
house in the Piney woods...

[Column 1]
Mary WHITE
Rebecca WHITE
James WHITE
Caleb WINSLO[?]
David WHITE
   [Column 2]
Sarah WHITE
Hosea SMITH
Exum NEWBY
John CORNWELL
Mary ALBERTSON
   [Column 3]
John TRUBLOOD
James GRIFFIN

[Column 3 cont.]
William GRIFFIN
Exum NEWBY
Josiah WHITE
   [Column 4]
Joshua PERISHO
Elizabeth X PERISHO
        her mark
Joshua PERISHO
Joshua PERISHO
Miriam LAMB
Gulielma COPELAND
Mary TRUBLOOD
Esther COPELAND

Page 193   Josiah TRUBLOOD, and Abigail OVERMAN dau
of Ephraim decd both of Pasquotank...26, 12m,
1795...at a publick meeting...near the narrows of
Pasquotank County...

[Column 1]
Timothy COTTEN
Thamar OVERMAN
Isaac OVERMAN
Ruth OVERMAN
   [Column 2]
Joshua TRUBLOOD
Mary TRUBLOOD
Stephon TRUBLOOD
John TRUBLOOD

[Column 2 cont.]
John TRUBLOOD
Mary TRUBLOOD
   [Column 3]
Josiah TRUBLOOD
Abigail TRUBLOOD
Josiah TRUBLOOD
Abel TRUBLOOD
Caleb TRUBLOOD

Page 195   John PRICE, and Elizabeth PALIN relict of
Thomas decd both of Pasquotank...22, 9m, 1790...in
their publick Meeting place near New Biggin Creek...

[Column 1]
Benjamin PRICE
[?] LACY[?]
   [Column 2]
John PRICE
Elizabeth PRICE
Page 196
   [Column 3]
Miriam WHITE
Susannah LACY

[Column 3 cont.]
Francis WHITE
Elizt. THOMBLINSON
Elizabeth SYMONS
Absala SYMONS
   [Column 4]
M John SYMONS
Isaac BOSWELL
Thomas SAINT
Elias ALBERTSON

[Column 3 cont.]
Mary SQUIRS
Mary TOMES
Mary NEWBY
Mary WINSLOW
Miriam PRICHARD

[Column 4 cont.]
Elizabeth EARL
Josiah GILBERT
Christopher NICHOLSON
Frances WHITE
Abraham SYMONS

Page 199   Josiah GILBERT son of Jeremiah of
Pasquotank, and Dorothy NIXON dau of John of
Perquimons...19, 4m, 1797...at their Meeting House
near the head of Little River in Perquimons...

[Column 1]
James NEWBY
Thomas GILBERT
Aaron L. GILBERT
Nathan MORRIS
George BUNDY
Samuel BUNDY
Naomi NEWBY
Thomas NICHOLSON
Mariam WHITE
[Column 2]
Mary OVERMAN
William NIXON
Enoch NEWBY
Mary NEWBY
John NIXON
Jeremiah GILBERT
Rebeckah GILBERT

[Column 2 cont.]
Sarah NIXON
Josiah BUNDY
Mary BUNDY
Abigal GILBERT
John BELL
Nathan MORRIS
[Column 3]
Josiah GILBERT
Dorothy GILBERT
Mary MORRIS
Charles OVERMAN
Nathan BUNDY
Gulielma MORRIS
Benjamin MORGAN
John MORRIS
Lydia MORGAIN

Page 200   John WILSON son of Joseph of Perquimons,
and Milisent TRUEBLOOD dau of Fisher decd of
Pasquotank...1, 8m called August, 1799...in their
publick Meeting House near the narrows of
Pasquotank...

[Column 1]
Myriam OVERMAN
Elizabeth TRUEBLOOD
Joseph PERISHO
Elizabeth TRUEBLOOD Junr
Aaron TRUEBLOOD
Joshua PERISHO
James TATLOCK
Mary GLASCO
Peter FORBES
Stephen TRUEBLOOD
Elizabeth JACKSON

[Column 2]
Isaac OVERMAN
Isabel OVERMAN
Lydia WILSON
Isaac TRUEBLOOD
Jonathan TRUEBLOOD
Abel TRUEBLOOD Senr
Kezia BOWLES
Josiah TRUEBLOOD Senr
Caleb TRUEBLOOD
Joshua TRUEBLOOD
Naomi TRUEBLOOD

[Column 3]
John WILSON
Milesent WILSON

Page 201   Jonathan TRUEBLOOD son of Fisher decd of
Pasquotank, and Miriam WILSON dau of Joseph decd of
Perquimons...22, 12m, 1799...in their publick
Meeting House at Piney woods...

[Column 1]
David WHITE
Exum NEWBY
Caleb WINSLOW
[Column 2]
William WHITE
Polly RATCLIFF
Robert WHITE
Joseph WILSON
Saml. WILSON
Thos. WHITE
Thos. MOORE
Seth WHITE
Jonathan WHITE
Josiah GRIFFIN
[Column 3]
Caleb WINSLOW

[Column 3 cont.]
Samuel MOORE
Reuben PERRY
Isaac BYRIAN
Martha NEWBY
Sarah WHITE
Margaret MOORE
Pharabe PARKER
Penninah PARKER
Thomas WHITE
Exum NEWBY
[Column 4]
Jonathan TRUEBLOOD
Miriam TRUEBLOOD
Elizabeth WILSON
Sarah ELLIOTT
John WILSON

Page 202   Josiah GILBERT son of Thomas decd of
Pasquotank, and Sarah OUTLAND dau of Joseph decd of
Perquimons...31, 12m called december, 1794...in
Perquimons County in their public meeting place near
the head of Little River...

[Column 1]
Josiah BUNDY
Jas. NEWBY
Wm. OVERMAN
Matthew SYMONS
Sarah SYMONS
Thomas NICHOLSON
Charles OVERMAN
[Column 2]
* Aaron MORRIS Senr[?]
Gabriel COSAN
Mary MORRIS minr[?]
Thomas MORRIS
William MURPHY
Elizabeth NIXON
Benjamin PRICE
Mary PRICE

[Column 3 cont.]
Jonathan MORRIS
Martha MURPHY
Mary MORRIS
John NIXON
Ann NIXON
Sarah WILSON
Sarah NICHOLSON
[Column 4]
Elizabeth SYMONS
Jeremiah GILBERT
Samuel ANDERSON
Lydia EVANS
Josiah GILBERT
Rebecca GILBERT
Nathan MORRIS
John MORRIS

[Column 2 cont.]
* Z.[?] NIXON
[Column 3]
Thomas GILBERT
Abigail GILBERT

[Column 5]
Josiah GILBERT
Sarah X GILBERT
    her mark

Page 203-204 Joseph PARKER son of Job, and
Elizabeth MORRIS dau of Aaron, both of
Pasquotank...9, 3m called March, 1800...at the
Meeting House near Newbeggin Creek...

[Column 1]
Thomas JORDAN
Will: NIXON
Benjn. PRITCHARD
Toms WHITE
Will: T. MUSE
Jos. [?] SHANNONHOUSE
Jn[?] MCDONALD
David FOSTER
Will: SYMONS
[Column 2]
Will: ROBBINSON
Wm. ALBERTSON
[?] WHITE
Josiah ROBINSON
Lydia MORRIS
John PARKER

[Column 2 cont.]
Aaron ALBERTSON
Joseph BUNDY
[Column 3]
Aaron MORRIS
Mary WHITE
Margt. MORRIS
Ann NIXON
M[?] NIXON
Phara. PARKER
Easther WHITE
Aaron MORRIS Junr
Abigah[?] MORRIS
Mordecai MORRIS
[Column 4]
Joseph PARKER
Elizabeth PARKER

Page 204-205 Seth MORGAN son of Benjamin of
Pasquotank, and Elizabeth OVERMAN dau of John of
Perquimons...15, 8m, 1799...at the Meeting House at
Suttons Creek...

[Column 1]
Joseph COX
Nathan TRUEBLOOD
Anderson TOMS
Thos. OVERMAN
Eliza: BOGUE Junr.
Nancy OVERMAN
[Column 2]
Mary GRIFFIN
Mary BUNDY
Reuben OVERMAN
Robert PERREY
Caleb WHITE
Phinehas ALBERTSON

[Column 3]
Benja. ALBERTSON
Sarah ALBERTSON
Benja. MORGAN
Sarah MORGAN
Lemuel MORGAN
Meriam MORGAN
Gabriel COSAND
Sarah COSAND
[Column 4]
Seth X MORGAN
    his mark
Elizabeth X MORGAN
        her mark
Caroline OVERMAN
John OVERMAN

Page 207-208 Henry DELON son of Mark of Pasquotank,
and Mary BUNDY dau of Josiah of Perquimons...10,
11m, 1799...at their publick meeting place near the
head of Little River...

[Column 1]
Zachary NIXON
Sarah SYMONS
Mary SYMONS
Pharaby BUNDY
Mary SANDERS
Reubin DELON
Esther WHITE
William ROBINSON
Lydia SYMONS
Zachary NIXON Junr
Josiah GILBERT
Dorothy GILBERT
Jehoshaphat MORRIS
Isaac MORRIS
[Column 2]
Josiah BUNDY
Mary BUNDY
Mark DELON

[Column 2 cont.]
Ann DELON
Jeremiah GILBERT
Charles OVERMAN
Caleb BUNDY
Lyddia MORGAN
John BELL
Nathan BUNDY
Penninah BUNDY
Elizabeth MORRIS
George BUNDY
Thomas SYMONS
Ruth BUNDY
Christopher MORRIS
Josiah BUNDY
[Column 3]
Henry DELON
Mary DELON

Page 209 Jehoshaphat SYMONS son of Nathan decd, and
Sarah NEWBY dau of Thomas decd, both of Pasquotank
...24, 4m called April, 1800...at their publick
meeting place near Symons's creek...

[Column 1]
Absala SYMONS
Sarah COSAND
[Column 2]
Jehoshaphat SYMONS
Sarah SYMONS
Page 210
[Column 3]
Thomas JORDAN
Margaret JORDAN
Sarah JORDAN
Margaret JORDAN Junr
John PRICE Junr
John WHITE
Lydia NEWBY
Elizabeth NEWBY
[Column 4]
Caleb TRUEBLOOD
Joseph WILSON
Sarah WILSON

[Column 4 cont.]
Lydia MORGAN
Miriam TRUEBLOOD
Sarah TRUEBLOOD
Lydia MORRIS Junr
Joseph PRITCHARD
Toms WHITE
Jehoshaphat MORRIS
[Column 5]
Naomi NEWBY
Mary SYMONS
Jesse SYMONS
James NEWBY
Jacob SYMONS
Lydia MORRIS
Nathan MORRIS
Mary MORRIS
Elizabeth TRUEBLOOD
Sarah OVERMAN

Page 212 Thomas WHITE son of William decd of
Perquimons, and Susannah PALIN dau of Thomas decd of
Pasquotank...29, 4m, 1801...at Newbegun Creek in
their publick meeting place...

[Column 1]

Lydia MORRIS
Sarah SYMONS
Edmd. WHITE
Toms WHITE
James WHITE
Thos. JORDAN

[Column 2]

Caleb WINSLOW
Esther ROBINSON
Elizabeth SYMONS
Wmn. TOWNSEND

[Column 2 cont.]

Wmn. ROBINSON

[Column 3]

Jesse WHITE
Benj. PRITCHARD
Penninah PRITCHARD
Betty WHITE
Pharabe SYMONS
Peggy MORRIS

[Column 4]

Thomas WHITE
Susannah WHITE

Page 213 Thomas MORRIS son of Aaron decd, and
Rebeckah WHITE dau of James, both of Pasquotank
...16, 7m, 1801...at their publick meeting place
near Symons's Creek...

[Column 1]

Myriam EVANS
Sarah JORDAN

[Column 2]

Caleb TRUEBLOOD
Aaron MORRIS
John OVERMAN
Thomas MORRIS
Hannah MORRIS
Mary SYMONS
Mary WHITE
Mary JORDAN

[Column 3]

Lydia SYMONS
Myriam TRUEBLOOD
Sarah TRUBLOOD
Nathan MORRIS
Tamer[?] MORRIS
[?] MORRIS

[Column 4]

Abigale MORRIS
Thos. JORDAN

[Column 4 cont.]

Margt. JORDAN
Ann WHITE
Joshua MORRIS
Margt.[?] MORRIS

[Column 5]

Penninah BUNDY
Isaac MORRIS
Ruth BUNDY
James WHITE
Milscent[?] SYMONS

[Column 6]

James WHITE
Elizabeth WHITE
Chris[?] MORRIS
Christopher[?] MORRIS
[?] MORRIS

[Column 7]

Thos. MORRIS
Rebeckah X MORRIS
        her mark

Page 214-215 Thomas MORRIS son of Mordecai, and
Sarah JORDAN dau of Thomas, both of Pasquotank...
1, 4m called April, 1802...at the Meeting House at
Symons's Creek...

[Column 1]
M. M. OVERMAN
Anderson MORRIS
John OVERMAN
B. PRITCHARD Junr.
James BANKS[?]

[Column 2]
Mary WHITE
Abigale MORRIS
Will: T. MUSE
[?] WHITE
Edmd. WHITE
Aaron MORRIS
L[?]a MORRIS
[?] PRITCHARD
[?] JORDAN
Aaron MORRIS
Caleb TRUEBLOOD
[?] OVERMAN
[?] OVERMAN
[?] OVERMAN

[Column 3]
Margt. MORRIS
Joshua MORRIS
Nathan MORRIS
Pharaba PARKER[?]

[Column 3 cont.]
Mordecai MORRIS
C. SHEPPHERD
Margt. JORDAN
Jacob SYMONS
Mary SYMONS
Sarah SYMONS
Eliza OVERMAN
Eliza. WHITE

[Column 4]
Mordecai MORRIS
Abigale MORRIS
Thomas JORDAN
Margaret JORDAN
Joseph PRITCHARD
Toms WHITE
Margt. WHITE
Joseph WILSON
Sarah WILSON
Hannah MORRIS
Huldah[?] WHITE
Margt. MORRIS

[Column 5]
Thomas MORRIS
Sarah MORRIS

Page 215-216 Joseph PRITCHARD son of Benjamin, and
Margaret JORDAN dau of Thomas, both of Pasquotank
...30, 12m called December, 1802...at the Meeting
House at Symons's Creek...   [Column 3]

[Column 1]
Elisa. OVERMAN
James OVERMAN

[Column 2]
Jacob SYMONS
Mordecai MORRIS
Phinehas ALBERTSON
Sarah ALBERTSON
Rebecka ALBERTSON
Mordecai MORRIS
Lydia MORGAN
Sarah MORRIS
Aaron MORRIS
Thomas WHITE
Nathan MORRIS
Bennomy MORRIS
Jesse[?] MORRIS

[Column 3]
Thomas JORDAN
Benja. PRITCHARD
Josiah WHITE
Miriam JONES
Sarah NICHOLSON
Thomas MORRIS
Sarah MORRIS
Chalkley ALBERTSON
Hannah MORRIS
Abigale MORRIS
Toms WHITE
Aaron MORRIS Junr
Lydia MORRIS
Lydia MORRIS
Joseph JORDAN
William[?] NICHOLSON[?]
Benj. ALBERTSON[?] Senr

[Column 2 cont.]
John HENLEY[?]
Elizabeth WHITE

[Column 4]
Joseph PRITCHARD
Margaret PRITCHARD

Page 217-218   Jesse MOORE son of Samuel, and Mary
ANDERSON dau of Joshua decd, both of Perquimons...
2, 3m, 1803...at the Meeting House at Little River
in Perquimons...

[Column 1]
Mary GRIFFIN
Mary MORGAN
Margaret[?] GRIFFIN
Martha GRIFFIN
[Column 2]
Exum NEWBY
John BELL
Sarah BELL
Benja. MORGAN
Jehoshapht [?]
Lancelot BELL
Mary OVERMAN
Lydia MORGAN
Rebecka TRUEBLOOD
[Column 3]
George BUNDY
Thos. SYMONS
Melicent MORGAN
Penninah BUNDY

[Column 3 cont.]
Jesse MORRIS
Thos. COPELAND
Joshua MORRIS
Joel GILBERT
Aaron L[?]GILBERT
[Column 4]
Rebeckah GILBERT
Mordecai MORRIS
Nathan MORRIS
Josiah BUNDY
Mary MOORE
Melicent MOORE
Charles OVERMAN
Mary OVERMAN
Will: ROBINSON
[Column 5]
Jesse MOORE
Mary MOORE

Page 218-219   Exum OUTLAND son of Josiah of
Northampton, and Miriam OVERMAN dau of Isaac of
Pasquotank...20, 2m called February, 1803...At the
Pasquotank monthly meeting at the Narrows...

[Column 1]
Sarah TRUEBLOOD
Abel TRUEBLOOD
Stephen TRUEBLOOD
George R. HENLEY
Sarah JACKSON
Malachi SAWYER
Edward B. TRUEBLOOD
Thomas RELF
Rhoda JANING[?]
Caleb SAWYER
Joseph H. TRUEBLOOD
Abigail X TRUEBLOOD
Josiah TRUEBLOOD
Rebecka FORBES

[Column 2 cont.]
David BOWLES
Keziah BOWLES
Abner NICHOLS
Naomi NEWBY
Margt.[?] NICHOLS
Jonathan TRUEBLOOD
John WILSON
Abbijah TRUEBLOOD
Eliza. TRUEBLOOD
Mary TRUEBLOOD
Naomi TRUEBLOOD
Jane PLEAS
Isaac PLEAS
Joshua TRUEBLOOD

[Column 1 cont.]
Will: FORBES
Aron TRUEBLOOD
Milesent TRUEBLOOD
John TRUEBLOOD
Miriam TRUEBLOOD
Joseph TRUEBLOOD
Peter FORBES
  [Column 2]
Isaac OVERMAN
Isbell OVERMAN
John OUTLAND
Seth GRIFFIN

[Column 2 cont.]
Ann ANDERSON
Joshua PERISHO
Eliza. PERISHO
John ANDERSON
Caleb TRUEBLOOD
Joshua TRUEBLOOD
David BOWLES
Mary TRUEBLOOD Junr
  [Column 3]
Exum OUTLAND
Miriam OUTLAND

Page 220   Joseph JORDAN son of Thomas, and Sarah
SYMONS dau of Thomas decd, both of Pasquotank...10,
7m, 1803...at Symons' Creek in their publick Meeting
place...

[Column 1]
John HENLEY
John LOWRY
Eliza. JORDAN
  [Column 2]
Mordecai MORRIS
Margaret MORRIS
Abigale[?] MORRIS
Abigale[?] MORRIS Junr
Sarah OVERMAN
Aaron MORRIS
Mary TRUEBLOOD

[Column 3]
Thomas JORDAN
Thomas MORRIS
Sarah MORRIS
Jos. PRITCHARD
Margt. PRITCHARD
Toms WHITE
Mordecai MORRIS Junr.
Sarah LOWRY
  [Column 4]
Joseph JORDAN
Sarah X JORDAN
    her mark

Page 224   John SYMONS son of Thomas, and Ann MORRIS
dau of Joseph, both of Pasquotank...24, 11m, 1750/1
...at John MORRIS'S dwelling House...

[Column 1]
Stephen SCOTT
Samuel NEWBY
Aaron MORRIS
John MORRIS
Mary MORRIS
William ALBERTSON

[Column 2]
John SYMONS
Ann X SYMONS
 her mark
Joseph MORRIS
Thomas SYMONS
Elisabeth MORRIS
Ann SYMONS

and Several Other names, but the original being so
much Worn out, could not be Inserted with any degree
of Certainty, Thomas JORDAN Register

Page 226   John SYMONS son of Thomas and Ann, and
Miriam PRICHARD widow and Relict of Benomi
decd...29, 9m, 1774...in their publick Meeting place
at Symons's Creek...

[Column 1]
David DAVIS
Edwd. EVERIGIN
Rob. J BURDEN[?]
Myles SNOWDON
Caleb SAWYER
Edmd. CHANCEY
Ruth PRICE
Abram SYMONS
Miriam WHITE
Mary SYMONS

[Column 2]
Ann OVERMAN
Devotion DAVIS
Henry HAUGHTON
Joseph SYMONS
Thomas SYMONS
Benjamin MORRIS
Miriam MORRIS
Henry PALIN
Mordecai MORRIS
Abigail MORRIS
Nathan OVERMAN
Elisabeth SQUIRES
Silas DRAPER
Mary DRAPER
Benjamin MORRIS
Nathan MORRIS
John TRUEBLOOD
Rouland ROBINSON

[Column 3]
Mary TRUEBLOOD
Matthew PRICHARD
Miriam SANDERS
Sarah PRICHARD

[Column 3 cont.]
Clarkey MORRIS
Caleb TRUEBLOOD
Lyddia DAVIS
Joshua MORRIS
Rebecah MORRIS
Aaron MORRIS Junr
Nathan SYMONS
James WHITE
Joseph MORRIS Senr
Ruth OVERMAN
Rachel WILSON
Sarah NICHOLSON Senr
Richard WOOD
John SYMONS Junr

[Column 4]
John SYMONS
Miriam SYMONS
Chalkley ALBERTSON
Aaron MORRIS Senr
Josiah WINSLOW
Ralph FLETCHER
John HENLEY
Thomas NICHOLSON
John MORRIS
Ruth MORRIS
Elizabeth GILBERT
Benjamin WHITE
Anney WHITE
Martha OVERMAN
Huldah WHITE
Joshua WHITE
Rebekah PEARSON
Melisent MORRIS
Miriam MORRIS

Page 227   Christopher MORRIS son of Aaron of
Pasquotank, and Gulielma BUNDY dau of Josiah of
Perquimons...8, 3m, 1797...at their public meeting
place near the head of little river...

[Column 1]
[?] NIXON
John MORRIS
George BUNDY

[Column 2 cont.]
Nathan NIXON
Thomas SYMONS
Zach. NIXON

[Column 1 cont.]
[?] WHITE
Naomi NEWBY
Josiah GILBERT
Aaron MORRIS Junr
Joshua MORRIS
Isaac MORRIS
Charles OVERMAN
John NIXON
   [Column 2]
Mary BUNDY
John BELL
Sarah NICHOLSON
Nathan MORRIS
Mary MORRIS
Benjamin BUNDY
Josiah SYMONS

[Column 2 cont.]
Joseph NIXON
Rebecca GILBERT
   [Column 3]
Josiah BUNDY
Lydia MORRIS
Nathan BUNDY
Sarah BELL
Mary BUNDY
Mark MORRIS
Mary SANDERS
Mary OVERMAN
Thomas NICHOLSON
   [Column 4]
Christopher MORRIS
Gulielma MORRIS

Page 228 Samuel BOGUE son of Joseph of Perquimons,
and Elizabeth MORGAN dau of Benjamin of
Pasquotank...26, 7m called July, 1797...in their
public meeting house near the head of little
river...

[Column 1]
Stephen WHITE
Sarah NICHOLSON
James MORGAN
Joseph GRIFFIN
Lemuel MORGAN
Ann SANDERS
James NEWBY
Benja. WHITE
Charles OVERMAN
Mary OVERMAN
   [Column 2]
Joseph BOGUE
Mary BOGUE
Elizabeth BOGUE
Miriam BOGUE

[Column 2 cont.]
Benj. COSAND
Mary COSAND
John MORRIS
Charles MORGAN
Josiah BUNDY
Mary BUNDY
Mary GRIFFIN
Nathan MORRIS
   [Column 3]
Samuel X BOGUE
      his mark
Elizabeth X BOGUE
        her mark
Benjamin MORGAN
Sarah MORGAN

Page 229 Henry PALIN son of Henry decd of
Pasquotank, and Sarah NIXON dau of John of
Perquimons...21, 1m, 1798...at their meeting house
near Little river in the County of Perquimons...

[Column 1]
James NEWBY
Zach. NIXON Junr.
James OVERMAN

[Column 3]
Za. NIXON Senr.
Mary NIXON
Josiah BUNDY

[Column 1 cont.]
John PERRY
   [Column 2]
Miriam HASKET
Thomas NICHOLSON
Sarah NICHOLSON
William NIXON
George BUNDY
Mary BUNDY
Lydia MORGAN
Phinehas NIXON
John MORRIS
Josiah SYMONS
Martha GRIFFIN

[Column 3 cont.]
Mary BUNDY
Josiah GILBERT
Mary BUNDY
Nathan MORRIS
Mary MORRIS
Abigail NIXON
Caleb BUNDY.
   Column 4]
Henry PALIN
Sarah PALIN
John NIXON

Page 230   John PIKE, and Sarah SMALL relict of
Obadiah, both of Pasquotank...10, 3m, 1802...at
their Meeting House near the head of Little River...

   [Column 1]
Thos. NICHOLSON
Thos. SYMONS
Geo: BUNDY
Jereh. GILBERT
Nathan BUNDY
Lydia MORGAN
Mary ANDERSON
Becky GILBERT
   [Column 2]
Mary NEWBY
Nathan MORRIS
Mary MORRIS
Lydia EVANS
Sarah BUNDY
Milesent MORGAN
Elizabeth NIXON
Penninah TATLOCK
Chs. OVERMAN

   [Column 3]
Joshua BUNDY
Josiah ROBINSON
Enoch NEWBY
Lydia WILSON
Eliza. ALBERTSON
Miriam ALBERTSON
Kiziah ALBERTSON
Jno. ANDERSON
Aron[?] ANDERSON
Thos. MOORE[?]
   [Column 4]
Jonan. TRUEBLOOD
Saml. ALBERTSON
Eliza. ALBERTSON
Saml. WILSON
Myriam TRUEBLOOD
Eliza. PARISHO
   [Column 5]
John PIKE
Sarah X SMALL her mark

Page 234   Aaron MORRIS Jun son of John decd, and
Lydia DAVIS dau of William decd, both of
Pasquotank...19, 7m called July, 1797...at Newbiggin
Creek in their public meeting place...

   [Column 1]
Nathan BUNDY
Ruth BUNDY
Jehoshaphat SYMONS

   [Column 2 cont.]
Joshua MORRIS
Mary MORRIS
Margaret MORRIS

[Column 1 cont.]
John MORRIS
Mary SYMONS
Edmd. WHITE
Thomas MORRIS
Thomas NICHOLSON
Sarah JORDAN
Margaret JORDAN Junr
Pritchard MORRIS
Isaac MORRIS
    [Column 2]
Gulielma MORRIS
Mary WHITE
Lydia MORGAN
Nathan MORRIS
Mark MORRIS
Toms WHITE
Benjamin PRITCHARD

[Column 2 cont.]
Joseph MORRIS Junr
    [Column 3]
Lydda MORRIS
Margaret JORDAN
Thomas JORDAN
Aaron MORRIS
Benjamin PRICE
Josiah BUNDY
Sarah OVERMAN
Pennina PRITCHARD
Mary NICHOLSON
Aaron MORRIS
Mary BUNDY
    [Column 4]
Aaron MORRIS
Lydia MORRIS

Page 235 William NEWBY son of William of Perquimons, and Hannah BUNDY dau of Caleb of Pasquotank...25, 1m, 1797...at their usual meeting place near the head of little River...

[Column 1]
Christopher BUNDY
John BUNDY
Charles MORGAN
Charles OVERMAN
Sarah NICHOLSON
    [Column 2]
Sarah BELL
Mary MORRIS
Nathan MORRIS
Thomas NICHOLSON
John NEWBY
Naomi NEWBY
Mary OVERMAN

[Column 3]
Benjamin BUNDY
Mary BUNDY
James MORGAN
Benjamin MORGAN
Moses BUNDY
Miriam WHITE
Samuel BUNDY
Josiah BUNDY
    [Column 4]
William NEWBY
Hannah X NEWBY
    her mark

Page 236 Jacob MORRIS son of Benjamin decd, and Mary TRUEBLOOD dau of Caleb, both of Pasquotank... 1, 3m, 1798...near Symons Creek in their public meeting place...

[Column 1]
Betty STANTON
J LANE Junr
Miliscent PIKE
Jacob SYMONS
Rebeccah WHITE

[Column 3 cont.]
John PRICE
Elizabeth TRUEBLOOD
Toms WHITE
Margaret WHITE
Joseph WILSON
Sarah WILSON

[Column 2]
Gabriel TRUEBLOOD
Wm. TRUEBLOOD
Thomas HENBY
Ely MORRIS
Josiah SYMONS
Lydia SYMONS
Mary SYMONS
Samuel PRICE
[Column 3]
Jehoshaphat SYMONS

[Column 3 cont.]
Elizabeth SYMONS
Mordecai MORRIS
Miriam TRUEBLOOD
Sarah TRUEBLOOD
[Column 4]
Jacob MORRIS
Mary MORRIS
Caleb TRUEBLOOD
Miliscent SYMONS
Jesse SYMONS

Page 238   Jesse SYMONS son of Jehoshaphat of
Pasquotank decd, and Sarah BUNDY dau of Josiah of
Perquimons decd...27, 9m called September, 1775...at
their publick meeting house near the head of Little
River...

[Column 1]
Benjamin MORRIS
Joseph SYMONS
Nathan MORRIS
Jos. JONES
Elizabeth ALBERTSON
Peirce NIXON
Mourning WILSON
Barnabe NIXON
[Column 2]
Caleb TRUEBLOOD
Joseph NICHOLSON
Mary NICHOLSON
Hannah NIXON J
Jemima NIXON
Matthew PRICHARD
Abram SYMONS
Eliza. GILBERT
Ann OVERMAN
Penelope SYMONS
Nathan PEARSON
Joshua ALBERTSON
[Column 3]
Chalkley ALBERTSON
Zachariah NIXON

[Column 3 cont.]
Thomas NICHOLSON
Moses BUNDY
Jane BUNDY
Thomas OVERMAN
Sarah BARROW
Margaret JORDAN
Thos. JORDAN
Jane JORDAN
Mary NIXON
Mourning BUNDY
[Column 4]
Jesse SYMONS
Sarah X SYMONS
   her mark
Joshua BUNDY
Sarah HOLLOWELL
Josiah BUNDY
John SYMONS
Nathan SYMONS
Sarah PRICHARD
Lyddai SYMONS
John NIXON
Jane NIXON

Page 239   William NEWBY of Perquimons, and Mary
WHITE dau of Joshua of Pasquotank...21, 1m called
January, 1802...at Symons's Creek in their publick
meeting place...

[Column 1]
Caleb TRUEBLOOD
Robert MOORE
Thomas MORRIS
Thos. JORDAN
Margaret JORDAN
James OVERMAN
Mordecai MORRIS
    [Column 2]
Aaron MORRIS Junr
Toms WHITE
Saml. PRICE
Susannah NEWBY

[Column 2 cont.]
Huldah WHITE
Milesent SYMONS
Eliza. SYMONS
Sarah JORDAN
    [Column 3]
Eliza. WHITE
Eliza. OVERMAN
Marg [?] JORDAN
    [Column 4]
Wm. NEWBY
Mary X NEWBY
    her mark

Page 240   John WHITE son of Benjamin of Perquimons, and Mary OVERMAN dau of Charles of Pasquotank...20, 4m, 1803...at their publick meeting place at Little River in Perquimons...

[Column 1]
Aaron ALBERTSON
Josiah ROBINSON
Thos. ALBERTSON
Abagale GIBBERSON[?]
Mary NEWBY
Abraham SAUNDERS
Jesse MORRIS
George BUNDY
    [Column 2]
Will ROBINSON
Ann ROBINSON
Robert WHITE
Nathan MORRIS
Mary MORRIS
Stephen WHITE
Demsey WHITE
Aaron L. GILBERT

[Column 2 cont.]
Joel GILBERT
Joshua MORRIS
    [Column 3]
Charles OVERMAN
Mary JONES
Margaret MORRIS
Miriam JONES
Josiah BUNDY
Joshua BUNDY
Sarah JONES
John OVERMAN
Martha GRIFFIN
Joseph GRIFFIN
Josiah WHITE
    [Column 4]
John WHITE
Mary WHITE

Page 241   Levi MUNDEN son of Joseph decd, and Kezia BOGUE dau of William, both of Perquimons...21, 8m, 1776...at the Week day meeting house on Suttons Creek...

[Column 1]
Martha WINSLOW
John MOORE
Sarah ALBERTSON
Gabriel COSAND
Mary MOORE
John ANDERSON

[Column 2 cont.]
John OVERMAN
Hannah OVERMAN
Sarah ALBERTSON
Wm. ALBERTSON
    [Column 3]
Levi MUNDEN

[Column 1 cont.]
Simon BOSWELL
Aaron COSAN
Duke BOGUE
[Column 2]
Francis ALBERTSON
Hannah MUNDEN Senr.
Benjn. ALBERTSON
Elisha PARKER
Moses BUNDY

[Column 3 cont.]
Kezia U MUNDEN
  her mark
William BOGUE
Elizabeth BOGUE
Sarah BOGUE
Miriam BOGUE
Margret KINYON
Elisabeth PARKER
Robert BOGUE

Page 243 Levi MUNDEN son of Joseph decd, and Rhoda
ALBERTSON dau of Nathaniel, both of Perquimons...
19, 4m, 1780...at their Week-day Meeting house near
Suttons Creek...

[Column 1]
Joseph KINYON
Saml. STAFFORD
[Column 2]
Elisabeth BOGUE
Elisabeth HALL
Sarah HALL
[Column 3]
Mary ANDERSON
Gulielma SAINT
Sarah CHARLES
Silas HASKITT
John ANDERSON
Chalkley ALBERTSON
Moses BUNDY
John ANDERSON
Aaron COSAND
Joshua BUNDY

[Column 3 cont.]
Elisabeth CHARLES
Hannah COSAND
Sarah BOGUE
[Column 4]
Levi MUNDEN
Rhoda X MUNDEN
  her mark
Nathaniel ALBERTSON
William MUNDEN
Anna MOORE
Miriam PEIRCE
John PEIRCE
Aaron MOORE
Ann CORNWELL
Isaac WILLIAMS
Joseph ANDERSON
(We Concur with the above

said parties proceedings as afore-said in witness
where-of we hereunto Subscribe our names)
Hannah MUNDEN Senr   Mary ALBERTSON

Page 252 Josiah WHITE son of Caleb decd of
Perquimons, and Elizabeth WHITE dau of Benjamin decd
of Pasquotank...1, 3m, 1804...at Symon's Creek
Meetinghouse...

[Column 1]
A. ALBERTSON
Benja. ALBERTSON
Thos. JORDAN
Jesse WHITE
James MCADAMS

[Column 2 cont.]
Abigale WHITE
Elizabeth OVERMAN
Sarah TRUEBLOOD
Joseph PARKER
[Column 3]
Sarah TRUEBLOOD

[Column 1 cont.]
Will TRUEBLOOD
Binnoni WHITE
Toms WHITE
Margarett WHITE
Patsey SAUNDERS
Stephen WHITE
   [Column 2]
Barneby NIXON
Joshua BUNDY
Betty WHITE
Nathan MORRIS
Mordecai MORRIS
Rachel WHITE

[Column 3 cont.]
Sarah ALBERTSON
P. ALBERTSON
Rebecca ALBERTSON
Rachel PRICE
Saml. PRICE
Toms WHITE
Eliza. WHITE
Josiah WHITE
Doratha JORDAN
Nixon ALBERTSON
   [Column 4]
Josiah WHITE
Eliza. WHITE

Page 253   Joseph JONES, and Miriam PRICE widow,
both of Perquimons...27, 2m, 1805...in their publick
meeting house near the head of Little River....
   [Column 1]
Jonathan ARNOLD
Sarah BELL
Rebecca GILBERT
Charles OVERMAN
Mary OVERMAN
Joshua MORRIS
George BUNDY
Aaron L. GILBERT
   [Column 2]
Jonathan NEWBY

   [Column 2 cont.]
Mourning NEWBY
Sarah CHARLES
Elizabeth BUNDY
Chalkley ALBERTSON
Joshua BUNDY
Josiah BUNDY
Nathan MORRIS
   [Column 3]
Jos. JONES
Miriam JONES

Page 254   Isaac MORRIS son of Aaron decd of
Pasquotank, and Pharaby BUNDY dau of Josiah of
Perquimons...3, 3m, 1802...at their Meeting House
Near the head of Little River in Perquimons...
   [Column 1]
Isaac MORRIS
Pharaby MORRIS
Page 255
   [Column 2]
Mark MORIS
John BELL
Rebecca GILBERT
Nathan MORRIS
Mary MORIS
Charles OVERMAN
Jesse MORRIS
   [Column 3]
Josiah BUNDY

   [Column 3 cont.]
Joshua MORRIS
William OVERMAN
Josiah BUNDY
Mary BUNDY
Lydia MORRIS
George BUNDY
Joshua BUNDY
   [Column 4]
Thomas [?]
Mary ANDERSON
Mary SANDERS
Nathan BUNDY
Ruth BUNDY

Page 255-256 Henly NICHOLSON son of Christopher decd, and Sarah OVERMAN dau of William, both of Pasquotank...23, 4m called April, 1800...at their publick meeting house at Newbegun Creek...

[Column 1]
Wm. ROBINSON
Wm. T MUSE
R. HOWETT
Joseph MULLEN
Michl. T. H. DOWE[?]
Thomas MORRIS
Benjamin PRITCHARD
Joseph MORRIS
Saml. S. JORDAN
Thos. Ell. HENLEY
Mary OVERMAN
Joseph BUNDY
Thomas NICHOLSON
Elizabeth PENDLETON
[Column 2]
Josiah ROBINSON
John MULLEN
G. J. HAM
John NIXON
Mordecai MORRIS
Mariam TRUEBLOOD
Thomas MORRIS

[Column 2 cont.]
Joseph PRITCHARD
Elizabeth OVERMAN
William OVERMAN
Eliza PARKER
Lydia MORRIS
Wm. SYMONS
William NICHOLSON
[Column 3]
Henly NICHOLSON
Sarah NICHOLSON
Ester WHITE
John OVERMAN
Sarah SYMONS
Job BROTHERS
Aaron MORRIS
Abigail OVERMAN
Mary NICHOLSON
Mary WHITE
Pharaby SYMONS
Sarah SYMONS
Joshua MORRIS

Page 257-258 Aaron MORRIS son of Aaron decd, and Sarah DRAPER dau of Thomas...2, 10m, 1805...at Newbegun Creek...

[Column 1]
Benjamin PRITCHARD
Will. ROBINSON
Mary SYMONS
Margaret MORRIS
Peninah BUNDY
Joseph BUNDY
Lydia MORRIS
Jehoshaphat MORRIS
Sarah MORRIS
[Column 2]
Mordecai MORRIS
Wm. SYMONS
Thomas SYMONS
Joshua MORRIS
Caleb SYMONS

[Column 2 cont.]
Eli MORRIS
Christopher MORRIS
Pritchard MORRIS
Lydia SYMONS
Sarah SYMONS
[Column 3]
Aaron MORRIS
Sarah MORRIS
Aaron MORRIS
Sarah SYMONS
Benjamin PRITCHARD
John SYMONS
Ruth BUNDY
Margaret MORRIS
Jehoshaphat SYMONS

Page 259-260 Joel GILBERT son of Jeremiah, and
Lydia MORGAN dau of James, both of Pasquotank...
25, 1m, 1804...at their public meeting place near
Little River...

[Column 1]
Charles OVERMAN
John BELL
Josiah ROBINSON
James PRITCHARD
Benjamin BUNDY
Caleb MORRIS
Rebecah GILBERT
George BUNDY
Joshua MORRIS
Mary MORGAN

[Column 2]
Joshua BUNDY
Sarah BUNDY
Reubin OVERMAN
Thomas GRIFFIN
Joshua SMALL

[Column 2 cont.]
Benjamin MORGAN
Lancelot BELL
Millecent MORGAN
Peninah MORGAN
Martha GRIFFIN

[Column 3]
Joel GILBERT
Lydia GILBERT
Jesse MORRIS
Joseph COX
Jeremiah GILBERT
John BUNDY Junr.
Mary GRIFFIN
Aaron Lan. GILBERT
Mary BELL

Page 261 Samuel PRICE, and Rachel WHITE Junr, both
of Pasquotank...1, 12m called December, 1803...near
Symons Creek in their publick meeting place...

[Column 1]
Rachel WHITE
Eliza. WHITE
Sarah TRUEBLOOD
Eliza. OVERMAN
Sarah PRICE
Patience NEWBY
A. ALBERTSON
John PRICE
Mary TOMES
Melecent TRUEBLOOD

[Column 2]
Caleb WHITE
Abigal WHITE
Mordecai MORRIS
Tomes WHITE
Parthena WHITE
B. ALBERTSON Junr
Foster TOMES
Nixon ALBERTSON

[Column 2 cont.]
John Anderson TOMES
Josiah WHITE
Fras. WHITE

[Column 3]
Jacob SYMONS
P. ALBERTSON
Aaron MORRIS
James MCADAMS
William TRUEBLOOD
Caleb SYMONS
Charlotta MCADAMS
Thomas JORDAN
Benjamin LAZELL[?]
Naomi NEWBY
Mary WHITE

[Column 4]
Samuel PRICE
Rachel PRICE

Page 262   Caleb SYMONS son of Jesse[?] of Pasquotank, and Peninah BUNDY dau of Benjamin of Perquimons...29, 1m, 1806...at a publick meeting place at little river...

[Column 1]
John BELL
Jessee[?] MORRIS
Mary MORRIS
Chas. OVERMAN
Aaron S. GILBERT
Caleb MORRIS
Josiah BUNDY
John BUNDY
Mary MORRIS
Mary OVERMAN
Mary BELL
Thomas SYMONS
Melicent SYMONS

[Column 2]
Joshua BUNDY
Josiah ROBINSON
Joshua MORRIS
Jessee[?] SYMONS
Benjamin BUNDY
Sarah BUNDY
Lydia SYMONS
Benjamin MORGAN
Jehosapaht MORRIS
Jeremiah GILBERT
Lancelot BELL
George BUNDY
Melicent BUNDY

[Column 3]
Sarah SYMONS
Melescent SYMONS

[Column 4]
Caleb SYMONS
Peninah SYMONS

Page 263   Thomas MORRIS son of Mordecai, and Ann HENLY dau of Joseph decd, both of Pasquotank... 30, 4m, 1807...at their publick Meeting place near Symons Creek...

[Column 1]
Phinehas ALBERTSON
Rebecca ALBERTSON
Joseph JORDAN
Sarah JORDAN
John WHITE
Benja. BAILEY
John MULLEN
John HENLEY

[Column 2]
Margaret MORRIS
Sarah TRUBLOOD
Mordecai MORRIS
Abigail MORRIS
Margaret PRICHARD
Melicent HENLEY
Nixon ALBERTSON
Sally SYMONS

[Column 2 cont.]
Joseph BUNDY
Joseph H. TRUEBLOOD
Joshua MORRIS

[Column 3]
Thomas MORRIS
Ann MORRIS
Lucretia MORRIS
Naomi JORDAN
Miriam TRUEBLOOD
Nathan MORRIS
Mary MORRIS
~~Thomas MORRIS~~
~~Ann MORRIS~~
Joseph BANKS[?]
Sarah BANKS[?]
Mark MORRIS

Page 264   Benjamin PRITCHARD son of Benjamin, and
Abigail MORRIS dau of Mordecai, both of Pasquotank
...2, 6m, 1808...at their publick meeting place near
Symons Creek...

[Column 1]
Nathan OVERMAN
Rebeckah MORRIS
Tomes WHITE
Mordecai MORRIS
Hannah MORRIS
Elisha WHITE
Nathan MORRIS
Nathan MORRIS
Mordecai MORRIS Junr
Sarah NICHOLSON
Joshua MORRIS of Nn.
Margaret MORRIS
Margaret PRITCHARD
Caleb PRITCHARD
Paul S. POOL
Joseph SMALL

[Column 2]
Benjamin PRITCHARD
Peninah PRITCHARD
Margaret WHITE
Mary WHITE
Thomas MORRIS
Miriam MORRIS
Mary MORRIS
Benoni MORRIS
Jehoshaphat MORRIS
Aaron MORRIS Senr
Joshua MORRIS
Joseph PRITCHARD
Soloman POOL Jr.
Mordecai OVERMAN
Joseph PIKE
Samuel PRICE
Josiah WHITE

[Column 3]
Benjamin PRITCHARD
Abigail PRITCHARD

Page 265   Joshua MORRIS son of Nathan, and Mary
MORGAN dau of Charles decd, both of Pasquotank...
21, 5m, 1806...at their publick Meeting house at
litle River...

[Column 1]
Benjamin MORGAN
Joshua SMALL
Josiah ROBINSON
William WOOD
John OVERMAN
Isaac MORRIS
Jean BUNDY Junr
Josiah BUNDY
Mary MORRIS Junr
Jehosaphat MORRIS
John BUNDY
Nathan BUNDY

[Column 2]
Nathan MORRIS
Mary MORRIS Senr
Josiah BUNDY
Joshua BUNDY
Aaron La. GILBERT
George BUNDY
Rebeckah GILBERT
Miliscent MORGAN
Jerimiah GILBERT
Elizabeth MORGAN
Jesse MORRIS
Caleb MORRIS

[Column 3]
Joshua MORRIS
Mary MORRIS

Page 266 Mordecai MORRIS, and Miliscent MORGAN
widow, both of Pasquotank...19, 10m, 1808...at
Little River Meeting house...

[Column 1]
Benjamin MORGAN
Margaret MORGAN
Mary MORGAN
George BUNDY
Jehosaphat MORRIS
Josiah BUNDY
John BUNDY Junr
Lancelot BELL
Nathan SYMONS
Mary ALBERTSON
John BELL
Josiah BUNDY
Nathan BUNDY

[Column 2]
Jesse SYMONS
Mordecai MORRIS Junr
Nathan MORRIS
Rueben OVERMAN
William WOOD
Thomas MORRIS
Ann MORRIS
Anderson MORRIS
Toms WHITE
Chalkley ALBERTSON
Martha GRIFFIN
Aaron MORRIS
Ruth BUNDY
Phinehas NIXON

[Column 3]
Mordecai MORRIS
Miliscent X MORRIS
      her mark

Page 267 Nathan TRUEBLOOD son of John decd of
Pasquotank, and Patience NEWBY dau of Joseph of
Perquimons...28, 2m, 1805...at Symonses Creek
Meeting house...

[Column 1]
Miriam TRUEBLOOD
Mary OVERMAN
Rebeckah TRUEBLOOD
Sarah TRUEBLOOD
Margaret MORRIS
Joshua PERISHO
Toms WHITE
Mordecai MORRIS
Mary NEWBY
Joseph NEWBY
Miliscent NEWBY
Phinehas ALBERTSON
Joseph PARKER
Josiah WHITE
Aaron ALBERTSON

[Column 2]
Isaac OVERMAN
Isabel OVERMAN
Benjamin PRITCHARD Junr
Mordecai MORRIS Junr
William TRUEBLOOD
John OVERMAN
George R HENLY
Samuel PRICE
Aaron MORRIS
William WATSON
Benjamin ALBERTSON
William ALBERTSON
Thos. ALBERTSON

[Column 3]
Nathan TRUEBLOOD
Patience TRUEBLOOD

Eastern Quarterly Meeting, Minutes, Vol. I, 1708-
1792. (Inserted at the end of the book)

To thee monthly meating of friends and breathren
[torn] Noarth of Iraland or else whear to whom this
may com[torn] befoure it being from our quarterly
meating in litle river in noarth caralinah ye 25 &
26 days of ye 10th month/1708...the farther ocation
of our wrighting to you at this time is concerning
our deare friend Pattricke HANDORSON yt came from
amongst you and visited ye meatings in this
province...sined by us whose names are
underwriten...

[Column 1]
William EVERIGIN
Benjamen PRICHARD
Stephen SCOTE
Peter SYMONS
Rebaca SYMONS
Damaris WHITE
Elezebeth NIXON
Ann SYMONS

[Column 2]
John SYMONS

[Column 3]
Henery WHITE
William NEWBY
Gabriel NEWBY

[Column 3 cont.]
Mathew PRICHARD
Zachariah NIXON
Timothy CLARE
Jeremiah SYMONS
Agustin SCARBORA
Jeams DAVISE
Caleb BUNDEY
Hanry KEATON
Samuel NICKLESON
Edward MAYO
John MORIS
Joseph JORDAN
Jacob OVERMAN
Jeams TOOKE
John WHITE

North Carolina Yearly Meeting, Vol. I, 1704-1793.
(Inserted at the end of the book, with no page
number, but following page 304.)

Joseph ROBINSON of Perquimings County, and Sarah
PENDLETON of Pasquotanck County...5, 11m, 1752...at
our Meeting House at Simons's Creek...

[Column 1]	[Column 2]
John EVEREGIN	Daniel SAINT
William SYMONS	Samuel ANDERSON
Stephen SCOTT	Thomas SMALL
Samuel NEWBY	Joshua ELLIOT
John ROBINSON	[Column 3]
Charles OVERMAN Ser.	Joseph ROBISON
Jehosaphat SYMONS	Sarah ROBINSON
Joseph JORDAN	Ann ELLIOT
John HENLY	Sarah ROBINSON
Aaron MORRIS	Penelope JORDAN
Robert JORDAN	Mary CONNER
Joseph JORDAN	Naomi NEWBY
William ALBERTSON	Mary NICHOLSON
Josiah TRUELOOD	Elizabeth JORDAN
Joshua MORRIS	Mary SCOTT

Matthias JORDAN son of Matthew, late of Isle of
Wight County in Virginia decd, and Elizabeth
PENNLETON dau of Thomas of Pasquotank County
decd...5, 11m, 1752...at our Meeting House at
Simons's Creek...

[Column 1]	[Column 2]
Stephen SCOTT	Daniel SAINT
Samuel NEWBY	Samuel ANDERSON
Charles OVERMAN	Thomas SMALL
Jehosaphat SIMONS	Joshua ELLIOT
John EVERIGIN	Joseph ROBINSON
Joseph JORDAN	Sarah ROBINSON Senr
John HENLY	[Column 3]
Aaron MORRIS	Matthias JORDAN
Robert JORDAN	Elizabeth JORDAN
Joseph JORDAN S:Masr.	Ann ELLIOT
William ALBERTSON	Penelope JORDAN
Josiah TRUEBLOOD	Mary CONNER
Joshua MORRIS	Naomi NEWBY
	Sary ROBINSON
	Mary NICHOLSON
	Elizabeth JORDAN
	Mary SCOTT

Minutes and Records Perquimans Monthly Meeting of
the Religious Society of Friends in North Carolina
1680-1762. [Page 45] "Transcribed out of an old Book
...By Thos. PEIRCE Senr, Thos. JESSOP & Robt.
WILSON, this sixth day of ye fourth month 1728."

Page 1/2 William BUNDY of Paquimance River, and
Mary PEIRCE of ye same place...15, 10m, 1683...at ye
house of Mary PEIRCE...

[Column 1]

Hannah PHELPS

Mary [?]

[Column 2]

Ann WILSON

Hannah HILL

Mary SCOT

Ann NICHOLSON[?]

[Column 3]

Jno. THUSSTANE

John JOHNSON

[Column 3 cont.]

Jno. WILKISON

Jona. PHELPS

[Column 4]

Christor. NICHOLSON

Joseph SCOT

Joshua SCOT

[Column 5]

William BUNDY

Mary BUNDY

Robert WILSON

Page 2/2-3 John BELMAN of Paquimance, and Sarah
WILSON of ye Same place...19, 8m, 1687...at ye house
of Jona. PHELPS...

[Column 1]

Hannah HILL

Hannah PHELPS

Johanah JENKINS

Elizabeth WHITE

[Column 2]

Robert BEASLY

Isaac WILSON

[Column 2 cont.]

Jona. PHELPS

Ann WILSON

[Column 3]

John BELMAN

Sarah BELMAN

Robert WILSON

William BUNDY

Page 3 Saml. NICHOLSON and Elizabeth CHARLES both
of Paquimance...6, 10m, 16[88?]...at a Meeting at
Jona. PHELPSES house...

[Column 1]

Mercy STEPNEY

Susanah GEORGE

Mary TOMES

Mary KENT

Hannah KENT

Margaret BOGUE

[Column 2]

John THUSTONE

Joseph SUTTON

Richd. STANDERWICK

Caleb BUNDY

[Column 2 cont.]

John KINSEY

George AMES

John HARLOE

[Column 3]

Saml. NICHOLSON

Elisabeth NICHOLSON

Robert WILSON

John STEPNEY

Gabriel NEWBY

Giles LONG

Saml. CHARLES

Page 3-3/2 Gabriel NEWBY son of William of
Nancemond in Virginia, and Mary TOMES dau of Francis
TOMES of Paquimance in ye County of Arlbemarle...1,
4m, 1689...Quarterly meeting at Ann NICHOLSON house.

[Column 1]
Hannah HILL
Ann WILSON
Ann NICHOLSON
Mary CLEARE
Hannah GOSBY
Sarah BELMAN
Deliverance SUTTEN
[Column 2]
Thos. LEPER
Timothy CLEARE
Eve BELONGEY
Robert BEASLEY
Robert HARMON
Thos. PEIRCE
Saml. NICHOLSON
Caleb CALLOWAY
Wm. HOGBEN

[Column 2 cont.]
Wm. TURNER
John KINSEY
John WHIDBY
Saml. CHARLES
[Column 3]
Gabriel NEWBY
Mary NEWBY
Francis TOMES
William NEWBY
William BUNDY
Robert WILSON
Zachariah NIXON
James HOGG
Gearge AMES
Caleb BUNDY
John GOSBEY
Francis TOMES

Page 4/2-5 John NICHOLSON son of Christopher late
of North Carolina, and Priscila TOMES dau of Francis
of ye Same place...20, 9m, [1700]...at ye house of
her father Francis TOMES...

[Column 1]
Ann WILSON
Mary NEWBY
Mercy STEPNEY
[Column 2]
Saml. NICHOLSON
Nathaniel NICHOLSON
Mary TOMES
Ann DORMAN

[Column 3]
John NICHOLSON
Priscila TOMES
Francis TOMES
John STEPNEY
Joshua TOMES

pr Gabriel NEWBY
recorder

Page 5-5/2 Francis TOMES son of Francis of ye place
aforesd., and Margaret LAWRANCE widdow of ye
deceased Wm. LAWRANCE of ye Same place...8, 4m,
1696...at ye house of Margaret LAURANCE...

[Column 1]
Mary TOMES
Ann WILSON
Jane BYAR
Eliner BOGUE
Elisabeth NICHOLSON
Elisabeth CALLOWAY

[Column 2 cont.]
Richd. DORMAN
John NICHOLSON
Saml. NICHOLSON
Timothy CLEARE
[Column 3]
Francis TOMES

[Column 1 cont.]
Rachel WILSON
Elisabeth CLARE
[Column 2]
Caleb CALLOWAY
Willm. MOOR
John LAURANCE
Willm. BUTLER
Richd. CHEASTON

[Column 3 cont.]
Margaret TOMES
Francis TOMES
Joshua TOMES
Gabriel NEWBY
Robert WILSON
Isaac WILSON
Israel SNELLING
William BOGUE

Page 5/2 William BOGUE and Eliner PERISHO both of
Paquimance...5, 6m, 1689...At a Meeting at Jona.
PHELPS old Plantation...

[Column 1]
Hannah HILL
Hannah SNELLING
Ann WILSON
Margaret TOMES
Ann WILSON Junr
Elisabeth EVANS
[Column 2]
Richd. BYAR
Robt. BEASLY
Caleb BUNDY
James WHITE

[Column 2 cont.]
David SHEARWOOD
James LOADMAN
Richd. EVANS
[Column 3]
Willm. X BOGUE
   his marke
Eliner A BOGUE
   her mark
Saml. NICHOLSON
John THUSTON
John LILLY

Page 6 William MORE and Elezebeth MAKEBRIDE both
[torn]equimens...10, 9m, [1697]...at the house of
Janne[torn]...

[Column 1]
[torn]ll NEWBY
[torn]s TOMES
[torn] TOMES
[torn]y CLEAR
[torn]muell CHARLES
[torn]saac WILLSON
Richard CHESTON
[torn]acob OVERMAN
[torn]illiam BUTLER
[torn]ichard FOX
[torn]zekiel MOLDEN

[torn]ecorded pr. me
   Thomas PEIRC

[Column 2]
Mary NEWBY
Elezebeth CLEAR
[Column 3]
William MORE
Elezebeth MORE
Janne BYER
Francis TOMES Snr
William BOOGE
Margratt [torn]
Eliner [torn]
Ann [torn]
Mary [torn]
Dority [torn]
Kathiran[?] [torn]

Page 6/2 Timothy CLARE and Hanah SNELING Relict of
Isreall SNELLING Late of paquiman...[?], 1m,
[170?]...

[Column 1]
[torn]eres PIRCE
[torn]th NICOLESON
[torn]th PRITLOE
[torn] CLEAR
[torn] CLEARE
[torn]RMAN
  [Column 2]
Francis TOMES
John NICOLESON
Joseph PIERCE
John SHAW[?]

[Column 2 cont.]
Mary TOMES
Mary NEWBY
Margret TOMES
  [Column 3]
[T]imothy C[torn]
Hanah CLEA[torn]
Francis[?] T[torn]
Samuell NICO[torn]
Wm. MORE
Thomas WINSLOE[?]
John[?] [torn]

Page 7-7/2 William NEWBY and Jane BYAR...3, 7m,
1701...
  [Column 1]
Margaret TOMES
Elisabeth CHARLES
Dameris PEIRCE
  [Column 2]
Nathaniel NICHOLSON
Saml. NICHOLSON
Gearge BATES
Benja. NICHOLSON

[Column 2 cont.]
John PRITLOWE
  [Column 3]
William NEWBY
Jane NEWBY
Wm. MOOR
Francis TOMES Junr
Isaac WILSON

Page 7/2 John NEWBY of Little River, and Elisabeth
NICHOLSON of Paquimance...11, 6m, 1701...in publick
meeting at ye house of Francis TOMES...
  [Column 1]
Ann DORMAN
Hannah FORSTER
Sarah NEWBY
Mary NEWBY
Elisabeth CLEARE
Elisa. PRITLOWE
Ann WILSON
Dameris PEIRCE
Elisa. THICKPEN
Rebecca SEBRIEL
  [Column 2]
Isaac WILSON
Wm. NEWBY
Zachariah NIXON

[Column 2 cont.]
Francis TOMES Junr
Timothy CLARE
Peter JONES
Joshua TOMES
Mary TOMES
  [Column 3]
John NEWBY
Elisabeth NEWBY
John NICHOLSON
Francis TOMES
John ANDERSON
John PRITLOWE
Benja. NICHOLSON

Page 8 Joshua TOMES and Sarah GOSBEY...23, 9m,
1701...at a publick meeting at ye house of Francis
TOMES...

[Column 1]
Ann DORMAN
Margaret TOMES
Dameris PEIRCE
Elisabeth MOOR
Rebecca SEBRIEL
Ann WILSON
Hannah LAURANCE
[Column 2]
Saml. NICHOLSON
Nathaniel NICHOLSON
Francis BEASLY
Nathaniel ALBERTSON
Saml. CHARLES

[Column 2 cont.]
Peter ALBERTSON
Wm. BOGUE
Benja. NICHOLSON
[Column 3]
Joshua TOMES
Sarah TOMES
Francis TOMES
Gabriel NEWBY
Francis TOMES
Isaac WILSON
Joseph PEIRCE
Christopher NICHOLSON

Page 8-8/2 Temothy WINSLOW son of Thos. of
Perquemens, and Rachell WILLSON of the place
aforesaid...9, 1m, 1736/7...at ye house of Mary
NEWBYS...

[Column 1]
Joseph MAYO
Zachariah NIXON
Joseph NEWBY
Samuell BUNDY
Abram SANDERS
Judeth SANDERS
Savery[?] BAGLEY
Thos. HOLLOWELL
John GRIFIN
Samuell NEWBY
Thos. BAGLEY
[Column 2]
Timothy WINSLOW
Rachel WINSLOW

[Column 2 cont.]
Rt. WILSON
Joseph WINSLOW
Thomas WINSLOW
Joseph WILSON
Thomas JESSOP
Jane JESSOP
Mary NEWBY
Lovy[?] ELLIOT
John WINSOWE
John WINSLOW
[?]
Elisabeth WINSLOW
Recorded the 25 of the
first month 1737 By
Zachariah NIXON Clarke

Page 10/2 Peter JONES of Yopen in paquimans
precint, and [Ame] HANCOCK ye dau of Staven of ye
same place...18, 8m, [1704]...att a forth day [torn]
at ye New metting house...

[Column 1]
William NEWBY
Gabriell NEWBY
Isaac WILSON
Samuell NICOLESON
John NICOLESON
Francis WELES
Richard CHESTEN
William MORE

[Column 2]
Peter PI J[torn]
Ame X H[torn]
Jane NEW[torn]
Hanah [torn]
Hanah C[torn]
Mary NEWBY
Elizabeth MORE
Ann WILSON

[Column 1 cont.]   [Column 2 cont.]
Thomas WINSLO   Ann DORMAN
Jose[?torn] PIRCE   Mary CLEARE
Recorded by me G N   Elizabeth CLEARE
ye 18 of ye 8 mth 1704

Page 11 Thomas WINSLOE ye son of Timothy of
paqu[torn], and Elizabeth CLEARE ye dau of Timothy
of [torn]...2, 9[torn], 1704...att Timothy CLEARS...
      [Column 1]   [Column 2]
Timothy WINSLOE   Thomas W[torn]
Sarah WINSLOE   Elizabeth WIN[torn]
Hanah CLEARE   Timothy CL[torn]
Mary CLEARE   Wm. NEW[TORN]
Jane LANE   Isaac WILS[torn]
Mary TOMES   Wm. MOR[torn]
Mary NEWBY   John NICOLES[torn]
Ann WILSON   Nath. ALBERT[torn]
Elizabeth MOORE   Wm. BOOG
Arther JONES   Wm. NEWBY Jr
Jane CLARE   Edward NEWBY
Sa[torn] CLEAR   Joseph NEWBY
Recorded pr me   Joseph NEWBY[This name
Gabriell NEWBY   written in a different
This 7th of ye   hand. Part of later
12th 1704/5   notes on the page?]

Page 13 Nathanell ABERTSON son of Albert ALBERTSON
Lat of paq[torn], and Abigall NICOLESON dau of
Samuell...[torn], 5m, 1705...a meeting att her
father Samuell NICOLESON [torn]...
      [Column 1]   [Column 2]
Mary ALBERTSON   Nathanell ALB[torn]
Mary TOMES   Abigall ALB[torn]
Mary NEWBY   Samuell NICOLESON
Ann DORMAN   Elizabeth NICOLESON
Marcy STEPNEY   Timothy CLEARE
Hannah CLEARE   John NICOLESON
Dameris PIRCE   Nath. NICOLESON
Sarah BAROW   Albert ALBERTSON
Recorded   Asue ALBERTSON
by me   Peter ALBERTSON
Gabriell NEWBY   Francis WELES
[torn]   Isaac WILSON
                          [?]   [? NY]

Page 14 At a quarterly meeting in Pequimens the
29th of ye [torn] 1707 thare friends fulring into

thare mature concill [torn] the great ocation to
preventing disorders have tharefore [torn] good if
[?] of the body of the sd meeting men wh[torn] to
stand from time to time to ye yearly meeting with
[torn] Judgment in truth...

[Column 1]

Mathew PRICHARD
James DAVIS
Hanry KEETON
Staven SCOTT
Edward MAYOE
Agustin SCARBOROUG
John KINSEY
Emanuel LOW
Zachariah NIXON
John MORISS
Benjamin PRICHARD
John WHITE
Caleb BUNDY

[Column 2]

Francis TOM[torn]
William NEWB[torn]
John BARO[torn]
Gabriel NEWBY
Timothy CLEARE
Thomas PEIRC
Isaac WILLSON
Ralph FLETCHER
Francis WEELLS
John PRITLOE
Samuell NICEL[torn]
John NICELSON
Francis TOMES Junr
John HAWKINS

Page 15/2 From our Monthly Meeting in
Pequimons...2, 11m, 1711/2...whare as Sarah BUNDY
the dau of William and Mary BUNDY hath Contrary to
the Councell of her mother and her Relations and
friends Joyned her selfe in maridge to a man that is
of another Profession in Religon Contrary to the
good order Astablished... She is not in unity with
us... Signed in behalf of ye Sd Meeting...

[Column 1]

Mary TOMES
Elesebeth PRITLOE
Margreat TOMES
Ann DORMAN
Elezabeth NICOLESON
Ravci[?] PEIRC
[?] NICOLESON

[Column 2]

Reachell LARRANC
Reachell PRITLOE
Ann WILLSON

[Column 3]

Richard RATLIFF
William MORE
William BOOG
Elezebeth MORE

[Column 4]

Francis TOMES
Timothy CLEAR
Isaac [W]ILLSON
Samuell [torn]
Francis [torn]
Samuel [torn]

Page 17 [1707?] [Gabriel NEWBY] and Ralph BOSEMAN
a man not [torn] to our meetings the said meeting
chuses seven friends of the sd meeting to End the
diferance ... We give it as our Judgement that thay
Aought to Live in Love and younity as mutch as if
this diferance had not been.

[Column 1]
John PRITLOWE
Samuell NICOLSON

Thomas PEIRC recorder

[Column 2]
Francis TOMES
John BARROW
Timothy CLEAR
Isaac WILLSON

Page 18 Arthar JONES of Prquimens, and Rachal
SNELLEN dau of Israel late of ye same...4, 1m,
1707/8...att Timothy CLEARS house hir fathar in
[torn]...

[Column 1]
Francis TOMES
William NEWBY
Gabriel NEWBY
Samuel NICELSON
John NICELSON
Ralph FLETCHER
William BOOGE
William MORE
Richd. CHESTON
Mary NEWBY
Mary PEIRC Siner
Rebekah PEIRC
William NEWBY
Edward NEWBY
Steven GIBENS
Joseph NEWBY

[Column 2]
Arthar A JONES
Rachal R JONES
Mary BEESLY
Hannah CLEAR
Elesebeth CALLOWAY
Timothy CLEAR
Daniel JONES
Francis JONES
Ann ALBERTSON
Elesebeth JONES
Sarah JONES
Elesebeth WINSLOE
Jann LARRANC
Mary CLEAR
Jann CLEAR
Sarah CLEAR

Recorded pr Thomas PEIRC this 5th ye 1m 1707/8

Page 18/2 George BARROW Sonn of John of Pequimens,
and Elezebeth TURNER the dau of [torn]rd of the same
place...10, 6m, 1710...at the aforesd John BARROWS
house...

[Column 1]
Johanah WILLIAMS
Mary PEIRC
Ame JONES
Margett PAVILL
Ann WILLSON

[Column 2]
Jenkins WILLIAMS
John WILLIAMS
Francis FOSTER
Samuell NICELSON
Isaac WILLSON
Thomas PEIRC
Timothy CLEAR
Peter JONES

[Column 3]
Joseph SMITH
Robart HARMON
John PEIRC
Thomas PEIRC Juner

[Column 4]
George BARROW
Elezebeth BARROW
John BARROW
Richard TURNER
John BARROW Jun
James BARROW
Joseph BAR[torn]
John [torn]

Page 19/2 Stephen GIBBENS of Pequimens, and Janne
LARRANC the dau of William [torn]sed of the same
place...9, 12m, 17[0]8/9...att a 4th day meeting att
the Lower meeting house Att Francis [TOM]ES...

[Column 1]
Isaac WILLSON
Timothy CLARE
Samuel NICELSON
John PRITLOE
John NICELSON
Richd. RATCLIF
Thomas PEIRC
John PEIRC
Recorded Pr Tho.
PEIRC this 21st of
ye 2cn mot. 1709

[Column 2]
Stephen GIBBENS
Jane LARRANC GIBBENS
Francis TOMES Junr
Arthur JONES
Ann WILLSON
Damarus RATCLIF
Rebekah PEIRC
Elezebeth NIXSON
Elezebeth THIGBEN
Hannah NICELSON
Pricilah PRITLOE

Page 21 Edward MAYO of Pascota[nk] Cooper, and Mary
CLARE dau of Timothy of Pequimens...[?], 2m,
1709...house of Timothy CLARE in Pequimens...

[Column 1]
Hannah SMITH
Hannah FOSTER
Ann DORMON
Rebekah PEIRC
Elezebeth NICELSON
Pricelah PRITLOE
Leah PRITLOE
Isabell NEWBY
Mary NEWBY
Moses NEWBY
Joseph NEWBY
Gorge BARROW
Barnabey NIXSON
[torn]ESSEY[?]
[torn]BYROM[?]
[torn]iam EVERIGIN

[Column 2]
Francis TOMES
Mary TOMES
Mary CLARK
Thomas WINSLOE
Benjaman PRITCHARD
Samuel NICELSON
William NEWBY
Zachariah NIXSON
Gabriel NEWBY
Francis FOSTER

[Column 2 cont.]
Thomas PEIRC
Ann WILLSON
Mary BOSMAN[?]

[Column 3]
John NICELSON
Arthar JONES
Francis NEWBY
Thomas PEIRC
Wm. NEWBY
Edward NEWBY
Joseph NEWBY
Jesse[?] NEWBY

[Column 4]
Edward MAYO
Mary MAYO
Timothy CLARE
Hannah CLARE
Sarah PRITCHARD
Elezebeth SCOTT
Elezebeth WINSLOW
Matthew PRITCHARD
Janne CLARE
Sarah PRITCHARD
Caleb BUNDY
Sarah CLARE
Mary NEWBY
Janne BUNDY

[Column 2 cont.]   [Column 4 cont.]
Isaac WILLSON   Stephen SCOTT

Page 21/2 Richard CHESTEN Cooper of ye County of
Albemarle, and Ann DORMAN Relect of [torn]hard
DORMAN of the same place...2, 11m, [17]11/12 att our
meeting house in Pequimens...

[Column 1]   [Column 2 cont.]
Margreat TOMES   Ann A CHESTEN
Elezebeth NICELSON   her mark
Elezebeth MOORE   Christipher NICELSON
Elezebeth PRITLOE   Nathanell NICELSON
Rebekah PEIRC   Samuell NICELSON
Ann WILLSON   Samuell CHARLES
   [Column 2]   Nathan NEWBY
Richard R C CHESTEN   Gabriell NEWBY
      his mark   Isaac WILLSON
                         Timothy CLEAR

Page 22/2 Nathanell NICOLESON son of Christopher of
paquiman, and Sarah MARIS dau of John of ye same
place...[torn], 8m, 1704...att a Monthly Meeting att
ye new Metting hows[torn]...

[Column 1]   [Column 1 cont.]
Samuell NICOLESON   [?]GE[?]
John NICOLESON   [Column 2]
Isaac WILLSON   Francis TOMES
Christopher NICOLESON   Gabriell NEWBY
Joshua TOMES[?]   [Column 3]
Samuell CHARLES[?]   Nathanell N NICOLESON
Francis TOMES Jnr   by mark
[?]TLOE   Sarah S NICOLESON
[?]MES   her mark

Page 23 John KINZEY son of John Late of the Present
of [torn]mons In the County of Arlbemarle weaver,
and Presello NICELSON [torn]ct of the desesed John
NICELSON Late of the County and place aforesd...23,
6m, 1711...att the [hou]se of the Afore:sd Presello
NICELSON...

[Column 1]   [Column 2 cont.]
Dameres RATCLIF   Arthar JONES
Ann WILLSON   John PEIRC
Hannah CLEAR   [Column 3]
Elezebeth WINSLOE   Nathanell NICELSON
Elezebeth MORE   William NEWBY Juner
Alexander:ese:SUTEN   Edward NEWBY
Margret TOMES   Thomas PEIRC Juner

[Column 1 cont.]
Hannah NICELSON
Abigell ALBERTSON
Elizebeth[?] REED[?]
  [Column 2]
William NEWBY
Gabriell NEWBY
Francis FOSTER
Samuell NICELSON
Joshua TOMES
Thomas WINSLOE
Richard RATLIFF

[Column 4]
John KINZEY
Presello KINZEY
Francis TOMES
Mary TOMES
Mary NEWBY
Francis TO[torn] Jun
Samuell CH[?][torn]
Mary [torn]
Sarah [torn]

Page 23/2 [Advise to the women of the Meeting, no
date, probably between 1708 and 1710, signed by the
following:]
  [Column 1]
Ann DORMAN
Ann WILLSON
Elezebeth PRICLOE
Elezebeth MORE
Elezebeth WINSLOE
Mary CLEAR

[Column 2]
Mary TOMES
Sarah BARROW
Janne NEWBY
Mary NEWBY
Hanah CLEAR
Margret TOMES

Page 24 John HENBY of Paquimens, and Hanah DARMON
dau of Richard Late of ye place...24, 9m, 1714...a
forth day meeting At the Lower meeting hows by Mary
TOMESES...
  [Column 1]
Ann CHESTON
Ann NICKOLSON
Ann WILLSON
Hanah NICKOLSON
Elizabeth NICKOLSON
Elizabeth REED
Elizabeth MOUNTIGU
Damaris RATLIFF
Jane FLECHER
Sarah TOMES
Prissila KINSEY
Mary DARMON
Mary THOMES
Recorded
by Richard
  RATLIFF

[Column 2]
John I H HENBY
Hanah H H HENBY
Richard CHESTEN
Richard CHESTEN Jun[?]
[torn] NICKOLSON
Frances WELLS
Ralph [F]LEACHER
Thomas [P]EIRC
Tho[torn] WINSLOW
Samuell CHARLES
J[o]hn KINSEY
[S]amuell CHARLES Jun[?]
Frances FOSTER
James HENBY
Abraham GINIT
Thomas RATLIFF

Page 26 [Advice to the Meeting, Recorded the 15th
of the 9[?]m, 1712[?] by Thomas PEIRCE. Signed by:]

[Column 1]
Gabriell NEWBY
Francis WELS
[Column 2]
Isaac WILSON
Samuell BOND
William LACY
Thomas WINSLO
Francis JONES
Arther JONES

[Column 3]
Francis TOMES
William NEWBY
John BARROW
Gorg FORDICE
Timothy CLEARE
Richd. CHESTON
William BOOGE
John PRITLOE
William MORE
Francis TOMES Junr

Page 27 Benjamin WILLSON and Judah DOCKTON dau of
Thomas...15, 12m, 1721/2...at the house of Thomas
DOCTON in Paquimons...
[Column 1]
Mary DOCKTON
Jacob DOCKTON
Leah SMITH
Rachel DOCKTON
Joseph NEWBY
John SMALL
Thomas NEWBY

Recorded By R[? torn]

[Column 2]
Benjamin WILLSON
Judeth WILLSON
Thomas DOCKTON
Elisabeth DOCKTON
Elisabeth PRICE
John PRICE
Robert WILLSON
Isack WILLSON
[torn] SMALL

Page 27/2 John SIMONS of Pascotank, and Prissilla
KINSEY widdow of John KINSEY Late of Paquimons...8,
1m called March, 1721/2...at the Publik meeting hows
at Paquimons...
[Column 1]
Mary MORRIS
Elizabeth NICKOLSON
Mary NICKOLSON
Rebeckah SYMONS
Mary WHITE
Elizabeth PHELPS
Rebeckah PRITLOE
Mary NEWBY
Sarah MORGIN
Elizabeth NIXON
[Column 2]
Henry WHITE
Zachariah NIXON
Samuell NICKOLSON
Steephen SCOTT
Thomas PEIRCE
Samuell BUNDY

[Column 2 cont.]
John PRITLOE
Joseph NICKOLSON
Jesse NEWBY
Richard RATLIFF
Damaris RATLIFF
[Column 3]
John SIMONS
Prissilla P SIMONS
          her mark
Francis TOMES
Jer- SYMONS
Wm. SYMONS
Thomas SYMONS
Samuell CHARLS
John MORRIS
Joseph NEWBY Junr
Joshua TOMES

[torn]ed By Richard RATLIFF

Page 28/2 John NIXON son of Zachariah, and Elisa.
NEWBY dau of Gabriel all of Paquimance...10, 7m,
1729...at ye House of Gabriel NEWBY...

[Column 1]
Benja.} PRITCHARD
Isabel }
Mary TROTT[torn]
Mary N[torn]
Leah SMI[torn]
Joshua ELLIO[torn]
Thos. JESSOP
Thos. NEWBY
John SYMONS
[Column 2]
Francis NEWBY
[torn] SANDERS
Jan[torn]SSOP
Joseph [torn]BY
Mary NEWBY
Willm. HILL
[torn]HAIG
H[torn] BUNDY

[Column 2 cont.]
Phinihas NIXON
[Column 3]
John NIXON
Elisabeth NIXON
Gabriel NEWBY
Mary NEWBY
Zachariah NIXON
Elisabeth NIXON
Joseph NEWBY
John MORRIS
Mary MORRIS
Elisa. NEWBY
Rachel PEARSON
Jesse NEWBY
Saml. NEWBY
Recorded the 15th Day
ye 8th month 1729.
by Rt. WILSON

Page 29 John WINSLOE of Pequimins, and Esther
SNELLING dau of Hanah CLARE of the same...10, 8m,
1716...at the dwelling hows of Timothy CLARE...

[Column 1]
Mary NEWBY juner
Sarah CLARE
John HENLEY
Mary THOMES june
Mary NEWBY
Jane CHARLES
Damaris RATLIFF
William PLATO
John WILLIAMES
Elisabeth NICKOLSON
Peter ALBORDSON
Humphrey WADEY
[Column 2]
John WINSLOE
Esther WINSLOE
Thomas WINSLOE

[Column 2 cont.]
Timothy WINSLOE
Timothy CLARE
Hanah CLARE
Sarah WINSLOE
Arther JONES
Elisabeth WINSLOE
Jane LANE
Sarah LILLEY
Edward MAYO
Mary MAYO
Joseph NEWBY
Isabell NEWBY
Ann NEWBY
Elisabeth NEWBY
[torn] SMITH

Recorded By Richard RATLIFF

Page 29/2 John ANDERSON and Elizabeth NICHOLSON dau
of Samuell...28, 3m, 1719...at the Lower meeting
House...

[Column 1]
Elizabeth THOMES
Mary PEIRCE
Mary WHITE
Cateron ANDERSON
Mary THOMES
  [Column 2]
Hanah HENBY
Elizabeth CHARLES
Sarah MORGIN
Joseph NEWBY
Abraham[?] LARANCE[?]
Henry WHITE
Thomas MOUNTECUE
Nathan NEWBY
John WILLIAMS
Ralph FLETCHER
Joseph NICHOLSON
Mathew PRITCHARD

[Column 2 cont.]
Samuell CHARLS
  [Column 3]
John ANDERSON
Elizabeth ANDERSON
Know[?] NICHOLSON
Samuel NICHOLSON
Elisabeth NICHOLSON
Jane MORGIN
Jane MORGIN
Nathaniel NICHOLSON
Christopher NICHOLSON
George[?] HOLLOWELL[?]
Abigall ALBARDSON[?]
Hanah NICKOLSON
Ann NICKOLSON
Sarah THOMES
Recorded By
Richard RATLIFF

Page 30 John WHITE of Virginia, and Sarah CLARE dau
of Timothy of Paquimons...7, 8m, [1717]...At the
uper meeting howss at Paquimons...

[Column 1]
William SCOTT
William NEWBY[?]
Samuell NICHOLSON
Samuell CHARLES
William BOAGE juner
Nathan NEWBY
Arther JONES
Robert WILLSON
  [Column 2]
Hanah CLARE
Elisabeth WINSLOE
Jane ROBINSON
Rachel WILLSON
Leah SMITH

[Column 2 cont.]
Ann NICHOLSON
Mary THOMES
  [Column 3]
John WHITE
Sarah WHITE
Timothy CLARE
John WHITE
Nathanuell NICHOLSON
Thomas WINSLOE
John PRITLOE
Cornelious RATLIFF
Recorded By
Richard RATLIFF

Page 30/2 Edward NEWBY son of Gabriell of
Pequimins, and Mary HAGE dau to William and Mary
HAIGE decd of Pascotank...17, 1m, 1719/20...at the
uper meeting...

[Column 1]
Elezabeth SMALL
Elezabeth JORDAN
[?] SMALL
Presilah KINSEY
Mary THOMES
Elezabeth THOMES
[Column 2]
Robert JORDAN Junr
Joseph JORDAN
John PRITLOE
Paul PALMER
Samuell NICHOLSON
Ralph BUFKIN
John HOLLOWELL
John HENLEY
Ann[?] [torn]
[Column 3]
Elizabeth NEWBY
Sarah HAIGE
William HAIGE
Thomas NEWBY

[Column 3 cont.]
Joseph NEWBY
Nathan NEWBY
Jessey NEWBY
Samuell NEWBY
Zachriah NIXON
Thomas PEIRCE
[Column 4]
Edward NEWBY
Mary NEWBY
Gabriel NEWBY
Mary NEWBY
Mary NEWBY
Frances THOMES
Margret THOMES
Joseph NEWBY
Frances NEWBY
Ann NEWBY
Elizabeth NEWBY
Elizabeth NEWBY
Recorded By
[torn] RATLI[torn]

Page 31   Nathan NEWBY late of Nansemond in Virginia
sun of Nat[?] of ye same place, and Mary TOMES of
North Carolina the dau of Fr[ancis T]OMES of ye
place aforesd...1, 8m, 1720...at the meeting hous in
Paquimons...

[Column 1]
John HOLLOWELL
Thomas SMALL
John SMALL
[Column 2]
Joseph NEWBY
Ales SMALL
Mary NEWBY
Rachell PEIRSON
Sarah TOMES
Elisab. ELLIOTT
Sarah[?] MORGIN
Hanah NICHOLSON

[Column 3]
Nathan NEWBY
Mary NEWBY
Nathan NEWBY Se[torn]
Elisabeth NEWBY
Francis TOMES
Margret TOMES
Elisabeth NEWBY
Elisabeth TOMES
Thomas NEWBY
Ann NEWBY
Samuell NEWBY
Recorded By
Richard RATLIFF

Page 31/2   Peter JONES son of Peter of Paquimons,
and Mary PEIRCE dau of Thomas of the same place...
1, 7m, 1720...at the meeting house...

[Column 1]
Joseph NEWBY
Nathan NEWBY
Judah SANDERS
Rebeckah PRITLOE
Mary JONES
Elisabeth JONES
Rebeckah SUTTON
John ANDERSON
Samuell CHARLES
John PRITLOW
 Recorded By
Richard RATLIFF

[Column 2]
Peter JONES
Mary M JONES
Peater JONES
Thomas PEIRCE
Mary M PEIRCE
Mathew PRICHARD
Gabriell NEWBY
Zachry NIXON
Charls DENMAN
William JONES
Timothy CLARE
Samuell NICKOLSON

Page 32   Jonathan FELLPS ye sun of Jonathan of
paquimons, and Eliz. TOMES ye dau of Francis of ye
precinct afsd...16, 12m, 1720...at the Lower meeting
hows of paquimons...

[Column 1]
Frances TOMES
Joshua TOMES
Willam MORE
Henry CLATON
Thos. DAVIS[or PARIS]
Samll. CHARLS
Samll. PHELP
Samll. NICHOLSON
Thomas PEIRCE
John PEIRCE
Samuell SHARER[?]
Edward MAYO
    [Column 2]
Sarah MORGIN
Prissila KINSEY
Joseph NEWBY
   Recorded By Richard RATLIFF

[Column 2 cont.]
Gabriell NEWBY
Caleb PHENIX
Thomas NEWBY
John PRITLOE
Frances NEWBY
    [Column 3]
Jonathan PHELPS
Elizabeth PHELPS
Mary NEWBY
Ann PARRISS
Ann NEWBY
Judah SANDERS
Eliz. ELLET
Hanah NICHOLSON
Rebeckah PRITLOE
[torn] PEIRCE

Page 32/2   Stephen SCOTT of pascotank, and Hanah
NICHOLSON dau of Samuell in paquimons...13, 2m
called Aprill, 1721...At the publick meeting hows at
paquimons...

[Column 1]
Joshua TOMES
Sarah ALBORDSON
Joseph NEWBY
Elisabeth CHARLES
John WILLIAMS
Paul PAULMER

[Column 2 cont.]
Joseph BARROW
John HENLY
Henry WHITE
Edward MAYO Junr
[torn]th MOUNTICU
[torn]h [?]

[Column 1 cont.]
Peter DENMAN
Sarah MORGIN
Hepsibah CLARE
[?]har[?] WHITE
John SIMONS
[torn]nes[?] TO[torn]
[torn]ah [torn]
    [Column 2]
Ann NICHOLSON
Mary NICHOLSON
Thomas PRICHARD
Steephen DELEMAR
Mathew PRICHARD
Timothy CLARE

[Column 2 cont.]
[torn] [?]
[torn] [?]
  [Column 3]
Stephen SCOTT
Hanah H NICHOLESON
   mark now SCOTT
Samuell NICHOLSON
Elisabeth NICHOLSON
Abagall ALBORDSON
Jane BARROW
Christifer NICHOLSON
Samuell CHARLES
Joseph NICHOLSON

Page 33 Ralph BUFKIN of Paquimons, and Mary NEWBY
widdow of Edward NEWBY decd...15, 1m called march,
1721/2...At the publick meeting hows at Paquimons...

[Column 1]
John WILLIAMS
Joseph NEWBY Junor
Peter PEARSON
  [Column 2]
William HAGE
William TROTER
Thomas HARVEY
Henry CLAYTON
Thomas JESSOP

[Column 2 cont.]
Thomas WINSLOE
[?   ]
  [Column 3]
Ralph BUFKIN
Mary BUFKIN
Gabriell NEWBY
Mary NEWBY
Joseph NEWBY
[?] NEWBY

Page 33/2 Frances TOMES of Paquimons, and Rebeckah
PEIRCE of the same place... 5, 4m called June,
1722...at paquimons...

[Column 1]
Charls DENMAN
Samuell CHARLS
John SIMONS[?]
Elisabeth NEWBY
Thomas RICKS
John PEIRC
Thomas PEIRCE
Samuell PHELPS
  [Column 2]
Thomas PEIRCE
Gabriell NEWBY
Zachariah NIXON
Timothy CLARE

[Column 2 cont.]
Samuell NICHOLSON
Henry CLAYTON
Thomas DAVIS[or PARIS]
  [Column 3]
Frances TOMES
Rebeckah TOMES
Mary SIMMONS
Mary NEWBY
Mary PEIRCE
Prissilla SIMONS
Sarah PEIRCE
 recorded by
Richard RATLIFF

Page 36 George SUTTON of Paquimons, and Sarah PEIRC
dau of Thomas...25, 8m called October, 1722...att
the dwelling hows of Thomas PEIRC at Paquimons...

[Column 1]
Peter JONES
Joseph BARROW
John ANDERSON
Rachel BARROW
William TROTTER
Richard RATLIFF
    [Column 2]
Thomas PEIRC Junr
Henry CLATON
Charls DENMAN
John WAYTT
Peter JONES
Zachariah NIXON
Christipher NICHOLSON

[Column 2 cont.]
Samuell [torn]
Sarah [torn]
    [Column 3]
George SUTTON his mark
Sarah P SUTTON
    her mark
Thomas PEIRC
Mary PEIRC
John PEIRC
Rebeckah LONG
Mary SIMONS
[torn] SUTTON
[torn]

Page 36/2 Thomas JESSOP and Jane ROBINSON of
Paquimons...14, 12m, 1722/3...in the publick meeting
hows att Paquimons...

[Column 1]
Ruth GLASTER
Joseph WINSLOE
Mary WINSLOE
Henry CLAYTON
Elizabeth CLAYTON
Hanah CLARE
Frances WELS
Zachariah NIXON
Ann[?] BUNDY[?]
    [Column 2]
Mathew PRICHARD
Timothy CLARE
Joseph JESSOP
Mary MAYO
Margret JESSOP
Mary JESSOP

[Column 2 cont.]
Timothy JESSOP
Jesse NEWBY
Edward MAYO
    [Column 3]
Thomas JESSOP
Jane JESSOP
Elisabeth WINSLOE
Thomas WINSLOE
Sarah WHITE
Natha. NICHOLS[ON]
Huldah NEWBY
Mary NEWBY
Sarah GLASTER
Stephen SCOTT
  Rechstered By
Richard RATLIFF

Page 39 Richard DAVIS of Virginia, and Sarah
ALLBORDSON dau of Nathannell of Paquimons...31, 8m
called October, 1723...at the Lower meeting hows at
paquimons...

[Column 1]
Gabriell NEWBY
Zachariah NIXON
Stephen SCOTT

[Column 2]
Richard DAVIS
Sarah DAVIS
Nathanael ALBARDSON
Samuell NICHOLSON

[Column 1 cont.]
Samuell CHARLS
John SIMONS
Joseph NEWBY
Mathew PRICHARD
Thomas JESSOP
Recorded By Richard RATLIFF

[Column 2 cont.]
Elizabeth ALLBARDSON
Hanah SCOTT
Elizabeth ANDERSON
Prissilla SIMONS
[torn] ALLBARD[torn]

Page 39/2 Richard CHESTON of paquimance, and Eliz.
BARNS of ye precink and place aforesd...15, 10m,
1725...at ye lower meeting house in paquimance...

[Column 1]
Jerahmiah BARNS
Frans. TOMES
Samll. NICHOLSON
Samll. CHARLES
Joshua TOMES
Ralph FLETCHER
Nathan NEWBY
Tho. SMALL
Joseph NICHOLSON
Joseph THOMES
Recorded by Robert WILLSON

[Column 2]
Rebecah TOMES
Mary NEWBY
Penelope TOMES
Priscilla TOMES
Margreat TOMES
Pleasant TOMES
[Column 3]
Ricd. CHEASTON
Eliza. E CHEASTON

Page 40/2 Joshua TOMS of perquimons plantor, and
Eliz: CHARLES dau of Samll. of ye precinct afsd
spinster...9, 5m called July, 1724...in the meeting
hous at Francis TOMS...

[Column 1]
Mary NEWBY
Mary NEWBY
Ralph FLETCHER
Henry WHITE
[Column 2]
Thos. JESSOP
Eliz. NIXON
Jane BARROW
Joseph BARROW

[Column 3]
Eliz. NICKELSON
John MORRIS
Zack. NIXON
Samll. NICKELSON
[Column 4]
Joshua TOMS
Eliz. TOMS
Frans. TOMS
Gabriell NEWBY
Rebecco TOMS

Page 41 Samuel NEWBY of Little River, and Elisabeth
ALBERSON dau of Nathaniel of [?] Paquimance...11,
9m, 1725...at ye Lower Meeting House in
Paquimance...

[Column 1]
Ann NEWBY
Ann BUNDEY
Peter ALBERSON

[Column 2 cont.]
Joseph BARROW
Hannah SCOTT
Jane BARROW

[Column 1 cont.]
Esua ALBERSON
Richd. CHEASTON
Joseph NEWBY
Nathan NEWBY
Thos. JESSOP
Mary LACY
     [Column 2]
Abigal ALBERSON
Joseph NICHOLSON
Richd. DAVIS
Sarah DAVIS

[Column 2 cont.]
Hannah OVERMAN
Miriam NICHOLSON
     [Column 3]
Saml. NEWBY
Elis. NEWBY
James NEWBY
Saml. NICHOLSON
Elis. NICHOLSON
Nathl. ALBERSON
Elis. ANDERSON
Aaron ALBERSON

Recorded the 31 day of [torn] [1728]
     Rt. WILLSON

Page 41/2 Richd. SANDERS and Hannah NICHOLSON of
Paquimance...14, 8m, 1730...at ye lower Meeting
house in Paquimance...

     [Column 1]
Richard DAVIS
Thos. WINSLOW
Jos. BARROW
Nathaniel ALBERTSON
John BELMAN
Jos. NEWBY
Jos. PEIRCE
Wm. SHITTLETON
Peter JONES Junr
Joshua ELLIOT
     [Column 2]
Elisa NIXON
Mary PEIRCE
Elisa. PHELPS
Damaris RATTCLIFF

[Column 2 cont.]
Emme EVANS
Eliphal HARPER
Jane MORE
     [Column 3]
Richd. R SANDERS
     his mark
Hannah H SANDERS
     her mark
Thomas PEIRCE
Zachariah NIXON
Abraham SANDERS
Francis WELLS
Peter JONES
Joshua MORE
Saml. NEWBY

Recorded the 27 Day of
ye 8th month 1730 by Rt. WILSON

Page 43 Joseph WINSLOW and Plesent TOMES both of ye
countey of perquimons...22, 6m, 1729[?]...at the
house of Francis TOMESES...

     [Column 1]
Gabriel NEWBY
Mary NEWBY
Thos. JESOP
     [Column 2]
Mary NEWBY
Jos. NEWBY
Rich. EVERARD

     [Column 3]
Thos. WINSLOW
Elis. WINSLOW
Elis. PHELPS
     [Column 4]
Joseph WINSLOW
Plesant WINSLOW
Francis TOMES

Page 45 Cristopher NECHOLSON of Paquimance River in
ye County of arlbemarle, and Ann ATWOOD of ye same
County...11, 2m, 1680...in ye Meeting at ye House of
Francis TOMES where ye meeting is kept in
Paquimance...   [Column 2 cont.]
        [Column 1]   Francis TOMES
      Hannah HILL   Henry WHITE
      Mary PEIRCE   [Column 3]
      Dorothy PROWS   Christopher NICHOLSON
      Ann PROWS   Ann NICHOLSON
      Priscila TOMES   Charles PROWS
        [Column 2]   William BUNDY
      James HOGG   Jona. PHELPS
      Henry PROWS   Joseph SCOT
      James HILL   John PEIRCE

Page 47 John MORE son of William of Paquimance, and
Mary RATCLIFF dau of Dameris of ye place
aforesaid...10, 12m, 1729/30...in ye meeting House
at Francis TOMES in Paquimance...
        [Column 1]   [Column 2 cont.]
      Abraham SANDERS   [torn] MORE
      John ANDERSON   [torn] WINSLOW
      [torn] ELLIOT[?]   [Column 3]
      [column torn]   John MORE
        [Column 2]   Mary MORE
      Thos. WINSLOW   Dameris RATCLIF
      Joshua MORE   William MORE
      Jos. WINSLOW   Gabriel NEWBY
      Jos. NEWBY   Zachariah NIXON
      Saml. NEWBY   John MORRIS
      Elis. NIXON   Nathaniel NICHOLSON
      Elis. NEWBY   John LANE
      [torn]n PETIVER   John SYMONS
      [torn]ry NEWBY   William MORE
      [torn]garet TOMES
      [torn] 1732 by Rt. WILSON Clk.

Page 47/2 John NIXON son of Zachariah, and
Elisabeth [torn] dau of William MOORE all of
Paquimance...15, 4m, 1732...at ye upper Meeting
House...
        [Column 1]   [Column 2]
      Mary NIXON   Samuel MOORE
      John SYMONS   Jane BUNDEY
      Mary NEWBY   Joseph NEWBY
      Ann NEWBY   Thomas MOUNT[torn]
      Sarah WHITE   Thomas WINS[torn]

[Column 1 cont.]   [Column 2 cont.]
  Elisabet MAYO   Joseph RO[torn]
  William HILL   Mary NE[torn]
  Joseph NEWBY   Dameris [torn]
  Jesse NEWBY   [Column 3]
Recorded the 23 of   John N[torn]
ye 7th month [torn]   [torn]

Page 48 Wm. MORE and Rebecca TOMES of
Paquimance...10, 9m, 173[0]...at ye lower meeting
house in Paquimance...
    [Column 1]   [Column 3]
  Dameris RATCLIFF   William MORE
  Mary NEWBY   Rebecca MORE
  Sarah SCOTT   Thos. PEIRC
  Mary JONES   Jos. PEIRC
  Elis. WINSLOWE   Gabriel NEWBY
  Mary NEWBY   Zachariah NIXON
  Elis. NIXON   Joshua SCOTT
  Elis. PHELPS   Joseph NEWBY
    [Column 2]   Jesse NEWBY
  Robert WILSON   Joseph NEWBY
  Joseph JESSOP   Thos. JESSOP
  Thos. WINSLOWE   William MORE
  Jos. JESSOP Junr
  Joshua ELLIOT   Recorded the
26 Day of 9th Month 1730 by Rt. WILSON

Page 48/2 Josiah GILBERT and Sarah WILLIAMS both of
Paquimance...23, 10m, 1730...at ye house of Thos.
PEIRC...
    [Column 1]   [Column 3]
  Wm. SHITTLETON   Josiah GILBERT
  Peter JONES   Sarah P GILBERT
    [Column 2]   Thos. PEIRC
  Ann ALBERTSON   Mary PEIRC
  Jean ALBERTSON   Mary GILBERT
  Elisabeth PRATT   Zachariah NIXON
Recorded ye 3d Day of Jos. PEIRC
ye 12th month 1730/31 Aaron ALBERTSON
by Rt. WILSON   Alice PEIRC

Page 49 Thomas BINFORD of Virginia, and Elisa.
KINSEY of Paquimance...20, 11m, 1730/31...at the
lower meeting house in Paquimance...
    [Column 1]   [Column 3]
  Jos. PEIRC   Thos. BINFORD
  Nathan NEWBY   Elisabeth BINFORD

[Column 1 cont.]
Benja. WILSON
[Column 1 torn]
[Column 2]
Dameris RATCLIFF
Mary NEWBY
Judeth SANDERS
Alice PEIRC
Mary NEWBY
Sarah DAVIS
Mary TROTTER
[torn] NEWBY

[Column 3 cont.]
Zachariah NIXON
Elisa. NIXON
Ricd. SANDERS
Saml. NEWBY
Saml. NEWBY
Joseph NEWBY
Nathaniel NICHOLSON
William SHETTLETON
[torn]2th month 1730/31
[torn]By Rt. WILSON Clk

Page 49/2 Phinehas NIXON son of Zachariah, and Mary
[torn] widdow of William TROTTER both of
Paquimance...9, 12m, 1731/2...at ye House of Gabriel
NEWBY...

[Column 1]
Zachariah CHANCEY
Jos. MORRIS
Willm. SHUTTLETON
[Column 2]
Saml. NEWBY
Dameris RATCLIFF
Elisa. NEWBY
Benja. PRITCHARD
John MOR[torn]
Saml. NE[torn]

[Column 2 cont.]
Rebecca [torn]
Willia[torn]
Josep[torn}
[Column 3]
Phinehas NIXON
Mary NIXON
Zachariah NIXON
Gabriel N[torn]
Elisa. N[torn]
[Column 3 torn]

Recorded the first day [torn]

Page 51/2 John LACY and Jane FLETCHER of
Perquimans...28, 10m, 1743...at the meeting house in
the Old Neck...

[Column 1]
Isaac ELLIOT
Joshua DAVIS
Thomas JESSOP
Moses ELLIOT
Mary JESSOP
Mary JESSOP
Elizabeth NIXON
Margaret BARROW
[Column 2]
Rebecca TOMES
Henry PHELPS
Elizabeth KENYON
Thomas JESSOP
John GYER

[Column 2 cont.]
Francis TOMES
Zachariah NIXON
Nathan PEARSON
Thomas NEWBY
[Column 3]
John I LACY
  his mark
Jane + LACY
  her mark
Ralph FLETCHER
Mary FLETCHER
Elizabeth ALBERTSON
Arthur ALBERTSON
Elizabeth MORGAN
Joseph NEWBY

Page 52   Isaac ELIOT and Elizabeth MORGAN of the
county of Perquimans...18, 11m, 1743 ...at the house
of Caleb ELIOT of Perquimans...

[Column 1]
Tho. NEWBY
Eliz. NIXON
Joseph NEWBY
Caleb ELIOT
   [Column 2]
Zach: NIXON
John PEARSON
Mary JONES
Nathan PEARSON
Benjamin SANDERS

[Column 3]
Jacob ELIOT
John WHITE
Joshua ELIOT
Benjamin ELIOT
Charles JORDAN
   [Column 4]
Isaac I ELIOT his mark
Elizabeth E ELIOT
        her mark
Moses ELIOT
Charles ROBERTS

Page 52/2   Thomas TRUEBLOOD son of Amos of
Pasquotank, and Lydia ALBERSON dau of Nathan[iel]
ALBERTSON of Perquimons...14, 1m, 1743/4...at ye
meeting house In ye old Neck in Perquimons...

[Column 1]
Elizabeth NIXON
Rebeca TOMS
Mary NEWBY
Thomas NEWBY
   [Column 2]
Abel TRUEBLOOD
Joseph NEWBY
Silas CARPENTER

[Column 2 cont.]
Henry PHELPS
   [Column 3]
Thomas TRUEBLOOD
Lydia TRUEBLOOD
Amos TRUEBLOOD
Nathaniel ALBERTSON
Joshua ALBERTSON
Aaron ALBERTSON

Page 53   Pritlow ELLIOT son of William, and Sarah
CROXTON dau of Arther they both of perquimons
county...19, 7m, 1744...at the upper Meeting
House...

[Column 1]
Thomas HOLLOWELL
Joseph WILSON
   [Column 2]
Mary NEWBY
Joseph NEWBY
Thomas WINSLOW

[Column 3]
Pritlow ELLIOT
Sarah S ELLIOT
    her marke
Moses ELLIOT
Elizabeth PEARSON

Page 53/2   Samuel PARKS and Elisabeth HUDSON both of
ye County of Perquimons...9, 11m, 1744...at ye House
of Joseph MAYOS...

[Column 1]
Luke BONDS
Job WINSLOW

[Column 2 cont.]
John MOORE
Josiah BOGUE

[Column 1 cont.]
Jonathan PEARSON
John WILLSON
Jonathan PHELPS
    [Column 2]
Elisabeth WILSON
Elisabeth NIXON
Elisabeth WINSLOW
Elisabeth WINSLOW
Meriam WINSLOW
Thomas HOLLOWELL

[Column 3]
Samuel P PARKS
    his mark
Elisabeth X PARKS
    her mark
John HUDSON
Mary HUDSON
Thomas WINSLOW
Zach. NIXON
Joseph NEWBY
Nathan PEARSON
Joseph RATLIFF

Page 54   John WINSLOW son of Thomas of Perquimans Precinct, and Mary PEARSON dau of Peter Late of the same Province decd...20, 9m, 1740...at our meeting house near Leavin BUFKIN in Nancemund County in Virginia...

[Column 1]
Armiger TROTTER
Leavin BUFKIN
Edmund JORDAN
Thos. TROTTER
John MURDAUGH
Francis MACE
    [Column 2]
Joseph SMITH
Job WINSLOW

[Column 2 cont.]
Jonathan PEARSON
Sarah OVERMAN
Mor[?] MURDAUGH
    [Column 3]
John WINSLOW
Mary PEARSON
Thomas WINSLOW
Rachel PEARSON
Elizabeth WINSLOW

Page 54/2   Daniel SAINT and Margaret BARROW of the county of Perquimans...15, 6m, 1744...at the New meeting House in the old Neck in Perquimans...

[Column 1]
Nathan PEARSON
Peter JONES
Thomas NEWBY
Elizabeth PHELPS
Joseph RATLIFF
Joseph NEWBY Junr
Elizabeth BUNDY
Joseph BARROW
John BARROW
[?]
    [Column 2]
Elizabeth NIXON
Rebeckah TOMES
Zachariah NIXON
Aaron HILL

[Column 2 cont.]
Jesse HENDLEY
John ANDERSON
Joseph NEWBY
Samuel NEWBY
Abraham SAUNDERS
    [Column 3]
Daniel SAINT
Margret SAINT
Joseph BARROW
Sarah ASHLEY
Francis TOMES
Josiah BUNDY
Francis NEWBY
Mary NEWBY

Page 56/2-57 Robeart WILLSON son of Isack of
Pequimins, and Rachell PRITLOE dau of John of ye
precinct & place afsd...13, 6m, 1712...att ye Lower
meeting house att a fourth day meeting...

[Column 1]

Mary TOMS
Hanah FOSTER
Eliner BOAG
Elizabeth CHARLES
Sarah TOMMS
Hanah NICHOLSON
Rachell LAWRANCE
Ann CHESTEN
Mary TOMMS
Elizabeth PRITLOE Junr
Timothey CLARE
Francis WELLS
Samuell NICHOLSON
Jos. BARROW
Samuell CHARLES
Ralph FLETCHER
Joshua TOMMS

[Column 1 cont.]

Jno. BELLMAN
Isack WILLSON Junr

[Column 2]

Robeart WILLSON
Rachell WILLSON
Isack WILLSON
Ann WILLSON
John PRITLOE
Elizabeth PRITLOE
Priscilla PRITLOE
Sarah WARNER
Benjm. WILLSON
Esther BELLMAN
Ann WILLSON Junr
Wm. NEWBEY
Gabriell NEWBEY
Tho. DOCKTON

Page 58 [See page 40/2. This may continue the
witnesses to the marriage of Joshua TOMS and Eliz:
CHARLES on 9, 5m, 1724.]

[Column 1]

Mary NICHOLSON
Sarah DAVIS
Joseph NEWBY
Ralph FLETCHER Junr
Recorded the 10th Day
of the fifth month 1724 by

[Column 2]

Eliz. ALBORDSON
Abraham SANDERS
Joseph NICHOLSON
John WILLIAMS
John SIMONS
Thomas JESSOP

Page 59/2 Zach. CHANCY son of Edmund of Pascotank,
and Rebecca PRITLOWE dau of John of Paquimance...10,
11m, 1727/8...at ye house of Gabriel NEWBY...

[Column 1]

Gabriel NEWBY
Robert WILSON
Ruth BELMAN
Geo. SHARROW
Charles DENMAN
Saml. PHELPS
[Column 2]
Elisabeth NEWBY
Elisabeth NEWBY Junr
Joshua ELIOT

[Column 3]

Zachariah CHANCY
Rebecca CHANCY
Elisabeth PRITLOWE
Elisabeth ELIOT
Daniel CHANCY
Jacob CHANCY
William CHANCY
Leah SMITH
Judeth SANDERS

[Column 2 cont.]
Martha MACKY
Zach. ELTON   Recorded by
Moses ELIOT   Rt. WILSON

Page 60/2 Jeremiah BARNS of pequimance precinct, &
Sarah SHEARWOOD of ye place & precinct afsd...26,
10m, 1727...at ye lower Meeting House in
Paquimance...

[Column 1]   [Column 3]
Thomas JESSOP   Jeremiah BARNS
Joseph NEWBY   The marke of
Joseph NICHOLSON   Sarah S SHEARWOOD
Richd. CHEASTON   now BARNS
Saml. NICHOLSON   Elisabeth CHEASTON
Tho. WINSLOW   Mary SHEARWOOD
   [Column 2]   Ann MAYO
Dameris RATCLIFF   Elis. SHEARWOOD
Rebecca PRITLOWE   Jane JESSOP
Rachel PEARSON   Mary NEWBY
Francis TOMES
Zachariah CHANCY   Recorded on ye
Peter PEARSON   30th day of ye 2d mo.
Nathaniel NICHOLSON   1728 by Rt. WILSON

Page 61 John GRIFFIN son of James, and Elizabeth
HENBY dau of John they both of the County of
Perquimans...8, 12m, 1744...at the meeting house in
the old Neck...

[Column 1]   [Column 2 cont.]
Thomas JESSOP   Isaac SCRIVIN
Mary NEWBY   William ALBERTSON
Elizabeth NIXON   Joseph NEWBY
Margrate BARROW   Edward MAUDLIN
Francis JONES   [Column 3]
Jesse NEWBY   John GRIFFIN
Ralph FLETCHER   Elizabeth X GRIFFIN
Mary FLETCHER   her mark
Thomas PEIRCE   John HENBY
Mac. SCARBROUGH   James HENBY
   [Column 2]   Richard SKINNER
Mary JESSOP   William GRIFFIN
Rebeckah TOMES   Zach. NIXON
James HENBY   Henry PHELPS
Joseph ANDERSON   [?]athert PEARSON
Joseph RATLIFF   Thomas HOLLOWELL
Joshua DAVIS   Job WINSLOW

Page 61/2 Joseph RATLIFF and Mary FLETCHER dau of
Ralph both of Perquimons...13, 3m, 1747...at the
Meeting House at the Old Neck...

[Column 1]
Sarah SKINNER
Anne WILLIAMS
Matthew SMALL
Damaris SYMONS
Nathan NEWBY
Jonathan PHELPS
Cornelius MOORE
Thomas SMALL
Elizabeth PHELPS
Alice DAVIS
Mary ROBINSON
Miriam ANDERSON

[Column 2]
Henry PHELPS
Francis NEWBY
William SKINNER
Samuel MOORE
John Scott LAURENCE
Abram SANDERS
Richard SANDERS
Mourning PHELPS
Ralph FLETCHER
Elizabeth SANDERS
Isaac SCRIVEN
William BAGLEY
Joseph ANDERSON

[Column 3]
Jane FLETCHER
John GYER
John LASEY
Jonathan SKINNER
Daniel SAINT
Miriam GYER
Mary WILSON
Robert NEWBY
Jesse NEWBY
Judith SANDERS
Thomas PEIRCE
Rebeckah TOMS
Francis TOMS
Betty MOORE

[Column 4]
Joseph RATLIFF
Mary RATLIFF
Ralph FLETCHER
Mary FLETCHER
Sarah WINSLOW
Elizabeth NEWBY
Mary MOORE
Joseph NEWBY
John MOORE
Zachariah NIXON
Elizabeth NIXON
Joseph NEWBY Junr
Joseph WILSON
Joshua FLETCHER

Page 62 Isaac LAMB son of Henry, and Elizabeth
NIXON dau of Phineus both of Perquimons...18, 2m
called february, 1756...at the Meeting House in the
Old Neck in Perquimons...

[Column 1]
Fras. NEWBY
Nathan NEWBY
Fras. NIXON
Zach. NIXON
Jesse WINSLOW
Zach. TOMS
Joseph RATLIFF
Joshua MOORE
Ralph FLETCHER

[Column 2 cont.]
Hague ELLIOTT
Jos. SMITH
Kezia NEWBY
Thos. PEIRCE
Esau LAMB
Sarah FLETCHER
Miriam NIXON
Miriam NIXON

[Column 1 cont.]
Aaron MOORE
William CARRUTHERS
Mary MOORE
[Column 2]
Dorothy PHELPS
Fras. TOMS
Fras. TOMS Junr
William NEWBY
Matthew JORDAN
Registred the 18th Day
of the 4th Month 1756
Pr. Dan. SAINT Clk.

[Column 3]
Isaac LAMB
Elizabeth LAMB
Phineus NIXON
Joseph NEWBY
Patience NEWBY
Mary NIXON
John NIXON
Mary NIXON
Mary WILLIAMS
Thomas LAMB
Sarah LAMB

Page 65 Jacob HILL Late of Virginia, and Elisabeth BOGUE ye dau of William of North Carolina...17, 10m, 1719...at ye uper Meeting house...

[Column 1]
Mary MORGAIN
Richd. CHESTON
Timothy CLEARE
Saml. CHARLES
Robt. WILSON
Jona. PHELPS
[Column 2]
Joseph NEWBY
Mary TOMES
Elisabeth TOMES
[Column 3]
Gabriel NEWBY
Recorded ye 19 day
of ye Second month
1728 by Rt. WILSON

[Column 3 cont.]
John WILLIAMS
Abra. SANDERS
Benja. SANDERS
P. PALMER
Judeth DOCTON
[Column 4]
Jacob HILL
Elisabeth BOGUE
    now HILL
William BOGUE
Susanna HILL
William BOGUE
William HILL
James GRIFFIN
Sarah WHITE

Page 66 Benja. NEWBY of Pasquotank, and Susanna GRIFFING dau of James of Chowan...16, 12m called Febuary, 1731/2...in ye House of James GRIFFING in Chowan...

[Column 1]
Jos. NEWBY Senr
Will. BUNDY
Zachariah NIXON
Robert DAVIS
Ephr. BLANCHARD
Isabel BLANCHARD
Deborah NICHOLSON
Mary HILL

[Column 3]
Benja. B.N. NEWBY
    his mark
Susanna S.G. GRIFFING
    her mark
James GRIFFING
Sarah GRIFFING
James NEWBY
Saml. NEWBY
James GRIFFING

[Column 2]
Sarah HILL
Mary HILL
Naomi WHITE
James NEWBY Junr
Elis. WINSLOW
Guy HILL
Sarah WHITE
Mary NEWBY

[Column 3 cont.]
Jane GRIFFING
John GRIFFING
Will. HILL
[?   ] GRIFFING

Recorded the 19th Day
of 3d Month 1733
by Rt. WILSON Clk

Page 67/2 John WILLIAMS of pequimons, and Sarah
SUTTON Relict of Gorge of the place aforesd...22, 2m
called April1, 1725[?]...at the Dweling House of
Thomas PIERCE at Perquimons...

[Column 1]
Gabrill NEWBY
Rebaco LONG
Joseph BARROW
Jane BARROW
Rachell BARROW
Sarah BARROW
Abraham SANDERS
Char. DENMAN
Gord. SHARROW
Samll. NICKELSON
   [Column 2]
Eliz. NICKELSON
Jos. NICKELSON
Samll. PHELPS

[Column 2 cont.]
Jos. THOMAS
Judeth SANDERS
   [Column 3]
John WILLIAMS
Sarah WILLIAMS
Thos. PEARSE
Mary PEARSE
JonSarah[sic] WILLIAMS
Natthanial WILLIAMS
John PEARSE
Thos. PEARS Junear
Sarah PEARSE
Joseph PEA[torn]
Peter JONES

Page 68/2 Gall. NEWBY and Isaac WILLSON and Ann his
wife [a judgement]...9, 3m, 1709...att our metting
house att Francis TOMES In Pequimins...

[Column 1]
Joseph GLAISTER
Nathan NEWBY
Timothy CLEARE
Robt. JORDAN
Benjn. JORDAN
Matthew PRITCHARD
Francis WELLS
John SMITH
[?] SMALL

[Column 2]
Peter PEARSON
Caleb BUNDY
William MORE
Benjn. PRITCHARD
Stephen SCOTT
W. EVERIGIN
   [Column 3]
Gabriell NEWBY
Isaac WILLSON
Ann WILLSON

Page 69 Att a monthly meeting ye 6, 6m, 1712 Thair
friends took into their consideration the necesity

of a Companying traviling friends to Virgina and
hath freely subcribed their names to goe when need
shall require...

[Column 1]	[Column 2]
William NEWBY	Gabriell NEWBY
Richard RATCLEFF	Isaac WILLSON
Samuell NICELSON	Robert WILLSON
William NEWBY Jur.	Francis WELLS
Arther JONES	John KINSEY
Edward NEWBY	James LEATEN
Thomas PEIRC Jur.	

Page 69   Att the meeting Above Said advedance[?] was
Presented unto James BARROW and Pricela PRITLOE and
thay Chose men and women to Inspect the diferance as
followeth...

[Column 1]	[Column 2 cont.]
William NEWBY	Mary NEWBY
Timothy CLEAR	[Column 3]
Richard RATCLEF	Gabriell NEWBY
William MOORE	Isaac WILLSON
[Column 2]	Samuell CHARLES
Mary TOMES	Francis WELLS
Margreat TOMES	Elesabth MORE

Page 69/2   The Above sd friends inspected the
differance... friends that may have been concerned
in the aforesd [torn] may burie it in oblivien...

[Column 1]	[Column 2]
[torn]ell NEWBY	William NEWBY
[torn] WILLSON	Timothy CLEAR
[torn] CHARLES	Richard RATCLET
[torn]is WELLS	William MOORE
[torn] NEWBY	Mary TOMES
[torn]beth MOORE	Margreat TOMES

Page 70   Richard RATCLIFF his certificate a copy
insarted
To Friends Belonging to the monthly and quarterly
meeting Perquimons River in carolina or
elsewhere...Richd. RATTCLIFF Junor the Sonn of
Richd. [torn] of the Terascoe neckes in Chuckatuck
doth Intend by God [torn] to Take A woman to be his
wife A Liven in your P[torn]...wee did hear
approve...from our monthly meeting held att our
publick meeting house on Chuckatuck on the 14, 9m,
1706...Signed by us whose names are underwritten...

116

QUAKER MARRIAGE CERTIFICATES

[Column 1]
John MURDAUGH
Mathew SMALL
John RATTCLIFF
[Column 2]
James JORDAN
Mathew JORDAN
John JORDAN
Benjamin SMALL
John SMALL

[Column 3]
Isaac RICKES Senior
Richard RATTCLIFF Jun.
William SCOTT Senior
Benjamin JORDAN
Nathan NEWBY
Richd. JORDAN
Robart JORDAN
Recorded Pr me
Thomas PEIRCE this
8th of ye 10 month 1706

Page 70/2   Joseph ROBINSON of ye upper Parrish of
nanzemond County cordwinder, and Janne CLEAR dau of
Timothy of the County of Arlbemarle in Pequimons
River in North Carolina...12, 2m called [torn]l,
1711...at the house of Timothy CLARES...
[Column 1]
Mary TOMES
Hannah FOSTER
Ane WILLSON
Hannah NICELSON
Jane NICELSON
Richard RATCLIF
John HENLEY
Moses NEWBY
Joseph NEWBY
Ralph BUFKIN[?]
[Column 2]
Joseph GLAISTER
Gabriell NEWBY
Francis TOMES
Francis FOSTER
Samuell NICELSON

[Column 2 cont.]
Isaac WILLSON
William NEWBY
Thomas ROBINSON
Henry WHITE Jur
[Column 3]
Joseph ROBENSON
Jane ROBENSON
Timothy CLARE
Hannah CLARE
Thomas WINSLOE
Elezebeth WINSLOE
Edward MAY[torn]
Mary MA[torn]
Sarah CLA[torn]
Arthar [torn]

Page 71-71/2   Richard RATCLIFF Sonn of Richard of
Chuckatuck in the Terascoe neckes in Virginia, and
Damarus PEIRC Ralect of the desesed Joseph Late of
Pequimens...9, 11m, 1706/7...att the sd Damarus
PEIRCS house...
[Column 1]
[torn] SIMMONS
[torn TOMES
[torn] WHITE
[torn] CLARE
[torn]SON
[torn]RMAN
[torn]h PEIRC

[Column 3]
Richard RATCLIFF
Damarus RATCLIFF
Elizabeth NIXON
Zachrias NIXON
Barnebe NIXON
Francis TOMES
John MORIS

[Column 1 cont.]
[torn][?]
[torn]LOE
  [Column 2]
Samuel CHARLES
Francis WELLES
John PRICTLOE
Richd. TURNER
Edward NEWBY
John PEIRC
Thomas PEIRC Juner
James NEWBY

[Column 3 cont.]
Gabriell NEWBY
Timothy CLARE
William NEWBY
Isaac WILLSON
John NICELSON

[torn]rded Per me
Thomas [torn]RC
the 13th of ye 11
month [torn]1706/7

Page 72/2 Joseph BARROW Son of John of ye Precinct
of Peq[torn], and Jane NICELSON dau of [torn]uel]
NICELSON of ye foresd precinct...17, 5m, 1712...at
the house of ye foresd Samuell NICELSONS...
  [Column 1]
Mary TOMES
Damerus WHITE
Elesabeth NICKSON
Damarus RATCLEF
Mary NEWBY
Elinor BOOGE
[?]able NEWBY
Elesabeth CHARLS
  [Column 2]
Hannah FOSTER
Abigall ALBERTSON
Hannah NICELSON
Presello KINSEY
Ann NICELSON
Elesabeth REED
Sarah NEWBY
Mary MARIS[?]

  [Column 3]
Zacharies NICKSON
Gabriell NEWBY
John KINSEY
Richard RATCLEF
Samuell CHARLES
Ann BOSELL
Mary DORMON
James NEWBY[?]
  [Column 4]
Joseph BARROW
Jane BARROW
Samuell NICELSON
Elesabth NICELSON
James BARROW
Nathanell NICELSON
Benja. N[torn]
Christopher [torn]

Page 73/2 Peter HUNNICUT son of Robert of Virginia,
and Sarah HAIG dau of William of North Carolina...2,
8m, 1728...at ye house of Gabriel NEWBY...
  [Column 1]
Joseph NEWBY Jur
Margaret HUNNICUT
Elisabeth NEWBY
Rachel PEARSON
Elisabeth NEWBY
Leah SMITH
  [Column 2]
Jesse NEWBY

  [Column 2 cont.]
Mary NEWBY
  [Column 3]
Peter HUNNICUT
Sarah HUNNICUT
Robert HUNNICUT
Gabriel NEWBY
Wyke HUNNICUT
William HAIG

[Column 2 cont.]
Joseph NEWBY   Recorded ye 16 day
Fracis NEWBY   of ye 8th month 1728
Huldah NEWBY   By Rt. WILSON
Mary BUFKIN

Page 74   Joshua SCOTT of ye Precinct of Pascotank,
and Sarah PETITT of ye precinct of Paquimance...13,
10m, 1726...at ye publick meeting house in
Paquimance...

[Column 1]   [Column 2 cont.]
Edward MAYO   Saml. NEWBY
Richd. CHEASTEN   Joseph NICHOLSON
John WILLIAMS   [Column 3]
Jane JESSOP   Joshua SCOTT
Saml. NICHOLSON   Sarah PETITT
Saml. CHARLES   now SCOTT
Jesse NEWBY   Stephen SCOTT
  [Column 2]   Anna Letitia LOW
Tho. PEIRCE   John SCOTT
Mary PEIRCE   Jean BARROW
Rebecca TOMES   Recorded ye first day
Francis PETITT   of ye 11th mo 1726
Gabriel NEWBY   By Rt. WILSON

Page 79   From our Monthly Meeting at Paquimance 7,
10m, 1726...Concerning Marriage feasts and the Evils
that too Commonly atends them...

[Column 1]   [Column 3]
William JONES   Thomas PEIRCE
Joshua ELLIOT   Gabriel NEWBY
R: WILSON   Samuel NICHOLSON
  [Column 2]   Thomas JESSOP
Nathan NEWBY   Ralph FLETCHER
Peter JONES Junr   Peter JONES Sen
Thomas WHITE   Tho. WINSLOE
John WILLIAMS   Francis TOMES
Abraham SANDERS   Nathaniel NICHOLSON
William HILL
James GRIFFIN   Recorded ye 11th of
Francis NEWBY   ye 10th mo 1726
Joseph NICHOLSON   By R: WILSON
Jesse NEWBY

Page 81/2   Thomas WINSLOW son of Thom[torn] dau of
Richard RATLIFF of Paquimons...21, 11m called
January, 1734/5...at the meeting house in
paquimans...

[Column 1]
Phenahas NIXON
Joshua MORE
John ANDERSON
Joseph WILLSON
Joseph RATTLIFF
Recorded by me
Joseph NEWBY
[Column 2]
Timothy WINSLOW
Peter JONES
John WINSLOW
[Column 3]
Elizabath MAYO
Sarah MAYO
Joseph NEWBY

[Column 3 cont.]
Jane JESSOP
Thomas JESSOP
Elizabeth NEWBY
John MORE
[Column 4]
Thomas WINSLOW
Sarah WINSLOW
Thomas WINSLOW
Damures RATLIFF
Joseph NEWBY
Zachariah NIXON
Elisabeh[?] NIXON
Joseph WINSLOW
Nathaniel NICHOLSON

Page 82   Jacob ELIOT and Sarah WHIT dau of
Joh[?]...26, 4m called Jun, 1734...at ye house of
Sa[torn] WHIT in pequimons...

[Column 1]
William BACKHOUSE
Moses ELLIOT
Hanah ELLIOT
Nathan NEWBY
William ELLIOT
Caleb ELLIOT
Mary ELLIOT
Ann ELLIOT
Joseph WINSLOW
Tarans MECARDELL
James GRIFFIN
Ann NEWBY
Elizebeth NEWBY
Thomas WHIT
Joseph NEWBY
[Column 2]
Marget WHIT
Jocob PEIRY
Thomas WINSLOW
Joseph GRIFFIN
Zachriah NIXON
William WHIT
Elizebeth ELLIOT

[Column 2 cont.]
Uslese[?] ELLIOT
Efream BLANSHARD
Isbell BLANSHARD
Gabriel NEWBY
John BURTON
[Column 3]
Jacob I ELLIOT his mark
Sarah S WHIT her mark
Margrit ELIOT
Jane JESSOP
Mary JESSOP
Thomas JESSOP
Joshua ELLIOT
Abraham ELLIOT
Isaac ELLIOT
Mary NEWBY
Elisabeth MAYO
Sarah MAYO
Mary WHIT
Joseph NEWBY
Thomas WINSLOW
Leah SMITH
Recorded by Joseph HENBY

Page 84   John HENLY of Pasqotank In ye County of
Albemarle, & Isbell NEWBY of Pequimons In ye same
County dau of Gabriel...9, 11m, 1716...att ye

Dwelling house of Gabriell NEWBY In pequimons...

[Column 1]
Tho. HARVEY
Nathan NEWBY
Jos. NEWBY Senor
Tho. PARRIS[?]
Henry CLAYTON

[Column 2]
Mary MAYO
Ann HENLY
Mary TOMES
Sarah TOMES
Leah SMITH
Jno. SAUNDERS
Elesb. ELLIOTT
Sarah SCOTT
Hanah NICHOLSON
Eles. NICHOLSON

[Column 3]
Wm. NEWBY
Francis NEWBY
Wm. HAIGE

[Column 3 cont.]
Saml. NICHOLSON
Henr.[?] WHITE
Jno. MORRIS
Tho. NEWBY
Timo. CLARE
Tho. PEIRCE
Jno. KINSEY
[?   ]

[Column 4]
John HENLY
Isbell HENLY
Gabll. NEWBY
Mary NEWBY
Mathew PRITCHARD
Benjm. PRITCHARD
Edwd. MAYO
W. EVEREGIN
Ed. NEWBY
Jo[?] NEWBY

Page 86/2 Joseph SMITH of Pequimins, and Leah PRITLOE dau of John of Pequimons...on ye fifth day of the week being the 16, [6m, 1716]...at the hows of John PRITLOE aforesd...

[Column 1]
Humphrey WADEY
Peter DENMAN
Richard CHESTON
Thomas PEIRCE
Peter ALBORDSON
John WINSLOE
John TURNER

Recorded
By Richard RATLIFF[?]

[Column 2]
Henry CLAYTON
John WILLIAMS
Ann NICKOLSON

[Column 3]
Joseph SMITH
Leah SMITH
John PRITLOE
Elizabeth PRITLOE
Robert WILLSON
Ann WILLSON
Samuell CHAR[?]

Page 87-87/2 John SANDERS of nanzemond County in virginia, and Prissilla PRITLOE dau of John of ye County of Albamarl in Paquimns River in North Carolina...8, 1m called march, 1715/6...at ye house of John PRITLOE...

[Column 1]
Ezekiell MAUDLIN
Edward MAUDLIN

[Column 2 cont.]
William PLATO
Jesey NEWBY

[Column 1 cont.]
Abraham SANDERS
Elizabeth CHARLS
Jane CHARLS
Elizabeth NICKOLS
Rachel WILLSON
[Column 2]
Richard CHESTON
John PRITLOE
Thomas PERREC[?]
Humpher WADEY
Thomas PEIRC
Ralph FLETCHER
Robert WILLSON
Joseph NEWBY
John PEIRCE

[Column 2 cont.]
Thomas PAGE[?]
William BOAGE
[Column 3]
John SANDERS
Prissilla SANDERS
Elizabeth PRITLOE
Leeah PRITLOE
Rebeckah PRITLOE
Elizabeth PRITLOE
Damaris RATLIFF
Elizabeth NEWBY
Judeth PRITLOE
Hanah HENBY
Mary NEWBY

Page 88 Abraham SANDERS Late of Virginia, and Judah PRITLOE dau of John of Pequimons...the fifth day of ye week being the 6,[sic] [6m, 1716]...att the hows of sd John PRITLOE..

[Column 1]
Peter DENMAN
Thomas PEIRCE
Samuell CHARLS
[Column 2]
Rachel WILLSON
Ann WILLSON
Ann NICKOLS
John TURNER

[Column 3]
Abraham SANDERS
Judah SANDERS
John PRITLOE
Elizabeth PRITLOE
Richard CHESTON
John WINSLOE
Robert WILLSON

Recorded by Richard RATLIFF

Page 88/2 William ELLET of Paquimons, and Elisabeth PRITLOE dau of John of Paquimons...the fifth day of the week it being 16, [6m, 1716]...at the hows of John PRITLOE...

[Column 1]
Peter DENMAN
Thomas PEIRCE
Richard CHESTON
Samuell CHARLS
Peeter ALBORDSON
John WILLIAMS

Recorded
By Richard
RATLIFF

[Column 2]
William ELLETT
Elisabeth ELLETT
John PRITLOE
Elisabeth PRITLOE
Thomas ELLETT
Robert WILLSON
Ann NICKOLSON
John TURNER
Rachell WILLSON
Ann WILLSON

Page 89/2   Joseph PEIRCE of Paquimance, and Penelope
TOMES of ye same place...16, 2m called April,
1727...at ye publick Meeting House at Paquimance...

[Column 1]

Joshua TOMES
John WILLIAMS
Peter JONES
Sarah WILLIAMS

[Column 2]

John SYMONS
Tho. JESSOP
Will. JONES
Mary NEWBY
Jane JESSOP

[Column 3]

Joseph PEIRCE
Penelope PEIRCE
Tho. PEIRCE
Francis TOMES
Mary PEIRCE
Rebecca TOMES
William M[torn]
Recorded ye 19 of
ye 2d mo. 1718
by Rt. WILSON

Page 90   John NEWBY of Pascotank, and Elezebeth
BARROW Realect of ye decd [torn] BARROW Late of the
present of Pequimens...10, 4m called June, 1713...at
the meeting house in ye narrows of pequimens...

[Column 1]

Mary NEWBY
Ann CHESTON
Damarus RATCLEFF
Elezebeth NICELSON
Jane ROBERSON
Hannah NICELSON
Ann WILLSON

[Column 2]

John NEWBY

[Column 2 cont.]

Elezebeth NEWBY
Richard TORNER
Briget TURNER
William NEWBY
Gabriell NEWBY
Samuell NICELSON
Isaac WILLSON
Richard RATCLEF
John KINSEY

Page 91   John BARROE Junor of paquimins, and Rachell
LARANCE dau of William Late of ye sd place...5, 11m,
[1715]...at the Lower meeting hows...

[Column 1]

Mary THOMES
Mary DARMON
John WILLIAMS
[torn]nah HENBEY
[torn]ry MORGIN
[torn]hn WILLSON[?]

[Column 2]

Richard RATLIFF[?]

[Column 3]

Gabriel NEWBY
Ann CHESTON
Mary NEWBY
Damarus RATLIFF
[?] NICKOLSON

[Column 3 cont.]

[?] NEWBY

[Column 4]

Samuel NICKOLSON
Frances WLES
Arther JONES
Robert WILLSON
James[?] BAROW[?]

[Column 5]

John BARROW
Rachol BARROW
Wm. MORE
Wm. [?]
Peter[?] [?]
John P[?]

Piney Woods Monthly Meeting Minutes and Records,
Volume I. [Page 1 After a fire in 1851, a new
record was begun and "The marriage certificates
herein recorded are copied from the originals."]

Page 2 John WINSLOW son of John of Perquimans, &
Rachel WHITE dau of Thomas of the afsd...10, 3m,
1752...at the meeting House in the Piney Woods...

[Column 1]
Joseph WHITE
John WHITE
John MURDAUGH
Caleb ELLIOTT
Joseph MAYO
Joseph WINSLOW
Thomas WHITE
Thomas SMALL
Stephen SHEPHERD
Joseph WINSLOW
Francis JONES
John ROBINSON
William WHITE

[Column 2]
John WILSON
Margaret WHITE
Miriam NEWBY
Mary JONES
Hannah WINSLOW
Esther WINSLOW
William BAGLEY
Joshua PERISHO

[Column 3]
John WINSLOW
Rachel WINSLOW
Rachel WHITE
John WINSLOW
Benjamin ELLIOTT
Elizabeth WINSLOW

Page 4 John WINSLOW son of John of Perquimans, and
Margaret BELL dau of Lancelot decd of Pasquotank
...24, 11m called November, 1782...in their public
meeting place in the Piney Woods...

[Column 1]
Thomas NEWBY
Rebecca WHITE
Benjamin WHITE
Amos GRIFFIN
Thomas WHITE
Leah SANDERS
Sarah BELL

[Column 2]
Josiah WHITE
Mary WHITE
Isaac WILSON
John WINSLOW
Sarah NEWBY
Mary MORRIS
Sarah WHITE

[Column 3]
Miles WHITE
Mary WALTON
Nathan MORRIS
Sarah NICHOLSON
Nicholas NICHOLSON
Rache NICHOLSON
John BELL

[Column 4]
Seth WHITE
Pleasant WINSLOW
Caleb WINSLOW

[Column 5]
John WINSLOW
Margaret X WINSLOW
          her mark

Page 6 Jonathan SAUNDERS son of John decd & Mary
WHITE dau of John, both of Perquimans...14, 4m, 1814

...before a Monthly Meeting held at Piney Woods...

[Column 1]
Mourning WHITE
Robert WHITE
Nehemiah WHITE
John WHITE
Martha WHITE
Polly WHITE
George WHITE
Lancelot WINSLOW
Jemima BOYCE
Peggy WINSLOW
Mary RATLIFF
Ann NEWBY
David WHITE
Elizabeth WHITE

[Column 1 cont.]
Sarah WINSLOW
Mary BOGUE
Ann SAUNDERS
Thos. WHITE

[Column 2]
Betsey WHITE
Exum NEWBY
John NEWBY
Samuel L. WHITE
John WHITE Junr
John C. WHITE

[Column 3]
Jonathan SAUNDERS
Mary SAUNDERS

Page 8 Demsey WHITE son of Benjamin decd, &
Margaret SAUNDERS dau of Benjamin decd, both of
Perquimans...9, 3m, 1809...at their public Meeting
House at Piney Woods... [Column 2 cont.]

[Column 1]
Thomas WHITE
Robinson ELLIOTT
Josiah WHITE
David WHITE
Elizabeth WHITE
Lydia WINSLOW
Thomas SAUNDERS

[Column 2]
Josiah WHITE
George WHITE

Ann NEWBY
Margaret WHITE
Exum NEWBY
Jacob WHITE
Joshua ELLIOTT

[Column 3]
Moses BOYCE
Josiah BOYCE

[Column 4]
Demsey WHITE
Peggy WHITE

Page 10 Benjamin WHITE son of Thomas decd of
Perquimans, and Milicent HENLEY dau of John decd of
Pasquotank...25, 3m called March, 1767...at their
public meeting place at the Head of Little River...

[Column 1]
Joshua WHITE
Caleb WHITE
Thomas WHITE
John WHITE
John HENLEY
Sarah BARROW
Mary HILL
Joseph SCOTT
Ann METCALF
Mary HENLEY

[Column 2 cont.]
Joseph NICHOLSON
Mehetabel NICHOLSON
Zachariah NIXON
Joseph MCADAMS
Charles OVERMAN
Elizabeth WHITE
Miriam ROBINSON

[Column 3]
Benjamin WHITE
Patience NEWBY

[Column 1 cont.]
Miriam BELL
Samuel[?] NEWBY
    [Column 2]
Thomas NICHOLSON
Sarah NICHOLSON
Nicholas NICHOLSON
Mary NICHOLSON Junr
Mary NICHOLSON

[Column 3 cont.]
Joseph HENLEY
Aaron MORRIS
Thomas ROBINSON
Phineas NIXON
Thomas WINSLOW
    [Column 4]
Benjamin WHITE
Milicent WHITE

Page 12   John CORNWELL of Surry County, Virginia, and Leydia WHITE widow of John WHITE decd of Perquimans...15, 5m, 1788...at their public meeting house at the Piney Woods...

[Column 1]
Elizabeth WHITE
Caleb WINSLOW
Jacob WHITE
William WINSLOW
Josiah WHITE
Sarah WHITE
Exum NEWBY
Joshua WHITE
Seth WHITE
    [Column 2]
Samuel WINSLOW
Caleb WHITE
Rebecca WHITE

[Column 2 cont.]
Benjamin WHITE
Milicent WHITE
Samuel MOORE
Job BOND[?]
Jonathan WHITE
Francis WHITE
    [Column 3]
Thomas WHITE
Mary WHITE
Margaret MOORE
    [Column 4]
John CORNWELL
Leydia CORNWELL

Page 14   John WHITE son of Thomas, and Leydia WINSLOW dau of Joseph, both of Perquimans...15, 5m called May, 1757...in their public meeting place at the Piney Woods...

[Column 1]
Joseph NEWBY
Francis TOMS
Thomas NEWBY
Nathan NEWBY
Fras. NIXON
Isaac SAUNDERS
John WHITE
Jacob WINSLOW
Joseph SMITH
Stephen SHEPPARD
Cornelius MOORE
Joseph OUTLAND
James JORDON
Reuben PERRY

[Column 2 cont.]
Anne TOWNSEND
Jemima ROBINSON
Elizabeth WHITE
Kezia NEWBY
Robt. NEWBY
Karen MOORE
Jonathan PERSON
Caleb ELLIOTT
William WHITE
Danl. SAINT
John SMITH
John WILSON Junr
William MOORE
Benjamin PERRY

[Column 1 cont.]
Joseph MOORE
Joel HOLLOWELL
John WILSON
Wm. NEWBY
Joseph WHITE
Dennis DRISCOLL
Matthew JORDAN
Wm. WHITE
Jesse WINSLOW
Zachariah TOMS
[Column 2]
Benjn. HEATON
Joshua HASKETT
Joseph NICHOLSON
Samuel BARTLETT
Ezekiel PERRY
Deborah HEATON

[Column 2 cont.]
Thomas WHITE
Rachel WHITE
[Column 3]
Rachel WINSLOW
Pleasant WINSLOW
Joseph WINSLOW
Joseph WHITE Junr
Thomas WHITE
Matthew WHITE
Patience NEWBY
Elizabeth NIXON
Rachel SMITH
Sarah NEWBY
Elizabeth SAINT
[Column 4]
John WHITE
Leydia WHITE

Page 24   Joseph CHAPPELL son of John of Perquimans,
& Sarah SQUIRES dau of Rodger of afsd...21, 9m,
1788...at the meeting house at Newbegun Creek in
Pasquotank...
[Column 1]
Miriam PRITCHARD
Mary SQUIRES
Mary BARROW
Mary NICHOLSON
John SYMONS
Isaac CHAPPELL
Mordecai MORRIS
Sarah SYMONS
Mourning CHAPPELL
[Column 2]
Mark CHAPPELL
Aaron MORRIS Senr

[Column 2 cont.]
Benjamin PRITCHARD
Wm. CLARY
Thos. PALIN
Elizabeth CHAPPELL
Sarah COOKS
Isaac BOSWELL
Isaac CHAPPELL
[Column 3]
Joseph CHAPPELL
Sarah CHAPPELL
John CHAPPELL

Page 34   Thomas WHITE and Margaret WHITE both of
Perquimans...24, 1m, 1776...at their Meeting House
in Piney Woods...
[Column 1]
Caleb WINSLOW
Wm. MOORE
Francis JONES
Joseph NEWBY
Joseph WILSON
Wm. BOND
Jae[?] CANNON

[Column 2 cont.]
Anty[?] WHITE
Ann WINSLOW
Wm. WHITE
Wm. WHITE
Orpah WHITE
Margaret JONES
Sarah ROBINSON

[Column 1 cont.]
Thos. NEWBY
George WALTON
Mary WALTON
Jeremiah CANNON
[Column 2]
Elizabeth JORDAN
William ROBINSON
Leah HOLLOWELL
Josiah JORDAN

[Column 3]
Thomas WHITE
Margaret WHITE
Margaret WHITE
Caleb WHITE
Benjn. WHITE
Lydia WHITE
Sarah NICHOLSON
Matthew WHITE
Milicent WHITE

Page 36 Armejah LAMB son of Isaac decd, and Sarah
ANDERSON dau of Joseph decd, both of Perquimons
...24, 12m, 1795...at the Meeting House near Sutons
Creek...

[Column 1]
Thos. KIRSTEN[?]
Penina[?] HENBY
[Column 2]
Restore LAMB
Ben. ANDERSON
Abigail ANDERSON[?]

[Column 3]
Armejah LAMB
Sarah LAMB
Marry ANDERSON

Page 38 Samuel CHAPPEL son of John of Chowan, and
Miriam CHAPPEL dau of Isaac of Perquimans...14, 2m,
1805...at their Publick Meeting House at Piney
Woods...

[Column 1]
Mathew[?] NICHOLSON
Huldah CHAPPEL
Mary LAMB
Kesiah CHAPPEL
John CHAPPEL
Henry CHAPPEL
Sarah WHITE
Phereba CHAPPEL
Lydia LANE[?]
[Column 2]
Martha NEWBY
Reubin PERRY
John CORNWEL
Exum NEWBY Jur
Saml. S. WHITE

[Column 2 cont.]
Elisabeth LAMM
Keziah LAMM
Nathan CHAPPEL
Mark CHAPPEL
Elisabeth CHAPPEL
[Column 3]
Samuel CHAPPEL
Miriam CHAPPEL
Caleb WINSLOW Jur
Caleb GRIFFIN Jur
Thos NEWBY
Squires CHAPPEL
David[?] WHITE
Mirium CROTHERS

Page 40 William WINSLOW son of Jacob, and Pleasant
WHITE dau of John, both of Perquimans...18, 1m,
1787...at their Meeting House at Piney Woods...

[Column 1]
Jacob WINSLOW
Caleb WHITE
Benjamin WHITE
Thomas SANDERS
Thos. NEWBY
Jesse WINSLOW
Mary WHITE

[Column 2]
Mary WALTON
Orpha WHITE
Miles WHITE
Pleasant WHITE
Thomas WHITE
Jacob WHITE
Josiah JORDAN
Milosant LAMB

[Column 3]
William WINSLOW
Pleasant WINSLOW
Lydia WHITE
Caleb WINSLOW
Leah SANDERS
Mirium ELLIOTT
Ann WINSLOW
Elisabeth TOWNSEND

Page 43 Thomas JESSOP son of Jonathan decd, and
Rachael DRAPER dau of Joseph, both of Perquimons
...7, 3m, 1790... at Welses Meeting House...

[Column 1]
Racall[?] HASKET
Miriam[?] GUIER Jun
Thos. PEIRCE
Sarah BOGUE[?]
John EVANS
Joseph EVANS
Mary HOLLOWELL

[Column 2]
John GUYER
Mary LOWEY[?]
Cornelius MOOR
Sarah EVANS
Sarah GUYER
Keronhappuc MOORE
Benjamin WHITE
Barnabas BAGLEY

[Column 3]
Lydia EVANS
Robert EVANS
Robert EVANS Senior
Miriam DRAPER
Joseph GUYER
Pheribe BOGUE
Wm.[?] CORNWELL
Wm. NEWBY
Miriam GUYER
Ann[?] BOGUE

[Column 4]
Thomas JESSOP
Rachael JESSOP
Joseph DRAPER
Lydia DRAPER
Josiah DRAPER
Thomas DRAPER
Melosant MORRIS
Mary DRAPER
Nathan DRAPER

Page 46 William WINSLOW son of Jacob, and Pleasant
WHITE dau of John, both of Perquimans...18, 1m,
1787...at their Meeting House [at] Piney Woods...

[Column 1]
Pleasant WHITE
Thomas WHITE
Jacob WHITE
Josiah JORDAN
Elisabeth JORDAN
Milosant LAMB
Seth WHITE
William WHITE
Francis WHITE
[Column 2]
Caleb WHITE
Benjamin WHITE
Thomas SANDERS
Thomas NEWBY
Isaac WILSON

[Column 2 cont.]
Mary WHITE
Mary WALTON
Mary WHITE
Miles WHITE
[Column 3]
William WINSLOW
Pleasant WINSLOW
Lydia WHITE
Caleb WINSLOW
Leah SANDERS
Miram ELIOTT
Ann WINSLOW
Elisabeth TOWNSEND
Jacob WINSLOW

Page 54-55 Benjamin WINSLOW son of John decd, and
Abigail WHITE dau of John both of Perquimans...11,
4m, 1770...at the Meeting house in the Piney
Woods...

[Column 1]
Josiah WHITE
William WHITE
Mary WHITE
Josiah ELLIOTT
John WHITE
Sarah NICHOLSON
Robert WILSON
Charles OVERMAN
Sml. MC[?]
William BOND
Thomas NEWBY
Jacob JORDAN
Joseph SMITH
Thos. LANE
[Column 2]
Leah SMITH
Pritlow ELLIOTT
John WHITE
Sarah HOLLOWELL
Job ELLIOTT
Joshua WHITE
Jas. WHITE
Mathew WHITE

[Column 2 cont.]
Silas WHITE
William WHITE
William GRIFFIN
Margaret WHITE 1st
   "   "   2nd
Millicent WHITE
Margaret WHITE 3rd
[Column 3]
Benjamin WINSLOW
Abigail WINSLOW
Elizabeth WINSLOW
Sarah LILLY
Penninah SMITH
Saml. SMITH
Margaret SANDERS
Esther WINSLOW
John WHITE
Rachael WHITE
Eliza. WINSLOW
Esther PERRY
Keziah ELLIOTT
Reuben PERRY

Page 55   John BARROW son of Jno of Chowan, and
Margaret ELLIOTT dau of Isaac decd of
Perquimans...22, 12m, 1791...at a meeting house at
Welles...

[Column 1]
Joseph BOGUE
Samuel NIXON
Thomas ELLIOTT
Rebecah WHITE
Mary NEWBY
John SAUNDERS
Abraham ELLIOTT
Elizabeth NEWBY
Gabriel NEWBY

[Column 2]
Pleasant NEWBY
Rebecah ELLIOTT
Erie[?] BARROW
Joseph WHITE
Joshua ELLIOTT
Jos. JORDAN
Jos. BARROW
Delilah BARROW
Caleb WHITE

[Column 3]
John BARROW
Margaret BARROW
Elizabeth ELLIOTT
Leah SANDERS

Page 57   John BARROW son of John, and Sarah WINSLOW
dau of Benjamin decd both of Perquimons...2, 4m,
1797...at their public meeting house in the Piney
Woods...

[Column 1]
John BARROW
Sarah X BARROW
     her mark
Page 58
[Column 2]
Thomas WHITE
Sarah NICHOLSON
Thos. WHITE
Millicent WINSLOW
James WHITE
Robert WHITE
Miriam WHITE
Melicent WHITE
Miles ELLIOTT
Thos. REID

[Column 3]
Sarah WHITE
Mary RATLIFF
Phiraba PARKER
William WHITE
Hosea SMITH
Jemima WHITE
Penninah SANDERS
John WHITE
Halsey FLOYD
Seth WHITE

[Column 4]
Nathan NEWBY
Jacob WINSLOW
David WHITE
Anna BARROW
John WINSLOW
Rachael WINSLOW
John WINSLOW
~~John & Sarah BARROW~~

Suttons Creek Monthly Meeting Minutes and Records,
Volume I. [In 1794 Perquimans MM was divided into
Piney Woods MM and Suttons Creek MM.]

Page 1-2 William TRUBLOOD of the County of
Ran[torn], and Margaret SAINT of Perquimans...15,
3m, 1795... at a meeting near Suttons Creek...

[Column 1]
Edward TATLOCK
Francis WHITE
John HASKIT
Timothy COTTER
Joshua JONES
[torn] ALBERTSON

[Column 2]
Mary ANDERSON
Wm. ALBERTSON
Sarah BARBER
Hannah MOOR
John TRUBLOOD
Jos. MOOR

[Column 3]
Elizabeth JONES
Chalkley ALBERTSON
Elizabeth ALBERTSON
Miriam GUYAR
Sarah ALBERTSON
Sarah ANDERSON

[Column 4]
Willia[torn]
Marg[torn]
Jos. JO[torn]
Mary [torn]
Mar[torn]
Bet[torn]

Page 3-4 Jacob WILSON son of Ruben decd, and Miriam
GUYAR Junr dau of Joseph decd, both of Perquimans
...15, 4m, 1795...at the meeting house at Vosses
Creek...

[Column 1]
Nathan DRAPER
John CLARY
John GUYAR
William HASKIT
Thomas HOLLOWELL
Mary HOLLOWELL

[Column 2]
Ann CORNWELL
Lydda DRAPER
Susanna CLARY

[Column 2 cont.]
Jno. BOGUE
Abraham BUNDY
Richard WOOD

[Column 3]
Jacob WILSON
Miriam WILSON
Miriam GUYAR
Sarah GUYAR
Silvanus WILSON

Page 5-6 John ANDERSON and Anne CORNWELL, both of
Perquimans...15, 10m, 1795...at the Meeting House
near Suttons Creek...

[Column 1]
Wm. ALBERTSON
William ALBERTSON
Francis WHITE
Edward TATLOCK
Thomas HENBY
Josiah ALBERTSON

[Column 2 cont.]
John TOMS
Joseph NEWBY
Jesse WHITE
Elizabeth JORDAN
Sarah ALBERTSON
Miriam HARREL

[Column 1 cont.]
Levi MUNDEN
Jos JONES
Mary JONES
Thomas HOLLOWELL

[Column 2]
Benjamin ANDERSON
Mary ANDERSON
Elizabeth ALBERTSON
Chalkley ALBERTSON
Elizabeth ALBERTSON

[Column 3]
John ANDERSON
Anne ANDERSON
Charles CLARY
John CLARY
William CORNWELL
Susannah CLARY
Elizabeth CORNWELL
Penninah ANDERSON
Phinehas ALBERTSON
Samuel ANDERSON

Page 7-8 Benjamin EVANS son of Robert, and Rebekah WILLARD dau of Martin, both of Perquimans...23, 12m, 1795...at Wellses Meeting House...

[Column 1]
Thomas HOLLOWELL
John EVANS
Miriam PIERCE
Nathan DRAPER
John NEWBY
Nathan LACEY
John BAGLEY

[Column 2]
Joseph EVANS
John BOGUE
Peninah PEARSON
William PEARSON

[Column 2 cont.]
Barnea BAGLEY
Lydda DRAPER
Joseph WILLARD
Rhoda WILLARD

[Column 3]
Benjamin EVANS
Rebekah EVANS
Robert EVANS
Martin WILLARD
Sarah WILLARD
Elizabeth EVANS
Thomas EVANS

Page 9-10 Armejah LAMB son of Isaac decd, and Sarah ANDERSON dau of Joseph decd, both of Perquimans ...24, 12m, 1795...at the Meeting House near Suttons Creek...

[Column 1]
Thomas SANDERS
Thos. ALBERTSON
Nathan ALBERTSON
Francis WHITE
Zach. NIXON
Martha NIXON
Levi MUNDEN
Benjm. CHARLES
Josiah ALBERTSON

[Column 2]
Elizabeth ALBERTSON
Sarah ALBERTSON
Ann ANDERSON
Mary WHITE

[Column 2 cont.]
Mary BUNDY
P. ALBERTSON
Gabriel COSAND
Nathan NIXON
Wm. ALBERTSON

[Column 3]
Armejah LAMB
Sarah LAMB
Mary ANDERSON
Restore LAMB
Benjm. ANDERSON
Abigail ANDERSON
Chalkley ALBERTSON
B. ALBERTSON
Sarah ALBERTSON

Page 11-12 Thomas EVANS son of Robert, and Meriam
WILLARD dau of Martin, both of Perquimans...24, 2m,
1796...at Wellses Meeting House...

[Column 1]
Miles MURPHEY
Thomas DRAPER
Abraham BUNDY
John NEWBY
Mary DRAPER
Rachel JESSOP
Mourning BUNDY
Dorrithy MURPHEY
[Column 2]
Elizabeth BOGUE
Daniel WILLARD
Elizabeth EVANS
John BOGUE
William PEARSON

[Column 2 cont.]
Joseph EVANS
Joseph WILLARD
John EVANS
Thomas BOGUE
[Column 3]
Thomas EVANS
Miriam EVANS
Robert EVANS Senr
Martain WILLARD
Penninah PEARSON
Rebekah EVANS
Sarah WILLARD
Robert EVANS Junr
Stephen WHITE

Page 13-14 Joseph NEWBY and Mary WHITE [widow],
both of Perquimans...24, 8m, 1796...at Welses
Meeting House...

[Column 1]
Miriam DRAPER
Miriam GUYAR
Mornin BUNDY
Joel BARBER
Mary BOGUE
John NEWBY
Moses BARBER
Thos. HOLLOWELL
[Column 2]
Thomas WHITE
Jemima WHITE
Esther ROBINSON
Elizabeth BOGUE
Thos. ALBERTSON

[Column 2 cont.]
Thos. DRAPER
Mary DRAPER
Lida WHITE
Joseph DRAPER
[Column 3]
Joseph NEWBY
Mary NEWBY
Thomas NEWBY
Benjm. WHITE
Jno. BOGUE
Melisent WHITE
Jacob WHITE
Mary ELLIOT

Page 15-16 Benjamin COSAND son of Gabriel, and Mary
MORGAN dau of Lemmuel, all of Perquimans...17, 11m,
1796...at Suttons Creek Meeting House...

[Column 1]
Caleb WHITE
Nathan NIXON
Samuel BUNDY
Joseph LACEY

[Column 2 cont.]
Elizabeth TATLOCK
Susannah MORGAN
Stephen WHITE
Elizabeth MORGAN

[Column 1 cont.]
Charles MORGAN
Francis WHITE
Sarah ALBERTSON
Abigail ANDERSON
   [Column 2]
John COSAND
Chalkley ALBERTSON
B. ALBERTSON
John ANDERSON
Wm. ALBERTSON

[Column 3]
Benjamin COSAND
Mary + COSAND
Gabriel COSAND
Lemuel MORGAN
Miriam MORGAN
Hannah SANDERS
Lidia BUNDY
James NEWBY
Sarah COSAND
Sarah NEWBY

Page 17-18 Joseph WILLARD son of Martin, and
Peninah JESSOP dau of Enoch decd, both of Perquimans
...23, 11m, 1796...at Wellses Meeting House...

[Column 1]
Lyda DRAPER
Elizabeth EVENS
Thomas DRAPER
John GUYER
Thomas HOLLOWELL
   [Column 2]
Nathan DRAPER
Miriam GUYER
Thomas PIERCE
Elizabeth BOGUE

[Column 2 cont.]
Joseph EVENS
Abraham BUNDY
   [Column 3]
Joseph WILLARD
Peninah WILLARD
Martin WILLARD
Timothy JESSOP
Daniel WILLARD
Richard WOOD

Page 19-20 Jacob MORRIS son of Benja. decd, and
Elizabeth CORNWELL dau of Aaron decd, both of
Perquimans...22, 12m, 1796...at Suttons Creek
Meeting House...

[Column 1]
Abigail ANDERSON
Sarah COSAND
Thos. NEWBY
Wm. ALBERTSON
   [Column 2]
Elizabeth ALBERTSON
B. ALBERTSON
Gabriel COSAND
Sarah ALBERTSON Junr

[Column 3]
Charles CLARY
Francis ALBERTSON
Chalkley ALBERTSON
Christian SMALL
Sarah ALBERTSON Senr
   [Column 4]
Jacob MORRIS
Elizabeth MORRIS
Ann ANDERSON
John ANDERSON
William CORNWELL

Page 23-24 Levi MUNDEN son of Joseph decd, and Mary
ANDERSON dau of William ALBERTSON decd and widow of
Joseph ANDERSON, both of Perquimans...14, 9m,
1797...at their Meeting House...

[Column 1]
Sally TOMS
Francis WHITE
Benjamin CHARLES
Zach. NIXON
Anderson TOMS
James NEWBY
Naomi NEWBY
Zach. ALBERTSON
Susannah CLARY
Keziah NEWBY
Rachel NEWBY
　　[Column 2]
Chalkley ALBERTSON
William ALBERTSON
Thomas ALBERTSON
John OVERMAN
William ALBERTSON Junr
Sarah COSAND
Miriam HENBY

[Column 2 cont.]
Nathan NIXON
Jacob MORRIS
Mark MUNDEN
John TOMS
Mary TOMS
　　[Column 3]
Levi MUNDEN
Mary MUNDEN
Benjamin ALBERTSON
Sarah ALBERTSON
John ANDERSON
Anne ANDERSON
Benjamin ANDERSON
Abigail ANDERSON
Francis ALBERTSON
Armijah LAMB
Sarah LAMB
Gabriel COSAND

Page 25-26 Thomas ALBERTSON son of Benjamin, and
Milisent BAGLEY dau of Jhon, both of Perquimans
...14, 6m, 1797...at Welses Meeting House...
　　[Column 1]
Naomi NEWBY
Charles OVERMAN
Susan CLARY
Thomas DRAPER
Mary DRAPER
Thomas NEWBY
Thomas WHITE
James OVERMAN
Thomas HOLLOWELL
　　[Column 2]
William ALBERTSON
Mary OVERMAN
Nathan ALBERTSON
Mary ANDERSON

[Column 2 cont.]
Sarah ALBERTSON Junr
Abigail ANDERSON
Elizabeth BOGUE
Sarah ELLIOTT
Mary HOLLOWELL
　　[Column 3]
Thomas ALBERTSON
Milisent ALBERTSON
Benjamin ALBERTSON
Sarah ALBERTSON
John BAGLEY
Chalkley ALBERTSON
Phinehas ALBERTSON
Rebekah ALBERTSON

Page 27-28 Thomas ELLIOTT son of Pritlow decd, and
Peninah PEARSON dau of William, both of Perquimans
...13, 4m, 1796...at Welses Meeting House...
　　[Column 1]
Milisent BAGLEY
Barnea BAGLEY
John NEWBY

[Column 2 cont.]
Mary DRAPER
Rachel JESSOP
Lydia DRAPER

[Column 1 cont.]
Elizabeth PEARSON
Miriam EVANS
Elizabeth EVANS
John BOGUE
  [Column 2]
Mary LACEY
Elizabeth BOGUE
Robert EVANS
Miriam BAGLEY

[Column 3]
Thomas ELLIOTT
Peninah ELLIOTT
William PEARSON
Miriam PEARSON
Jonathan PEARSON
John ELLIOTT
Jobe ELLIOTT
Thomas DRAPER

Page 29-30 Joseph PERISHO son of John decd, and
Elizabeth ALBERTSON dau of Elihu decd, both of
Perquimans...14, 1m, 1798...at Suttons Creek Meeting
House...

[Column 1]
Sarah TOMS
Foster TOMS
Benjm. ALBERTSON
Thomas COSAND
Zach. NIXON
L. MUNDEN
Benjm. CHARLES
  [Column 2]
Chalkley ALBERTSON
Ann ANDERSON
Aaron ALBERTSON

[Column 2 cont.]
Gabriel COSAND
John TOMS
Joseph MOORE
Robert MOORE
  [Column 3]
Joseph PERISHO
Elizabeth PERISHO
Miriam ALBERTSON
Josiah ALBERTSON
Keziah ALBERTSON
Thomas MOORE

Page 31-32 Francis WHITE of Pasquotank son of John
decd, and Mary NEWBY of Perquimans dau of Joshua
MOORE decd and widow of Robert NEWBY...18, 1m,
1798...at Suttons Creek Meeting House...

[Column 1]
Sarah CANNON
Sarah WALTON
Josiah TOWNSEND
Nathan NEWBY
Francis WHITE
L. MUNDEN
Gabriel COSAND
  [Column 2]
B. ALBERTSON
Josiah JORDAN
John ANDERSON
Joseph SCOTT
Mary COLLEY

[Column 2 cont.]
Elizabeth BOGUE
Mourning NEWBY
Naomi NEWBY
  [Column 3]
Francis WHITE
Mary WHITE
Joseph MOORE
Joseph WHITE
Robert MOORE
Jno. BOGUE
Lydia BOGUE
Thomas WHITE

Page 33-34 James WHITE son of Caleb decd, and Sarah
COSAND dau of Aaron decd, both of Perquimans...25,
1m, 1798...at Suttons Creek Meeting House...

[Column 1]
Joseph MOORE
Sarah TOMS
John ANDERSON
John COSAND
Benjm. COSAND
Zachariah NIXON
Levi MUNDEN
Mary MUNDEN
Abigail ANDERSON
Thomas COSAND
Benjm. COSAND
    [Column 2]
Ann ANDERSON
Mary MOORE
William ALBERTSON
Sarah ALBERTSON Junr
Jemima WALTON
Phinehas ALBERTSON

[Column 2 cont.]
Rebeccah ALBERTSON
Mary WHITE
Nathan NIXON
Nathan MORRIS
Nathan ALBERTSON
    [Column 3]
James WHITE
Sarah WHITE
Rebeccah WHITE
Sarah ALBERTSON
Benjm. ALBERTSON
Gabriel COSAND
Sarah COSAND
Elizabeth ALBERTSON
Francis WHITE
Toms WHITE
Caleb WHITE

Page 35-36 Thomas NEWBY son of Joseph, and Mary
BOGUE dau of Duke decd, both of Perquimans...20,
12m, 1797...at Welses Meeting House...

[Column 1]
Josiah JORDAN
Mary LACEY
Rachel JESSOP
Mary HOLLOWELL
Thomas HOLLOWELL
Jacob WHITE
John WINSLOW
    [Column 2]
Peninah ELLIOT
Miles ELLIOT
Thomas BOGUE
Elizabeth BOGUE Junr
Elizabeth BOGUE Senr

[Column 2 cont.]
Mary DRAPER
Jemima WHITE
Esther ROBINSON
    [Column 3]
Thomas NEWBY
Mary NEWBY
Joseph NEWBY
John BOGUE
Joseph NEWBY Junr
Lydia BOGUE
Elizabeth JORDAN
Miriam GUYER

Page 39-40 William HASKIT son of Joshua decd, and
Gulielma GUYER dau of John, both of Perquimans...22,
2m, 1798...at Vosses Creek Meeting House...

[Column 1]
Chalkley DRAPER
Nathan WOOD

[Column 2 cont.]
Joseph SCOTT
Penina WOOD

[Column 1 cont.]
Joseph DRAPER
Lydia DRAPER
Miriam DRAPER
Rachel JESSOP
Josiah DRAPER
Dorcas BOGUE
Thomas HOLLOWELL
[Column 2]
Thomas PIERCE
Joseph WHITE
Mary GUYER
Sarah GUYER
Richard WOOD
Abigail WOOD

[Column 2 cont.]
Abraham BUNDY
Mary HOLLOWELL
[Column 3]
Wiliam HASKIT
Gulielma HASKIT
John GUYER
Joshua HASKIT
Jesse GUYER
Mirriam GUYER
Christian SMALL
John BOGUE
Miriam PIERCE
Robert BOGUE

Page 41-42   John EVENS son of Robert decd, and Sarah
WILLARD dau of Martin, both of Perquimans...15, 8m,
1798...at Welses Meeting House...

[Column 1]
Rachel JISSOP
Benjm. EVENS
Elizabeth EVENS
Miriam EVENS
Jos. WILLARD
[Column 2]
Mary DRAPER
Sarah WILLARD
Thos. DRAPER
Thos. BOGUE
Abraham BUNDY

[Column 2 cont.]
Mournin BUNDY
Thos. EVENS
[Column 3]
John EVENS
Sarah EVENS
Martin WILLARD
Rachel WILLARD
Daniel WILLARD
Miriam GUYER
Elizabeth BOGUE

Page 43-44   Thomas HENBY son of Thomas, and Hannah
HASKIT dau of John, both of Perquimans...17, 2m,
1799...at Suttons Creek Meeting House...

[Column 1]
Elisha HENBY
Foster TOMS
Isbel SCOTT
Francis WHITE
Abigail HENBY
Anderson TOMS
[Column 2]
Chalkley ALBERTSON
L. MUNDEN
Elizabeth ALBERTSON
Sarah ALBERTSON
B. ALBERTSON

[Column 2 cont.]
Zach. NIXON
Lemmuel MORGAN
Thomas HASKIT
[Column 3]
Thomas HENBY
Hannah HENBY
Thomas HENBY Senr.
William HASKIT
John ANDERSON
Anne ANDERSON
John HENBY
Betty BAGLEY

Page 45-46   Joseph ALBERTSON son of Josiah, and
Sarah ALBERTSON dau of Benjamin, all of Perquimans
...18, 10m, 1798...at Suttons Creek Meeting House...

[Column 1]
Joseph MOORE
Sarah ALBERTSON
Aaron ALBERTSON
Martha WEBB
Anne WEBB
L. MUNDEN
Demsey NEWBY
  [Column 2]
Peninah ALBERTSON
Elizabeth PERISHO
Benjm. ALBERTSON
John ANDERSON
William NEWBY

[Column 2 cont.]
Miriam ALBERTSON
Elizabeth ALBERTSON Senr
Gabriel COSAND
  [Column 3]
Joseph ALBERTSON
Sarah ALBERTSON
Benjm. ALBERTSON Senr
Marry ALBERTSON
Josiah ALBERTSON
Keziah ALBERTSON
Samuel ALBERTSON
Elizabeth ALBERTSON

Page 47-48   Nathan NIXON son of Thomas decd, and
Margaret BAGLEY dau of Nathan, all of Perquimans
...14, 6m, 1798...at Suttons Creek Meeting House...

[Column 1]
William HASKIT
Nathan BAGLEY
Phenehas NIXON
Sarah TOMS
Francis WHITE
Betty BAGLEY
Wm. ALBERTSON
Zach. NIXON
  [Column 2]
Thomas NICHOLSON
Sarah NICHOLSON
B. ALBERTSON
Sarah ALBERTSON

[Column 2 cont.]
John ANDERSON
Anne ANDERSON
Martha NIXON
Gabriel COSAND
  [Column 3]
Nathan NIXON
Margaret NIXON
Sarah COSAND
Phinehas ALBERTSON
Rebeca ALBERTSON
Sally NEWBY
Mary TOMS

Page 49-51   Nathan NICHOLSON son of Nicholas, and
Peniah PARKER dau of John, both of Perquimans...16,
5m called May, 1799...at Suttons Creek Meeting
House...

[Column 1]
B. ALBERTSON
Sarah ALBERTSON
John ANDERSON
John WHITE
L. MUNDEN
Thos. HASKITT
Rebecca ALBERTSON

[Column 2 cont.]
Stephen WHITE
Sarah LOW
Rachel PARKER
  [Column 3]
Nathan NICHOLSON
Peninah NICHOLSON
John PARKER

[Column 2]
Thomas NICHOLSON
Sarah NICHOLSON Junr
Enoch NEWBY[?]
Mathew NICHOLSON

[Column 3 cont.]
Ruth BUNDY
Francis WHITE
Sarah PARKER

Page 54-55 Thomas ELLIOTT son of Solomon decd, and
Abigail ANDERSON dau of Joseph decd, both of
Perquimans...17, 4m, 1800...at Suttons Creek Meeting
House...

[Column 1]
William ALBERTSON
Stephen WHITE
Sarah TOMES
Mary TOMES
Zach. NIXON
Sarah NEWBY
Mary ALBERTSON
Martha NIXON
Thos. HENBY
Hannah HENBY
Joseph SCOTT
Anderson TOMES
   [Column 2]
Mary ANDERSON
Ann ANDERSON
Jemima WALTON
Wm. HASKITT
Nathan ALBERTSON

[Column 2 cont.]
Sarah ALBERTSON
Francis ALBERTSON
Gaberel COSAND
Frances WHITE
Joseph MOORE
William ALBERTSON Senr
   [Column 3]
Thomas ELLIOTT
Abigail ELLIOTT
Levi MUNDEN
Mary MUNDEN
Miriam ELLIOTT
Mary ELLIOTT
James MAUDLIN
Miles TATLOCK
Chalkley ALBERTSON
Rebeca ALBERTSON
Phinehas ALBERTSON

Page 57-58 Joseph LACEY son of William decd, and
Elizabeth HASKIT dau of John, both of Perquimans
...17, 4m, 1800...at Suttons Creek Meeting House...

[Column 1]
James MAUDLIN
Zach. NIXON
Martha NIXON
Levi MUNDEN
Joseph MOORE
Miles TATLOCK
   [Column 2]
Thomas HASKITT
Betty HASKITT
Frances ALBERTSON
Joseph SCOTT
Stephen WHITE
Chalkley ALBERTSON

[Column 2 cont.]
Phinehas ALBERTSON
Nathan ALBERTSON
Frances WHITE
   [Column 3]
Joseph LACEY
Elizabeth LACEY
John HASKITT
Thos. HENBEY
Hannah HENBEY
William HASKITT
Elizabeth POOL
Mary MAUDLIN

Page 61   Joseph DRAPER son of Silas decd, and
Peninnah BUNDY dau of Abraham, both of Perquimans
...26, 2m, 1801...at the Meeting House near Vosses
Creek...

[Column 1]
Cynathia WOOD
Jos. WILLARD
Benj. DRAPER
John ANDERSON
Jessee DRAPER
John GUYER
Jessee GUYER
Joshua HASKITT
T. HOLLOWELL
[Column 2]
Elizabeth DRAPER
Moses BUNDY
Joseph DRAPER
Lydia DRAPER
Elizabeth BOGUE
Josiah DRAPER
Miriam DRAPER

[Column 2 cont.]
Polly WEBB
Nathan DRAPER
Samuel DRAPER
Nathan BUNDY
Richard WOOD
[Column 3]
Joseph DRAPER
Peninnah DRAPER
Abraham BUNDY
Mourin BUNDY
Milisent SYMONS
Chalkly DRAPER
Mary GUYER
Christian SMALL
Ann ANDERSON
Thos. DRAPER
Sarah DRAPER

Page 64-65   John NEWBY son of William decd, and
Susannah TATLOCK dau of Edward decd, both of
Perquimans...22, 10m, 1801...at Suttons Creek
Meeting House...

[Column 1]
Robert MOORE
Benja. ALBERTSON
Nixon ALBERTSON
Joseph MOORE
John COSAND
Aaron CORNWELL
John A. TOMS
[Column 2]
Mary DRAPER
Demcy TATLOCK
Miriam DRAPER
Jemima BOGUE
Peninah ALBERTSON
Gabriel COSAND
Ann TATLOCK
Mary WHITE

[Column 2 cont.]
Joseph TATLOCK
Josiah DRAPER
Sarah TOMS
Mary TOMS
[Column 3]
John NEWBY
Susannah NEWBY
Susannah TATLOCK
Miles TATLOCK
Joshua TATLOCK
Wm. NEWBY
Elizabeth BOGUE
Huldah WHITE
Ann ANDERSON
John ANDERSON
Jessee TATLOCK

Page 66-67 Jesse WHITE son of Benjamin, and Mary
ALBERTSON dau of Chalkley, both of Perquimans...25,
3m, 1802...at Suttons Creek Meeting House...

[Column 1]

Stephen WHITE
Benja. ALBERTSON Junr
Wm. ALBERTSON Snr.
Joseph JONES
George WALTON
Foster TOMS
Jacob SAUNDERS
John A. TOMS
Zach. NIXON
Demcy WHITE
Josiah WHITE
Francis WHITE
Seth WHITE
Nixon ALBERTSON

[Column 2]

Phinehas ALBERTSON
John OVERMAN
N. ALBERTSON
Margaret JONES
Margaret FLETCHER

[Column 2 cont.]

Miriam WHITE
Mary ANDERSON
Sarah TOMS
Ann ANDERSON
John ANDERSON
Mary TOMS
Betty WHITE
Miriam JONES
Mary TOMS

[Column 3]

Jesse WHITE
Mary WHITE
Chalkley ALBERTSON
Elizabeth ALBERTSON
John WHITE
Sarah ALBERTSON
Francis ALBERTSON
Gabriel COSAND
Levi MUNDEN
Mary MUNDEN

Page 68-69 Demcy MORRIS son of Benjamin decd of
Pasquotank, and Jemima BOGUE dau of Job decd...22,
12m, 1802...at Wellses Meeting House...

[Column 1]

Mary HOLLOWELL
Joseph EVENS
Jessee MOORE
Peter DRAPER
Joseph DRAPER
Thos. HOLLOWELL
Joseph BOGUE

[Column 2]

Demcy MORRIS
Jemima MORRIS
Elizabeth BOGUE
Milisent SYMONS
Thos. DRAPER
Chalkley DRAPER
Elizabeth BOGUE
Josiah DRAPER
Jessee DRAPER
Rachel JESSOP
Mark BOGUE

Page 70-71 Chalkley DRAPER son of Silas decd, and
Rhoda WILLARD dau of Martin, both of Perquimans
...27, 3m, 1803...at Wellses Meeting House...

[Column 1]
Elizabeth DRAPER
Sarah DRAPER
Josiah DRAPER
Jessee DRAPER
Benja. DRAPER
Nathan DRAPER
Jos. HASKETT
Wm. HASKETT
Marget WILLARD
[Column 2]
Jos. EAVENS
Moses BUNDY
Abraham BUNDY
Joseph DRAPER

[Column 2 cont.]
Thos. DRAPER
Mary DRAPER
Chalkly ALBERTSON
Miriam GUYER
Christian SMALL
[Column 3]
Chalkley DRAPER
Rhoda DRAPER
Martin WILLARD
Joseph WILLARD
Milesent SYMONS
John EAVENS
Samuel DRAPER
Elizabeth BOGUE

Page 72-73 Richard WILLIAMS of Guilford County, and
Susannah POINTER of Perquimans...14, 4m, 1803...at
Suttons Creek Meeting House...

[Column 1]
Jessee MOORE
Mary MOORE Junr
Sarah NEWBY
Benja. ALBERTSON Junr
Sarah PRICE
John A. TOMS
Francis WHITE
Joseph SCOTT
Moses CORNWELL
Jordan CLARY
Ann CLARY
Salley WEBB
[Column 2]
Chalkley ALBERTSON
Elizabeth ALBERTSON
Mary MUNDEN
Joseph JONES
Gabriel COSAND
Joseph MOORE
Mary MOORE Snr
Mary TOMS Snr

[Column 2 cont.]
Sarah TOMS
Mary TOMS Junr
Phillip POINTER
Foster TOMS
Caleb WHITE
Nathan NIXON
[Column 3]
Richard WILLIAMS
Susannah WILLIAMS
John CLARY
Peninah CLARY
James CLARY
Jessee WILLIAMS Junr
Ann ANDERSON
John ANDERSON
Priscilla SHEEPHERD
Sarah ALBERTSON
Susannah CLARY
Elizabeth CLARY
Sarah WHITE

Page 74 John Anderson TOMS son of John, and Phariby
BAGLEY dau of Nathan, both of Perquimans ...19, 12m,
1805...at Suttons Creek Meeting House...

[Column 1]
Benja. WHITE
William HASKIT
Charles SANDERS
William BAGLEY
Benja. ALBERTSON

[Column 2]
Sarah TOMS
Polley TOMS
Mary BAGLEY
Stephen WHITE
Foster TOMS

[Column 3]
John A TOMS
Phariby X TOMS
John TOMS
John ANDERSON
Mary TOMS Senr
Miriam WHITE

Carried Forward
Page 75
[Column 4]
Jesse COPELAND
Zach. NIXON
Gabriel COSAND
William JONES

[Column 5]
Christopher WILSON
James ELLIOTT
Zachariah TOMS
Zac. COPELAND

[Column 6]
Joshua TOMS
Nathan NIXON
Penina RATLIFF

Page 75-76 Jordan CLARY son of Charles decd, and
Catharine RATLIFF dau of Joseph decd, both of
Perquimans...18, 10m, 1804...at Suttons Creek
Meeting House...

[Column 1]
Peninah RATLIFF
Chalkley ALBERTSON
Jesse WILLIAMS
Benja. ALBERTSON
Benja. COSAND
Nathan COSAND
Charles CLARY

[Column 2]
Hannah COSAND
Mary ALBERTSON
Nancy NEWBY
Joseph MOOR
John ANDERSON
Richard WILLIAMS
Susannah WILLIAMS
Moses CORNWELL

[Column 3]
Jordan CLARY
Catharine CLARY
Joseph SCOTT
Ann CLARY
Ann ANDERSON
James CLARY
Mary RATLIFF
Benjm. ALBERTSON

A FAMILY HISTORY AND GENEALOGY OF WILLIAM BOGUE
(BOGE) AND SOME DESCENDANTS 1689-1978 AND ALLIED
FAMILIES, Compiled and Edited by Cordelia Bogue
Wright, Spiceland, Indiana, 1978, pp. 25-26. [This
is an exact copy as printed in the book. The names
of the witnesses were in paragraph form, from the
regular columnar form of the original certificate.]

The marriage certificate of Job Bogue, brother of
Joseph Bogue. Duke Bogue, another brother, attended
the wedding of Job and Elizabeth and was the fine
penman who wrote their wedding certificate. It is
now [1978] in the possession of Mrs. Elizabeth Bogue
Henly, Greenfield, Indiana.

        Whereas Job, son of Josiah and Deborah, and
Elizabeth, daughter of William Newby both of the
county of Perquimins, and Province of North
Carolina; hath laid their intentions of marriage
before several monthly meetings of the people
called Quakers, whose proceedings thereinafter
deliberate consideration and consent of parents and
relations being first had and being free from any
marriage entanglement with any other person and were
approved of by the aforesaid meeting; these are
therefore to certify all people for full
accomplishment of their said marriage, they, the
said Job Bogue and Elizabeth Newby appeared at a
public and solemn assembly of the aforesaid people
met together at Welles Meeting House in the
aforesaid county, according to good order. He, the
said Job Bogue, taking the said Elizabeth Newby to
be his wife, promising through Divine assistance to
be to her a kind and loving husband until death
separates us, or words to that effect. Then and
there, the said Elizabeth Newby, having the said Job
Bogue by the hand did openly declare as followeth:
"Friends, you are my witnesses that I take this, my
friend, Job Bogue, to be my husband, promising
through Divine assistance to be to him a kind and
loving wife, until death separates us," or words to
that effect--and for further confirmation hereof
they, the said Job Bogue and Elizabeth, his now
wife, hereunto these presents subscribed their
names, said Covenant and Superscription have as
witnesses hereunto subscribed our names this fifth
day of the third month in the year of our Lord, one
thousand, seven hundred seventy five:

Duke Bogue, Robert Bogue, John Maudlin, Thomas
Moore, Demsey Newby, Samuel Mayo, Sarah Hollowell,
Josiah Bogue, Nathaniel Albertson, Joseph Bogue,
Sarah Albertson, Joseph Bogue, Mary Bogue, Jemima
Newby, Jesse Bogue, Mark Bogue, John Pease, Sarah
Newby, Moses Bundy, Joseph Draper, William Newby,
Samuel Newby, Anne Delane, Huldah Newby, Elizabeth
Newby, Lydia Pease, Isabel Moore, Jonathon Pearson,
Job Bogue, Elizabeth Bogue.

Original marriage certificate of Benjamin White and
Meliscent Henley preserved in the family of the late
Charles Clarkson White, Belvidere, N.C. Xerocopy in
possession of Perquimans County Historical Society.
[Abstracted by Raymond A. Winslow, Jr.]

Benjamin WHITE Son of Thomas of Perquimons Deceased
and Meliscent HENLEY Daughter of John of Pasquotank
Deceased...25th of 3rd mo. called March 1767...in
Perquimons County in their Publick-Meeting Place at
the Head of Little-River...

[Column 1]
Joshua WHITE
Caleb WHITE
Thomas WHITE
John WHITE
Sarah NICOLSON
John HENLEY
Nicholas NICHOLSON
Mary NICHOLSON Junier
Sarah BARRER
Mary NICHOLSON
Mary HILL
    [Column 2]
Thomas NICHOLSON
Zachariah NIXON
Joseph MCADAMS
Samuel NEWBY
Joseph SCOTT

[Column 2 cont.]
Joseph NICHOLSON
Mehetabel NICHOLSON
Miriam BELL
Elesibeth WHITE
Miriam ROBINSON
Charles OVERMAN
Mary HENLEY
Ann METCALFE
    [Column 3]
Benjamin WHITE
Meliscent WHITE
Patience NEWBY
Joseph HENDLEY
Aaron MORRIS
Thomas ROBINSON
Phineus NIXON
Thomas WINSLOW

"Benjamin Whites' Certificate 1767 Recorded...
 Registered in New Record 1852-"

OVERMAN EXPRESS, by Gwen Barber. Lufkin, Texas,
[1977?], p.11. [Abstracted by Gwen Bjorkman]

"MARRIAGE CERTIFICATE OF EPHRAIM OVERMAN AND RACHEL
SMALL -- NORTH CAROLINA, PASQUOTANK CO."

Whereas Ephraim OVERMAN son of Isaac OVERMAN, and
Rachel SMALL daughter of Obadiah SMALL both of the
county aforesaid, having publickly declared their
intentions of taking each other in marriage before
several monthly meetings of the people called
Quakers in the County aforesaid according to good
order used among them, whose proceedings therein
after a deliberate consideration thereof with regard
unto the rightious law of God and Example of his
people recorded in the scriptures of the truth...
Now these are to certifie all whom it may concern
that for the accomplishment of their said intentions
this 6th day of the 7th month 1780, They the said
Ephraim OVERMAN and Rachel SMALL in a publick
assembly of the aforesaid people and others meet
together at their publick meeting House at Symones
Creek in the aforesaid County...

[Column 1]
Caleb TRUEBLOOD
Milisent MORRIS
Sarah BAILEY
Benjamin WHITE
Thomas SYMONS
Mary MORIS Sen.
Charles MORGAN
Obadiah SMALL
[Column 2]
Josiah WILSON
Sarah WILSON
Pricherd WOOD
Anne TRUEBLOOD
Jacob HILL
Miriam MORRIS
John SYMONS
Nathan MORRIS
Rachel WILSON
Miriam NICHOLSON
Elesebeth PRITCHARD
Benjamin PIKE
Robert HILL

[Column 2 cont.]
Ann OVERMAN
Jonathan MORRIS
Ephraim OVERMAN, Jr.
Zebulon OVERMAN
Nathan SYMONS
Penelope SYMONS
[Column 3]
Ephraim OVERMAN
Rachel OVERMAN
Obadiah SMALL
Lydia SMALL
Jane PIKE
Samuel SMALL
Demsey BUNDY
Nathan PEARSON
Miriam GILBERT
Miriam WHITE
Isaac OVERMAN
Sarah OVERMAN
Mary BUNDY
Elizabeth ALBERTSON
Henry PALIN

North Carolina State Archives. Caleb Winslow and
Family Papers 1712-1941, in the box Wills,
promissory notes, marriage certificates, bills,
bills of sale, receipts, accounts 1752-1904, n.d.,
shelf number P.C.90.14.
[Abstracted by Gwen Bjorkman from xerographic copy]

Caleb WINSLOW son of Timothy decd, and Ann PERRY dau
of Jacob, both of the County of Perquimons...
18, 10m, 1769...at the Meeting House in the Piney
woods...

[Column 1]
Josiah WHITE
~~Timothy~~
Timothy WINSLOW
Reuben WILSON

[Column 2]
Rachel WHITE
Ann WRITE
Gabriel NEWBY
James ELLIOT[?]

[Column 3]
Obed WINSLOW
Reuben PERRY
Mary WILSON
Bettey WINSLOW

[Column 4]
Caleb WINSLOW
Ann WINSLOW
Jacob PERRY
Ann PERRY
Rachel WILLIAMS

[next page]
[Column 5]
Thos. NEWBY
Wm. WHITE
Margaret WHITE
Elizth. WINSLOW
Jacob WINSLOW
Thomas SAINT
Rachel PERRY
Christian[?] HOLLOWELL
Mary HOLLOWELL

[Column 6]
Mary WINSLOW
Betty TOWNSEND
Sarah LILLY

Caleb and Ann WINSLOWS
Marriage certificate
Recorded Pr Seth WHITE

North Carolina State Archives.   Caleb Winslow and
Family Papers 1712-1941, in the box Wills,
promissory notes, marriage certificates, bills,
bills of sale, receipts, accounts 1752-1904, n.d.,
shelf number P.C.90.14.
[Abstracted by Gwen Bjorkman from xerographic copy]

Caleb WINSLOW of Perquimans County and Jemima CANNON
of Chowan County...11, 5m, 1797...at the Meeting
house at the Piney Woods in the County of Perqs...

[Column 1]
Exum NEWBY Junr.

[Column 2]
Margart MOORE
Exum NEWBY
Elias ALBERTSON
Milisant WINSLOW
Josiah TOWNSEND
Thomas WHITE
Betsey SANDERS
John WHITE
Thos. WHITE
Hosea SMITH
Thomas MOORE
Seth WHITE
Amos GRIFFIN

[Column 3]
John SMITH
John LEE
Jos. PARKER
Elisa. RATTCLIFF

[Column 3 cont.]
William WINSLOW
Jacob WINSLOW
Sarah WHITE
Martha NEWBY
Lydia CORNWELL
Joseph NEWBY
Elisabth NEWBY
Isabel PARKER
Reuben PERRY
Nathan NEWBY

[Column 4]
Caleb WINSLOW
Jemima WINSLOW
Rachel WHITE
Sarah CANNON
Jonathan WHITE
Mary RATLIFF
Caleb WINSLOW Junr.
Sarah WALTON
Mary NEWBY

Caleb & Jemima WINSLOW
Marriage Certificate
Recorded 1797

INDEX OF PERSONS

All names in the index are spelled as they were
originally spelled in the marriage certificate.
Names should be checked for all possible spellings.
In many cases, more than one entry for the same name
can be found on the page indicated. A page number
in parentheses indicates a marriage certificate on
that page for that person. If a woman's maiden name
and/or previous married name is given in a
certificate, it is indicated in parentheses and
indexed by her new married name.

ABERSON, Elizabeth 13
ABERTSON, Abigall
   (NICOLESON) 90
   Nathanell (90)
ACKISS, Thos. 57
ADAMS, Mary 32
AKEHURST, Danell 5 6
ALB., Chalkley 20
ALB[torn], Abigall 90
   Nathanell 90
ALBARDSON, Abigall 98
   Nathanael 102
ALBERSON, Aaron 104
   Abigal 104 Elisabeth
   (103) Esua 104 Lydia
   (108) Nathaniel 103
   Nathl. 104 Peter 103
ALBERT., Phinehas 20
ALBERT[torn], Nath. 90
ALBERTSON, [torn] 131 A.
   75 78 Aaron 63 74 81
   106 108 136 139
   Abigail 32 Abigall 117
   Abigell 95 Albert 90
   Ann 92 106 Arthur 107
   Asue 90 B. 20 132 134
   136 138 139 B. Junr 78
   Ben: 35 Benj. Senr 66
   Benja. 63 75 141 144
   Benja. Junr 142 143
   Benjamin 11 81 135 139
   Benjan. 54 Benjm. 136
   137 139 144 Benjm.

ALBERTSON (continued)
   Senr 139 Benjn. 11 17
   25 31 32 35 37 38 44
   75 Chalkley 11 13 15
   25 27 30-32 34-36 44
   46 51 55 56 58 66 69
   73 75 76 81 131 132
   134-136 138 140 142-
   144 Chalkly 143 Elias
   7 43 60 149 Elihu 10
   35 136 Elisabeth 31 35
   36 Eliza. 71 Elizabeth
   73 107 131 132 134
   (136)-139 142 143 147
   Elizabeth Senr 139
   Frances 140 Francis 27
   35 75 134 135 140 142
   Jean 106 Joseph (139)
   Joshua 23 35 37 44 45
   73 108 Josiah (35) 46
   131 132 136 139 Keziah
   136 139 Kiziah 71
   Lyddia 35 Lydia 108
   Marry 139 Mary (11) 20
   35 37 38 60 75 81 90
   (134) 140 (142) 144
   Milisent 135 Milisent
   (BAGLEY) 135 Miriam 35
   71 136 139 N. 142
   Nathan 132 135 137 140
   Nathaniel 75 89 104
   108 146 Nixon 76 78 79
   141 142 P. 76 78 132

ALBERTSON (continued)
Peninah 139 141 Peter
89 90 Phineas 11
Phinehas 19 23 63 66
79 81 132 135 137 139
140 142 Rebeca 139 140
Rebecca 76 79 139
Rebeccah 137 Rebecka
66 Rebekah 27 135
Rhoda (75) Saml. 71
Samuel 139 Sarah 11 17
25 31 32 35 37 46 51
54 63 66 74 76 131 132
134 135 137-(139)-140
142 143 146 Sarah
(ALBERTSON) 139 Sarah
Junr 134 135 137 Sarah
(NEWBY) 35 Sarah Senr
134 Thomas 11 (135)
Thos. 74 81 132 133
William 11 22 25 26 31
32 68 81 83 111 131
134 135 140 William
Junr 135 William Senr
140 Wm. 19 35 37 63 74
131 132 134 137 139
Wm. Snr. 142 Zach. 135
ALBORDSON, Abagall 101
Eliz. 110 Peeter 121
Peter 97 120 Sarah 100
ALLBARD[torn], [torn]
103
ALLBARDSON, Elizabeth
103
ALLBORDSON, Nathannell
102 Sarah (102)
ALLEN, Elisabeth 26
Matthew 12 36
AMES, Gearge 86 George
85
ANDERSON, Abigail 127
132 134 135 137 (140)
Ann 68 132 134 136 137
140-144 Anne 132 135
138 139 Anne
(CORNWELL) 131 Aron 71
Ben. 127 Benjamin (57)
132 135 Benjm. 132

ANDERSON (continued)
Benn. 11 Bettey (46)
Cateron 98 Elis. 104
Elisabeth 57 Elizabeth
98 103 Elizabeth
(NICHOLSON) 98 Jno. 71
John 10 22 28 32 35 37
38 46 50 55 56 68 74
75 88 (98) 100 102 105
109 119 (131) 132 134-
139 141-144 John. 57
Joseph 11 35 57 75 111
112 127 132 134 140
Joshua 67 Marry 127
Mary 11 32 46 57 58
(67) 71 75 76 131 132
134 135 140 142 Mary
(ALBERTSON) (134) Mary
(MORRIS) 57 Miriam 112
Penninah 132 Saml. 28
Samuel 10 11 35 46 62
83 132 Sarah 10 11 46
57 (127) 131 (132)
ARNOLD, Benjamin 37
Elisabeth (9) Jonathan
76 Mary 10 Rebekah 34
Sarah 35 37 William 9
10 17 20 23
ASHBURN, Nicholas 28
ASHLEY, Sarah 109
ATWOOD, Ann (105)

BACKHOUSE, William 119
BACON, Richard Senr 46
BAGLEY, Barnabas 128
Barnea 132 135 Betty
138 139 Ephraim 27
Jhon 135 John 132 135
Margaret (139) Mary
144 Milisent (135)
Miriam 136 Nathan 41
45 139 144 Phariby
(144) Savery 89 Thos.
89 William 112 123 144
BAILEY, Bathsheba 24
Benja. 79 Hannah 22 29
Martha 22 Sarah 147
Susannah 13 24 54

CHARLES (continued)
Samuell 94 95 98 100
101 110 115 117
[S]amuell Jun 95 Sarah
(56) 75 76
CHARLLS, Elezabeath
(MORISON) 1 Elezabeth
1 Elizabeath 2 Samuell
(1) Willam 1
CHARLS, Elesabeth 3 4
117 Elezabeath 5
Elizabeth 121 Jane 121
Samll. 100 Samuel 4
Samuell 96 98 101 103
121
CHEASTEN, Richd. 118
CHEASTON, Elisabeth 111
Eliza. 103 Ricd. 103
Richd. 87 104 111
CHESTEN, Ann 94 110 Ann
(DORMAN) 94 Richard 89
(94) 95 Richard Jun 95
CHESTON, Ann 95 122
Eliz. (BARNS) 103
Richard 87 (103) 120
121 Richd. 92 96 113
CL[torn], Timothy 90
CLA[torn], Sarah 116
CLARE, [torn] 116
Elisabeth 87 Hanah 97
98 102 Hanah (SNELING)
87 Hannah 93 116
Hepsibah 101 Jane 90
Janne 93 Mary (93)
Sarah 93 97 (98) Timo.
120 Timothey 110
Timothy 82 (87) 88 93
97 98 100-102 116 117
CLARK, Mary 93
CLARY, Ann 143 144
Barnes 42 Catharine
144 Catharine
(RATLIFF) 144 Charles
43 132 134 144
Elisabeth 43 Elisabeth
(PRICHARD NICHOLSON)
42 Elizabeth (17) 143
James 143 144 John 17

CLARY (continued)
43 58 131 132 143
Jordan 143 (144)
Miriam 43 Peninah 143
Susan 135 Susanna 58
Susannah 14 15 43 131
132 135 143 William 17
(42) 43 46 Wm. 56 126
CLATON, Henry 100 102
CLAYTON, Elizabeth 102
Henry 101 102 120
CLEA[torn], Hanah 88
CLEAR, [torn] 88 [torn]y
87 Elezebeth 87 Hanah
95 Hannah 92 94 Jann
92 Janne (116) Mary 92
95 Sa[torn] 90 Sarah
92 Timothy 90-92 94
115 116
CLEARE, [torn] 88
Elisabeth 88 Elizabeth
(90) Hanah 90 Hannah
90 Mary 86 90 Timothy
86 90 91 96 113 114
COLLEY, Mary 136
COLLISON, Hannah 49
COMANDER, Dorathy 6
Joseph 4 6
COMMANDER, Joseph 5 24
Sarah 47
COMMANDR, Joseph 1
CONNER, Demcy 10 Demsey
46 John 42 Mary (42)
83
COOKS, Sarah 126
COOPER, Saml. 16
COPELAND, Esther 60
Gulielma 60 Jesse 144
Sarah 17 58 Thos. 67
Zac. 144
CORNAL, Lydia 47
CORNWEL, John 127
CORNWELL, Aaron 134 141
Ann 46 58 75 131 Anne
(131) Elizabeth 132
(134) John 47 60 (125)
Leydia 125 Leydia
(WHITE) 125 Lidia 58

DRAPER (continued)
   Josiah 8 128 138 141–
   143 Lyda 134 Lydda 131
   132 Lydia 128 135 138
   141 Mary 69 128 133
   135 137 138 141 143
   Meliscent (30) Miriam
   8 128 133 138 141
   Nathan 128 131 132 134
   141 143 Peninnah 141
   Peninnah (BUNDY) 141
   Peter 30 142 Rachael
   (128) Rhoda 143 Rhoda
   (WILLARD) 143 Samuel
   141 143 Sarah (77) 141
   143 Silas 8 31 69 141
   143 Thomas 8 25 31 37
   77 128 133–136 Thos.
   133 138 141–143
DRISCOLL, Dennis 126

EAGAR, Sarah 3
EARL, Elizabeth 9 61
EARLL, Elisabeth 30 45
   John 45 Sarah (45)
EAVENS, John 143 Jos.
   143
EDEY, Benjamen 3
ELIOT, Benjamin 108
   Caleb 108 Elisabeth
   110 Elizabeth 108
   Elizabeth (MORGAN) 108
   Isaac (108) Jacob 108
   (119) Joshua 108 110
   Margrit 119 Moses 108
   111 Sarah (WHIT) 119
ELIOTT, Caleb 9 Miram
   129
ELLEOTT, Caleb 13
ELLET, Elisabeth
   (PRITLOE) 121 Eliz.
   100 William (121)
ELLETT, Elisabeth 121
   Thomas 121 William 121
ELLIO[torn], Joshua 97
ELLIOT, [torn] 105
   Abraham 119 Ann 83 119
   Caleb 119 Elizebeth

ELLIOT (continued)
   119 Hanah 119 Isaac
   107 119 James 148
   Joshua 83 104 106 118
   119 Lovy 89 Mary 119
   133 Moses 107 108 119
   Pritlow (108) Sarah
   108 Sarah (CROXTON)
   108 Uslese 119 William
   108 119
ELLIOTT, Abigail 140
   Abigail (ANDERSON) 140
   Abraham 130 Benjamin
   123 Caleb 123 125
   Elesb. 120 Elisab. 99
   Elisabeth 27 Elizabeth
   130 Hague 112 Hannah
   39 Helena 25 26 29 44
   54 Isaac 130 James 144
   Job 129 Jobe 136 John
   136 Joshua 39 124 130
   Josiah 129 Keziah 129
   Margaret (130) Mary
   140 Miles 130 137
   Miriam 140 Mirium 128
   Nixon 11 Peninah 136
   137 Peninah (PEARSON)
   135 Pritlow 129 135
   Rachel 46 Rebecah 130
   Robinson 124 Sarah 62
   135 Soloman 140 Thomas
   130 (135) 136 (140)
ELTON, Zach. 111
EVANS, Benjamin (132)
   Dorothy (59) Elezebeth
   31 Elisabeth 87
   Elizabeth 132 133 136
   Emme 104 John 128 132
   133 Joseph 59 128 132
   133 Lydia 48 59 62 71
   128 Meriam 133 Meriam
   (WILLARD) 133 Miriam
   136 Myriam 65 Rebekah
   132 133 Rebekah
   (WILLARD) 132 Richd.
   87 Robert 31 59 128
   132 133 136 Robert
   Junr 133 Robert Senior

EVANS (continued)
   128 Robert Senr 133
   Sarah 59 128 Thomas 59
   132 (133)
EVENS, Benjm. 138
   Elizabeth 134 138 John
   9 (138) Joseph 134 142
   Miriam 138 Robert 59
   138 Robrt. 9 Sarah 138
   Sarah (WILLARD) 138
   Thos. 138
EVERARD, Rich. 104
EVEREGIN, W. 120
EVERIGIN, [torn]iam 93
   Edwd. 7 69 John 83
   Mary 12 Mary (WHITE)
   12 W. 12 114 William
   (12) 82
EVINS, John 13
EXUM, Robert 13

FAULK, Wm. 57
FELLPS, Eliz. (TOMES)
   100 Jonathan (100)
FLEACHER, Ralph 95
FLECHER, Jane 95
FLETCHER, Jane (107) 112
   Joshua 27 46 112
   Margaret 142 Mary 107
   111 (112) Molley 46
   Ralph 27 46 69 91 92
   98 103 107 110-112 118
   121 Ralph Junr 110
   Sarah 112
FLOYD, Halsey 130
FORBES, Peter 61 68
   Rebecka 67 Will: 68
FORDICE, Gorg 96
FORSTER, Hannah 88
FOSTER, David 63 Fran.
   36 Frances 95 Francis
   92 93 95 116 Hanah 110
   Hannah 93 116 117
FOX, [R]ichard 87

GEORGE, Susanah 85

GIBBENS, Janne LARRANC
   93 Janne (LARRANC) 93
   Stephen (93)
GIBBERSON, Abagale 74
GIBENS, Steven 92
GILBERT, Aaron L. 61 67
   74 76 79 Aaron La. 80
   Aaron Lan. 78 Aaron S.
   79 Abigail 58 63
   Abigal 61 Becky 71
   Dorothy 61 64 Dorothy
   (NIXON) 61 Elisabeth
   10 25 30 (32) Eliza.
   73 Elizabeth 22 47 69
   Jereh. 71 Jeremiah 10
   15 16 25 32 40 49 52
   53 (56) 57 61 62 64 78
   79 Jerimiah 80 Joel 67
   74 (78) Josiah 8 9 14
   20 41 48 53 57 58
   (61)-(62)-64 70 71
   (106) Lydia 78 Lydia
   (MORGAN) 78 Mary 106
   Miriam 30 47 49 52 147
   Rebecah 78 Rebecca 62
   70 76 Rebeckah 67 80
   Rebekah 8 16 56-58 61
   Rebekah (MORRIS) 56
   Sarah 57 63 106 Sarah
   (OUTLAND) 62 Sarah
   (WILLIAMS) 106 Thomas
   10 25 32 57 61-63
   Thos. 30
GINIT, Abraham 95
GLAISTER, Joseph 114 116
   Mary 3 4 12 18 24 36
   38 Ruth 3 12 18 32 35
   36 Sarah 18 32 35
GLASCO, Mary 61
GLASGO, Vilette 55
GLASGOW, Vilaty 8
GLASTER, Mary 4 Ruth 102
   Sarah 102
GOODMAN, Joseph 1
GOSBEY, John 86 Sarah
   (88)
GOSBY, Hannah 86

GRIFFIN, Amos 9 13 47
    123 149 Anna 54 Caleb
    Jur 127 Elizabeth 47
    (60) 111 Elizabeth
    (HENBY) 111 Gulielma
    47 Hannah (9) (12) 32
    Hannah (KINNEON) 32
    James 23 (32) 48 60
    111 113 118 119 John 9
    13 (111) Joseph 9 12
    13 19 33 48 59 70 74
    119 Josiah 62 Josiah
    Junr 47 Leadoh 9 Lydia
    13 Margaret 67 Mariam
    9 Martha 13 19 48 59
    67 71 74 78 81 Mary
    (47) 63 67 70 78
    Miriam 13 48 Orpa 37
    Orpah 36 Reuben 9 13
    Seth 68 Susannah 39
    Thomas 78 William 9 13
    47 48 60 111 129
GRIFFING, [?] 114 James
    113 Jane 114 John 114
    Sarah 113 Susanna
    (113)
GRIFIN, James 13 John 89
GUIER, Miriam Jun 128
GUYAR, John 131 Joseph
    131 Miriam 131 133
    Miriam Junr (131)
    Sarah 131
GUYER, Gulielma (137)
    Jesse 138 Jessee 141
    John 128 134 137 138
    141 Joseph 128 Mary
    138 141 Miriam 128 134
    137 138 143 Mirriam
    138 Sarah 128 138
GYER, Miriam 112 John
    107 112
GYPSON, Elisabeth 43

H[torn], Ame 89
HAGE, Mary (98) William
    101
HAIG, [torn] 97 Sarah
    (117) William 39 117

HAIGE, Mary 98 Sarah 99
    William 98 99 Wm. 120
HALL, Elisabeth 42 44 51
    75 Eliza: 35 Lyda 55
    Sarah (44) 75 Stephen
    44 William 59
HALLAM, Elisabeth (47)
    Elisabeth (WHITE) 36
    Thomas (36)
HALLAN, Thomas 36
HALLEY, Grace (1) Grece
    1
HAM, G. J. 77
HANCOCK, [Ame] (89)
    Staven 89
HANCOK, Stephen 6
HANDORSON, Pattricke 82
HARBERT, Richard 16
HARLOE, John 85
HARMON, Robart 92 Robert
    86 Rosanna 44
HARPER, Eliphal 104
HARREL, Miriam 131
HARRELL, Mary 31
HARVEY, Tho. 120 Thomas
    101
HARVY, Dorathy 7
HASKET, Miriam 71 Racall
    128
HASKETT, Jos. 143 Joshua
    126 Wm. 143
HASKIT, Anna 22
    Elizabeth (140)
    Gulielma 138 Gulielma
    (GUYER) 137 Hannah
    (138) John 22 131 138
    Joshua 137 138 Thomas
    138 Wiliam 138 William
    131 (137)-139 144
HASKITT, Betty 140 Jesse
    43 45 John 43 45 140
    Joseph 35 Joshua 141
    Mary 43 Sarah (43)
    Silas 75 Thomas 140
    Thos. 139 William 43
    140 Wm. 140
HAUGHTON, Henry 69
HAWKINS, John 91

JENKINS, Johanah 85
JENNINGS, Miles 21
JEPSON, Eilizabeth 42
JESOP, Thos. 104
JESSOP, Enoch 134 Jane
  89 102 111 118 119 122
  Jane (ROBINSON) 102
  Jonathan 128 Jos. Junr
  106 Joseph 102 106
  Margret 102 Mary 102
  107 111 119 Peninah
  (134) Rachael 128
  Rachall (DRAPER) 128
  Rachel 133 135 137 138
  142 Tho. 122 Thomas 89
  101-(102)-103 107 110
  111 118 119 (128)
  Thos. 85 97 103 104
  106 Timothy 102 134
JISSOP, Rachel 59 138
JO[torn], Jos. 131
JOHNSON, John 85
JOHNSTON, John 40
JONES, Ame 92 [Ame]
  (HANCOCK) 89 Arthar
  (92)-94 Arther 90 96-
  98 115 122 Arthur 93
  Daniel 92 Elesebeth 92
  Elisabeth 45 100
  Elizabeth 131 Francis
  92 96 111 123 126 Jos.
  73 76 132 Joseph 11 22
  27 37 (76) 142 143
  Joshua 131 Margaret
  126 142 Mary 11 26 74
  100 106 108 123 132
  Mary (PEIRCE) 99
  Miriam 66 74 76 142
  Miriam (PRICE) 76
  Peater 100 Peter 88
  (89) 92 (99) 100 102
  104 106 109 114 119
  122 Peter Junr 104 118
  Peter Sen 118 Rachal
  92 Rachal (SNELLEN) 92
  Sarah 11 74 92 Will.
  122 William 100 118
  144

JONULE, Elisabeth 16
JORDAN, [?] 66 Benjamin
  116 Benjn. 114 Charles
  108 Doratha 76 Edmund
  109 Elezabeth 99
  Elisabeth 27 35 129
  Eliza. 68 Elizabeth 46
  58 83 127 131 137
  Elizabeth (PENNLETON)
  83 Jacob 129 James 116
  125 Jane 10 17 29 32
  36 40 56 73 John 116
  John Junr 46 Jos. 4 38
  130 Joseph 10 21 42 66
  (68) 79 82 83 99
  Joseph S:Masr. 83
  Josiah 58 127-129 136
  137 Marg 74 Margaret
  16 21 29 32 40 51 56
  57 64 (66) 72-74
  Margaret Junr 64 72
  Margaret (MORRIS) 21
  Margt. 37 65 66 Mary 4
  38 65 Mathew 27 116
  Matthew 83 113 126
  Matthias (83) Naomi 79
  Penelope 42 83 Richd.
  53 54 116 Robart 116
  Robert 46 83 Robert
  Junr 99 Robt. 10 114
  Saml. S. 77 Sarah (58)
  64 (65) 68 72 74 79
  Sarah (SYMONS) 68
  Thomas 15-17 19 (21)
  27 29 32 36 40 51 56-
  58 63-66 68 72 73 78
  Thos. 65 74 75
JORDEN, Phelocresta 5

KEATON, Hanry 82 Henry
  35 39 Miriam (39)
  Reub. 21 Reuben 57
  Rubn. 8 Ruth (35) 36
KEETON, Hanry 91 Miriam
  36
KENT, Hannah 85 Mary 85
KENYON, Elizabeth 107

MACKY, Martha 111
MADREN, Reuben 23
MAIDS, Timothy 1
MAKEBRIDE, Elezebeth
    (87)
MANERS, Jean 6 Jeane (6)
    Perigrene 6
MANN, Elisabeth 29
MARIS, John 94 Mary 117
    Sarah (94)
MARTIN, Jane 33 Jean 3
MATTHEWS, Lyddia 50
MAUDLIN, Edward 111 120
    Ezekiell 120 James 140
    John 146 Mary 140
MAY[torn], Edward 116
MAYO, Ann 18 111 Edward
    3 5 12 82 (93) 97 100
    102 118 Edward Jun 12
    Edward Junr 100 Edward
    Senr 18 Edwd. 32 35
    120 Edwd. Junr 18
    Elisabet 106 Elisabeth
    119 Elizabath 119
    Joseph 89 108 123 Mary
    3 12 18 32 35 93 97
    102 120 Mary (CLARE)
    93 Mary Junr 18 Samuel
    146 Sarah 119
MAYOE, Edward 91
MC[?], Sml. 129
MCADAM, Helena 37 Joseph
    25 27 29 31 34 37 44
    45 54
MCADAMS, Charlotta 78
    James 75 78 Joseph 14
    124 146
MCCORMICK, Wm. 37
MCDONALD, Jn. 63 John 8
MCKEEL, Sarah 55
MCMORINE, Robt. 16
MEADS, Timothy 6
MEAIDS, Ane 1 6 Ane
    (BLESSING) 7 Timothy
    (7)
MECARDELL, Terans 119
METCALF, Ann 8 124

METCALFE, Ann 146 Geo:
    41 George 51 Sarah 11
    13 15 16 19 26 40 41
    43 49 52
MOLDEN, [E]zekiel 87
MONTAGUE, Thomas 24
    Thos. 35
MOOR, Cornelius 128
    Elisabeth 89 Hannah
    131 Jos. 131 Joseph
    144 Willm. 87 Wm. 88
MOORE, [torn]beth 115
    Aaron 75 113 Abllam 39
    Anna 75 Betty 112
    Cornelius 112 125
    Elezebeth 46 94
    Elisabeth 105
    Elizabeth 90 Isabel 35
    146 Jesse 25 (67)
    Jessee 142 143 John 25
    31 39 74 108 112
    Joseph 58 126 136 137
    139-141 143 Joshua 22
    27 33 39 112 136 Karen
    125 Keronhappuc 128
    Margaret 47 62 125
    Margart 149 Mary 22 23
    27 31 67 74 112 113
    (136) 137 Mary
    (ANDERSON) 67 Mary
    Junr 143 Mary Snr 143
    Melicent 67 Robert 74
    136 141 Samuel 39 48
    62 67 105 112 125
    Sarah 31 Thomas 35 136
    146 149 Thos. 62 71
    William 39 (105) 115
    125 Wm. 126
MOR[torn], John 107 Wm.
    90
MORE, [torn] 105
    Elesabth 115 Elezebeth
    87 91 94 95 Elezebeth
    (MAKEBRIDE) 87
    Elizabeth 89 Jane (39)
    104 John (105) 119
    Joshua 104 105 119
    Mary 19 105 Mary

NEWBY (continued)
Susanna (GRIFFING) 113
Susannah 33 74 141
Susannah (TATLOCK) 141
Tamer 12 Tho. 108 120
Thomas 11 12 23 29 35
37 46 64 96 99 100
107-109 123 125 129
133 135 (137) Thos. 97
127 128 134 148 Will
34 William 12 35 (72)
(73) 82 86 (88) 89 92
93 95 96 98 113 115-
117 122 139 141 145
146 William Juner 94
William Jur. 115 Wm.
11 74 88 93 120 126
128 141 Wm. Jr 90 Wyke
14 Zach. 23 55
NEWTON, Ama 32
NICALLS, Samuell 6
NICEL[torn], Samuell 91
NICELSON, Ann 117
Christipher 94
Elesabth 117 Elezebeth
93 94 122 Hannah 93 95
116 117 122 Jane 116
(117) John 91-94 117
Nathanell 94 117
Presello (94) Samuel
92 93 Samuell 92 94 95
115-117 122
NICH:, Christopher 8 55
NICHN., Cristopher 7
Nicholas 59
NICHOL, Elizabeth 15
Rachel 13 Mary 55
NICHOLESON, Hanah 101
NICHOLIN, Sarah 13
NICHOLS, Abner 67 Margt.
67 Sarah 59 Thomas 55
NICHOLSON, Ann 24 85 86
101 105 Benja. 88 89
Carolina 30 37 Chas.
41 Chris. 21 Chrisr.
17 50 Christ. 24 28 40
43 45 49 51 58
Christifer 101

NICHOLSON (continued)
Christipher 102
Christopher 14 15 18-
20 22 24-28 31 36 37
43 47 50 55 57 61 77
86 89 98 105 Christor.
85 Chrsr. 9 Deborah
113 Eles. 120 Elis.
104 Elisabeth 12 19
(42) 49 52 85 86 (88)
98 101 Elizabeth (98)
Elizabeth (CHARLES) 85
Hanah 99 (100) 110 120
Hannah 12 (104) Henley
21 Henly 50 (77) John
8 9 19 55 (86) 88 Jos.
34 37 48 Joseph 10 16
17 20 22 24 25 (27)-
(29)-31 42 49 52 73 98
101 103 104 110 111
118 124 126 146 Know
98 Margaret (25) Mary
7 9 12 14-(18)-(20)-22
(24) 25 27 28 30 31 34
35 42 43 48-50 56 58
72 73 77 83 101 110
125 126 146 Mary Junr
24 25 28 34 125 146
Mary y Younger 28
Mathew 127 140
Mehetabel 22 124 146
Mehetable 28 Mehitabel
24 27 Mehitabel
(NIXON) 27 Melicent 56
Meliscent 19 43
Miliscent (55) Miriam
(22) (27) 52 104 147
Natha. 102 Nathan
(139) Nathaniel 33 86
88 89 98 105 107 111
118 119 Nathanuell 98
Nicholas 15 20 24-26
28 30 37 42 123 125
139 146 Peniah
(PARKER) 139 Peninah
139 Priscila (TOMES)
86 Rache 123 Rachel
(42) 51 52 Rebekah 10

NICHOLSON (continued)
30 (31) Rebekah (LOW)
29 Saml. (85)-89 104
111 118 120 Samll. 100
103 Samuel 20 24 98
118 Samuell 98-102 110
Sarah 8 10 11 13-15 17
19 20 22 25 26 37 42-
46 48 51 52 59 62 66
70-72 77 80 123 125
127 129 130 139 Sarah
Junr 140 Sarah (NIXON)
36 Sarah (OVERMAN) 77
Sarah Senr 69 Sarah
(SYMONS) 50 Susannah
28 Thomas 10 14 16 17
20-22 24-30 34 (36) 37
42 45 48 (50) 51 54 58
61 62 69-73 77 125 139
140 146 Thos. 48 71
Thos. Junr 41 46
William 66 77
NICHON., Chrisr. 55
Miliscent 8
NICKELSON, Eliz. 103 114
Jos. 114 Samll. 103
114
NICKHOLSON, Ann 98
NICKLESON, Samuel 82
NICKOLS, Ann 121
Elizabeth 121
NICKOLSON, [?] 122
[torn] 95 Ann 4 95 98
120 121 Christophar 4
Elisabeth 97 Elizabeth
95 96 Hanah 95 98
Joseph 96 Mary 96
Samuel 4 122 Samuell
96 100
NICKSON, Elesabeth 117
Zacharies 117
NICO[torn], Samuell 88
NICOLES[torn], John 90
NICOLESON, [?] 91
[torn]th 88 Abigall
(90) Christopher 94
Elizabeth 91 Elizabeth
90 John 88-90 94 Nath.

NICOLESON (continued)
90 Nathanell (94)
Samuell 89 90 94 Sarah
94 Sarah (MARIS) 94
NICOLSON, Sarah 146
NIKELLSON, Elezabeth 1
Samuell 1 2
NIKOLSON, Elesabeth 4
Hanah 4
NIXON, [?] 11 69 Abigail
17 20 22 41 51 71 Ann
21 48 59 62 63 Ann
(MORRIS) 21 Barnabe 27
28 37 50 53 54 73
Barnaby 14 17 Barnebe
116 Barneby 76 Damaris
(5) Dorithy 20 44 50
Dorothy 19 20 (61)
Elesabeth (3) 4
Elesabth Juner 4
Elezabeath 2 5 6 7
Elezabeath (PAGE) 1
Elezabeth 2 Elezebeth
82 Elis. 105 106
Elisa. 104 107 Elisa.
(NEWBY) 97 Elisabeh
119 Elisabeth 12 27 33
34 39 97 109 Elisabeth
(MOORE) 105 Elisabeth
Senr 36 Eliz. 103 108
Elizabeth (11) 17 20
(22) 59 62 71 96 107-
109 111 (112) 116 126
Elizabeth (MURPHEY) 19
Elizabeth (PRITCHARD
CLARY) 17 Ezra 29 45
54 Frances 17 Francis
27 Fras. 112 125
Frederick 17 Hannah 17
20 22 37 54 Hannah J
73 James 11 14 (17) 21
23 Jane 27 29 37 44 45
73 Jane (BUNDY SYMONS)
29 Jas. 59 Jemima (16)
26 29 36 54 73 Jno. 59
John 10 14 19-(21)-23
27-(29) 33 37 41 43-45
49 50 53 54 61 62 70

OVERMAN (continued)
58 (63) 75 77 Ephraim
10 15 23 36 53 (55) 60
(147) Ephraim Junr 23
147 Ephrm. 34 Hannah
24 32 74 104 Isaac
(15) 16 18 (23) 34 36
47 55 60 61 67 68 81
147 Isabel 61 81 Isbel
15 Isbel (TRUEBLOOD)
15 Isbell 18 68
[J]acob 87 Jacob 29 82
James 11 13 16 17 22
26 49 51-53 56 66 70
74 135 Jno. 38 John 4
(16) 19 24 28 32 35
37-40 42 47 63 65 66
74 77 80 81 135 142
Joshua 10 13 27 28 M.
M. 66 Martha 29 30 33
40 69 Mary 10 11 19 21
29 30 41 47 48 50 53
56 59 61 67 70 72 (74)
76 77 79 81 135 Mary
(ALBERTSON) 11 Miriam
9 23 28 30 39 42 47
(67) Miriam
(TRUEBLOOD) 23
Mordecai 80 Morgan 13
Mourning 29 Myriam 61
Nancy 63 Nathan 10 17
26 30 31 34 50 52 56-
58 69 80 Obadiah 34
Onias 9 Rachel 147
Rachel (SMALL) 147
Reuben 63 Reubin 78
Rueben 81 Ruth 17 22
30 60 69 Ruth
(TRUEBLOOD) 55 Sarah
14 16 19 21 32 40 42-
44 51 57 64 68 72 (77)
109 147 Sarah (HALL)
44 Sarah (PRICHARD) 16
Thamar 34 (38) 60
Thomas 9 10 13 16 22
27 30 31 34 37 38 41
42 (44) 47 50-52 54-58
73 Thos. 13 28 44 53

OVERMAN (continued)
63 William 9 11 14 40
76 77 Wm. 16 20 21 41
48 62 Zebulon 147

P[?], [?] 122
PAGE, Elezabeath (1)
Isaac 1 3 Thomas 3 12
121
PAILEN, Henry 56
PALIN, Ann 52 Ann
(OVERMAN) 52 Elisabeth
17 52 Elisabeth
(SQUIRES) 17 Elizabeth
(60) Henry 17 49 (52)
69-(70)-71 147 John 17
Mary 17 Miriam 52
Sarah 71 Sarah (NIXON)
70 Susannah (65)
Thomas 11 15-(17) 19
26 43 44 52 60 65
Thos. 126
PALMER, P. 113 Paul 99
PARIS, Thomas 101 Thos.
100
PARISHO, Eliza. 71
PARK, Sarah 48
PARKER, Elisabeth 75
Elisha 75 Eliza 50 77
Elizabeth 11 63
Elizabeth (MORRIS) 63
Isabel 149 Job 48 63
Joel 52 John 63 139
Jonathan 11 Jos. 59
149 Joseph (63) 75 81
Mary 53 54 Nathan 47
Peniah (139) Peninnah
54 Penninah 62 Phara.
63 Pharaba 66 Pharabe
62 Phiraba 130 Rachel
139 Sarah 48 140
PARKS, Elisabeth 109
Elisabeth (HUDSON) 108
Samuel (108) 109
PARRIS, Tho. 120
PARRISS, Ann 100
PAULMER, Paul 100
PAVILL, Margett 92

PHELPS (continued)
  Henry 107 108 111 112
  Jona. 85 87 105 113
  Jonathan 27 100 109
  112 Mourning 112 Saml.
  110 Samll. 114 Samuell
  101
PHENIX, Caleb 100
PIERCE, Joseph 88 Miriam
  138 Thomas 114 134 138
PIKE, Abigail 38 Ann 3
  (4) 18 38 Anne (38)
  Benjamin 147 Jane (3)
  147 Jean 3 John 3 5 38
  (71) Johnathan 5
  Jonathan 38 Joseph 80
  Mary 3 5 38 Miliscent
  72 Samuel 4 38 Sarah
  (SMALL) 71 Susana 5
  Susanna 38 Susannah 33
PIPER, Elizabeth (14)
  Nathan 14
PIRCE, [torn]eres 88
  Dameris 90 Jose[?torn]
  90
PLATO, William 97 120
PLATT, Henry 7
PLEAS, Isaac 67 Jane 67
POINTER, Phillip 143
  Susannah (143)
POOL, Clarkey 16 22 33
  56 Elizabeth 140 Paul
  S. 80 Richard 26
  Soloman Jr. 80
POOLE, Margreat 1
  Margrete (WHITE) 6
  Richard 6 Solloman (6)
  Soloman 1
POOLL, Solloman 6
POTTLE, Sarah 39
PRATT, Elisabeth 106
PRICE, Benjamin 15 60 62
  72 Bettey (ANDERSON)
  46 Betty 15 40 46
  Elisabeth 96 Elizabeth
  60 Elizabeth (PALIN)
  60 John 8 9 15 21 40
  (46) 52 53 (60) 72 78

PRICE (continued)
  96 John Junr 64
  Jonathan 9 14 (15) 42
  43 45 46 Mary 48 62
  Miriam (76) Rachel 76
  78 Rachel Junr (WHITE)
  78 Ruth 69 Saml. 74 76
  Samuel 73 (78) 80 81
  Sarah 78 143 Susanna
  (MORRIS) 15 Susannah
  15 44 46 53 William 46
PRICHARD, Ann (34)
  Benja. 5 12 Benjamen 3
  82 Benjamin (11) 17 91
  Benjn. 18 21 33 34 38
  Benomi 43 69 Elesabeth
  5 Elisabeth 15 18 34
  38 (42) 43 49 John 43
  Jos. 28 Joseph 11 42
  Margaret 79 Martha 38
  Mary (18) 19 (43)
  Mathew 30 82 91 100-
  103 Matthew 3 4 12 16
  18 24 34 36 69 73
  Miriam 10 16 40 61
  (69) Peninnah 11
  Peninnah (WHITE) 11
  Sarah 10 (16) 21 26 30
  31 33 34 47 49 53 56
  69 73 Thomas 3 5 18 21
  38 42 101 Thomas Junr
  43 Thos. 10 28 49
PRICHERD, Mary 3
PRICLOE, Elezebeth 95
PRICTHARD Elisabeth 4
  Elizabeth 14 John 14
  Martha 4
PRICTLOE, John 117
PRITCHARD, [?] 66
  Abigail 80 Abigail
  (MORRIS) 80 Anna 58 B.
  Junr 66 Benj. 65
  Benja. 66 97 107
  Benjaman 93 Benjamin
  66 72 77 (80) 126
  Benjamin Junr 81
  Benjm. 120 Benjn. 21
  63 114 Caleb 80

RO[torn], Joseph 106
ROBBINSON, Will: 63
ROBENSON, Jane 116
    Joseph 116
ROBERSON, Jane 122
ROBERTS, Charles 108
    Mourning 46 William 45
ROBINSON, Ann 46 74
    Elizabeth 15 Esther 65
    133 137 Jane 98 (102)
    Janne (CLEAR) 116
    Jemima 125 John 28 50
    83 123 Joseph 10 27 28
    45 49 (83) (116)
    Josiah 63 71 74 77-80
    Margaret 25 Mary 49
    112 Miriam 25 37 44
    (45) 124 146 Rouland
    69 Rowland 25 37 Sarah
    14 16 27 28 37 46 83
    126 Sarah Junr 10 28
    Sarah (PENDLETON) 83
    Sarah Senr 83 Sary 83
    Thomas 10 15 22 24-26
    29 37 42 54 116 125
    146 Thomas Junr 10
    Thos. 28 Thos. Junr 28
    Will: 50 67 74 77
    William 13 14 16 21 25
    44 46 58 64 127 Wm. 57
    77 Wmn. 65
ROBISON, Joseph 83
ROGERS, Stephen 57
ROTINSON, Thomas 58
RUSSELL, James 15

SAINT, Dan. 113 Daniel
    27 45 54 83 (109) 112
    Danl. 125 Elisabeth 27
    44 54 Elizabeth 126
    Gulielma 75 Hercules
    54 Margaret (131)
    Margaret (BARROW) 109
    Margret 109 Thomas 9
    13 23 44 54 60 148
SANDERS, [torn] 97 Abra.
    113 Abraham 59 104 105
    110 114 118 (121)

SANDERS (continued)
    Abram 89 112 Ann 31 70
    Benja. 113 Benjamin
    108 Betsey 149 Charles
    144 Elisabeth 42
    Elizabeth 112 Hannah
    42 104 134 Hannah
    (NICHOLSON) 104 John
    36 40 (120) 121 Judah
    100 121 Judah
    (PRITLOE) 121 Judeth
    89 107 110 114 Judith
    112 Leah 11 55 123
    128-130 Margaret 129
    Mary 64 70 76 Miriam
    10 69 Penninah 130
    Prissilla 121
    Prissilla (PRITLOE)
    120 Ricd. 107 Richard
    27 112 Richd. (104)
    Thomas 128 129 132
    William 33 38
SAUNDERS, Abraham 41 49
    74 109 Ann 124
    Benjamin 124 Isaac 125
    Jacob 142 Jno. 120
    John 123 130 Jonathan
    (123) 124 Margaret
    (124) Mary 124 Mary
    (WHITE) 123 Patsey 76
    Thomas 124
SAWER, Elizabeth 59
    Margaret 59
SAWYER, Caleb 10 17 67
    69 Fred B. 8 14 21
    Lovey 14 Malachi 14 67
    Margaret 19
SCARBORA, Agustin 82
SCARBOROUG, Agustin 91
SCARBROUGH, Mac. 111
SCOT, Joseph 85 105
    Joshua 85 Mary 85
SCOTE, Stephen 2 5 82
SCOTT, Elezebeth 93
    Eliphal 24 Eliphalet
    25 Eliphel 42
    Eliphelet 21 Hanah 103
    Hanah (NICHOLSON) 100

SNELLEN, Israel 92
    Rachal (92)
SNELLIN, Isarell 1
SNELLING, Esther (97)
    Hannah 87 Israel 87
    Isreall 87
SNODGRASS, Neil 37
SNOWDON, Myles 69
SPARLING, George 46
SQUIRES, Elisabeth (17)
    69 Mary 126 Rodger 126
    Roger 17 Sarah (126)
SQUIRS, Mary 61
STAFFORD, Abigail 52
    Abigail (COSAND) 52
    Josiah 52 Saml. 75
    Samuel 22 (52)
STANDERWICK, Richd. 85
STANTON, Betty 72
STEPNEY, John 85 86
    Marcy 90 Mercy 85 86
STIDHAM, Sarah 31
SUTEN, Alexander:ese: 94
SUTTEN, Deliverance 86
SUTTON, [torn] 102
    Elisabeth 32 George 32
    (102) Gorge 114 Joseph
    85 Nathaniel (32)
    Rebeckah 100 Sarah 102
    (114) Sarah (PEIRC)
    102
SYMONS, Abra 41 Abraham
    8 (9) 61 Abram 10 16
    30 33 69 73 Absala 8 9
    13 26 32 40 41 45 60
    64 Absalon 8 Ann 9 25
    28 30 33 39 50 68 69
    82 Ann (MORRIS) 68
    Anne 36 Caleb 77-(79)
    Damaris 3 4 24 50 112
    Damaris (WHITE) 2 33
    Elisabeth 16 26 29 30
    33 34 39-(41) (46) 49
    51-54 56 Elisabeth
    (GILBERT) 32 Eliza. 74
    Elizabeth 8 9 13-15 21
    48 57 58 60 62 65 73
    Jacob 64 66 72 78

SYMONS (continued)
    Jane 26 (29) 47 Jane
    (BUNDY) 25 Jehosaphat
    83 Jehoshaphat 26 28
    30 39 49 50 (64) 71 73
    77 Jehosophat 13 Jer:
    32 96 Jeremiah 5 6 7
    34 82 Jeremyah 1 Jesse
    (8) 13 40 51 64 (73)
    79 81 Jessee 79 John 3
    4 7-10 12 14 16 19 21
    24-26 28-(33)-34 36-41
    43 45 47 49 50 52 53
    56 57 (68) (69) 73 77
    82 97 105 122 126 147
    John H 15 John J 34
    John Junr 10 15-17 19
    21 25 26 30-32 40 43
    47 49 56 69 John Senr
    13 (32) Joseph 10 46
    50 69 73 Josiah 70 71
    73 Lyddai 73 Lyddia
    (26) (49) Lydia 64 65
    73 77 79 M. John 60
    Martha 3 Mary 9 29 30
    49 50 64-66 69 72 73
    77 Mary (CHARLES) 9
    Mary (MACE) 49 Mathew
    8 9 Matthew 45 62
    Melescent 79 Melicent
    26 79 Melisant
    (MORRIS) 8 Meliscen 8
    Milesent 74 143
    Miliscent 73 Milisent
    (13) 141 142 Milscent
    65 Miriam 50 69 Mirjam
    (PRITCHARD) 69 Nathan
    13 26 33 49 56 64 69
    73 81 147 Penelope 13
    16 26 34 (39) 41 51 52
    73 147 Peninah 79
    Peninah (BUNDY) 79
    Peter (49) (50) 82
    Pharaba 50 Pharabe 65
    Pharaby 77 Pressilla
    12 Priscilla 50
    Priscilla (BUFFKIN) 50
    Rachel 36 Rebaca 4 82

WHITE (continued)
Edmund 47 Elesabeth 3
4 Elesibeth 146
Elezabeath (7)
Elezabeth (NEWBEY) 2
Elisabeth 16 24 (36)
45 46 Elisabeth
(SYMONS) 46 Elisha 80
Eliza. 76 Eliza. 66 74
76 78 Elizabeth 14 65
67 (75) 85 124 125
Elizabeth (WHITE) 75
Ester 77 Esther 64
Frances 58 61 140
Francis 11 55 (58) 60
125 129 131 132 134-
(136)-140 142 143
Fras. 78 George 124
Guby 13 Guley 9 Henery
3 82 Henr. 120 Henry
1-7 12 18 22 24 33-
(35)-36 38 47 96 98
100 103 105 Henry Jur
116 Henry Sr. 33
Huldah 30 56 66 69 74
141 Jacob 19 124 125
128 129 133 137 James
16 (34) (39) 40 (46)
52 57 60 65 69 87 130
(137) Jane 38 Jane
(PIKE) 3 Jas. 129
Jeams 2 5 Jean 4 Jean
(PIKE) 3 Jemima 53 56
130 133 137 Jesse 65
75 131 (142) Jno. D.
59 John (2) 6 19 34 44
45 47 58 64 (74) 79 82
91 (98) 108 123-(125)-
126 128-130 136 139
142 146 149 John C.
124 John Junr 124
Johnathan (4) Jonathan
33 (38) 39 62 125 149
Jos. 54 Josaway 3
Joseph 4 13 14 35 38
45 58 123 126 130 138
Joseph Junr 126 Joshua
5 (18) 19 32 36 38 49

WHITE (continued)
55 69 73 124 125 129
146 Josiah 11 14 45 47
60 66 74-(75)-76 78 80
81 123-125 129 142 148
Josiah Junr 58 Leydia
(125) 126 Leydia
(WINSLOW) 125 Lida 58
133 Lyddia 11 Lydia
127-129 Margaret 54 57
59 72 80 123 124 (126)
127 129 148 Margaret
(SAUNDERS) 124
Margaret (WHITE) 126
Margarett 76 Margret
46 Margrete (6) Margt.
66 Mariam 61 Martha 30
53 124 Mary 3 4 6 7
(12) 14 19 21 36 (44)
47 49 55 60 63 65 66
72-(73)-74 77 78 80 96
98 (123) 125 128 129
132 (133) 136 137 141
142 Mary (ALBERTSON)
142 Mary (MOORE NEWBY)
136 Mary (NICHOLSON)
18 Mary (OVERMAN) 74
Mathew 129 Matthew 11
126 127 Melicent 130
Meliscent 19 55 146
Meliscent (HENLEY) 146
Melisent 133 Miles 11
123 128 129 Milescent
47 Milicent 125 127
Milicent (HENLEY) 124
Miliscent 7 Miliscent
(NICHOLSON) 55
Millicent 129 Miriam
11 19 20 26 30 33 34
38 39 42 47 51 52 60
69 72 130 142 144 147
Miriam (KEATON) 39
Moorning 55 Mourning
58 124 Naomi 18 (33)
36 114 Naomy 12 Nathan
11 Nehemiah 9 (38) 124
Orpah 126 128 Parthena
78 Peggy 124 Peninnah

WILSON (continued)
   Isaac 47 85 87-90 96
   123 129 Jacob (131)
   Jno. D. 59 John 56
   (61) 62 67 123 126
   John Junr 125 Joseph 9
   16 40 52 53 (56) 57 61
   62 64 72 89 108 112
   126 Josiah 147 Lydia
   61 71 Mal 21 Mary 112
   148 Milesent 62
   Milisent (TRUEBLOOD)
   61 Miriam (62) 131
   Miriam (GUYAR) Junr
   131 Mourning 73 R: 118
   Rachel 16 24 25 28 30
   31 53 56 69 87 147
   Robert 85-87 106 110
   129 Robt. 85 113 Rt.
   89 97 104-107 111 113
   114 118 122 Reuben 148
   Ruben 131 Ruth 31
   Saml. 62 71 Sarah 9 15
   40 53 56 57 62 64 72
   (85) 147 Sarah
   (CHARLES) 56 Silvanus
   131
WIN[torn], Elizabeth 90
WINS[torn], Thomas 105
WINSLO, Caleb 60 Thomas
   90 96
WINSLOE, Esther
   (SNELLING) 97
   Elezebeth 94 95 116
   Elisabeth 97 98 102
   Elizabeth (CLEARE) 90
   Esther 97 John (97)
   120 121 Joseph 102
   Mary 102 Sarah 90 97
   Tho. 118 Thomas 88
   (90) 93 95 97 98 101
   102 116 Timothy 90 97
WINSLOW, [torn] 105
   Abigail 129 Abigail
   (WHITE) 129 Ann 48 126
   128 129 148 Ann
   (PERRY) 148 Benjamin
   (129) 130 Bettey 148

WINSLOW (continued)
   Caleb 47 62 65 123 125
   126 128 129 (148)
   (149) Caleb Jur 127
   149 Elezebeth 93 Elis.
   104 114 Elisabeth 39
   89 109 Eliza. 129
   Elizabeth 109 123 129
   Elizth. 148 Esther 123
   129 Hannah 123 Jacob
   47 125 128-130 148 149
   Jemima 149 Jemima
   (CANNON) 149 Jesse 112
   126 128 Job 108 109
   111 John 10 25 28 50
   51 89 (109) 119 (123)
   129 130 137 John Junr
   48 Jos. 105 Joseph 39
   89 (104) 119 123 125
   126 Josiah 10 15 22 28
   69 Lancelot 124 Leydia
   (125) Lydia 124
   Margaret 123 Margaret
   (BELL) 123 Martha 74
   Mary 9 (28) 61 148
   Mary (PEARSON) 109
   Meriam 109 Milisant
   149 Miliscent 14
   Millicent 130 Obed 148
   Peggy 124 Pleasant 45
   123 126 128 129
   Pleasent (WHITE) 128
   129 Plesant 104
   Plesent (TOMES) 104
   Rachael 130 Rachel 11
   89 123 126 Rachel
   (WHITE) 123 Rachell
   (WILLSON) 89 Samuel 25
   125 Sarah 112 119 124
   (130) Temothy (89)
   Tho. 111 Tho[torn] 95
   Thomas 11 39 89 108
   109 (118) 119 125 146
   Thos. 89 104 105
   Timothy 89 119 148
   William 125 (128)
   (129) 149